WOMEN OF THE CHURCH

For all the monastic women, living and dead, who have been an inspiration and encouragement to me over the years, especially for Sr Bernard as she celebrates sixty years of faithful living as a 'woman of the Church'.

Patricia M. Rumsey

Women of the Church
The religious experience of monastic women

the columba press

First published in 2011 by
the columba press
55A Spruce Avenue, Stillorgan Industrial Park,
Blackrock, Co Dublin

Cover by Bill Bolger
Origination by The Columba Press
Printed in Ireland by Gemini International Limited

ISBN 978 1 85607 748 4

Contents

ABBREVIATIONS

CCSL	Corpus Christianorum (Series Latina)
CSEL	Corpus Scriptorum Ecclesiasticorum Latinorum
HEGA	Historia Ecclesiastica Gentis Anglorum
PG	Patrologia Graeca
PL	Patrologia Latina
SC	Sources Chrétiennes

Foreword

Why should we read history? Why in particular should theologians and people concerned for the church read history? Is it just a question of curiosity, of a desire to be generally well-informed, to be a little less ignorant? What should we expect of history: what does it do?

This volume by Sr Patricia Rumsey shows very clearly, I would suggest, that history can do at least three things: illuminate, liberate, and inspire.

Knowledge of the past illuminates the present. We can make better sense of the situation in which we find ourselves when we have some idea of the story of reversals and changes, tension and conflict, development and adaptation, which has led to it. Why do we use these words, divide things up in this way, make these associations, have these struggles, lead these kinds of lives? History may not provide the only kind of answer to these 'why' questions, but it does provide an indispensable one. Sr Patricia's book, then, by making accessible an overview of the history of women's monasticism, puts us in a position to understand and think constructively about the current situation of women religious – and perhaps of women in the church more generally – with all the richness, potential and tension that this holds.

History also liberates. In books like this one we learn that the tradition we have inherited is rich and long and varied; that it is not, and never has been, fixed and unchanging. A longer sense of the past can play a vital role, in particular, in freeing us from excessive bondage to the immediate past: it can liberate us from the feeling that fidelity means simply continuing to do what the previous generation, or the one before that, did. So if, as Sr Patricia shows, women's monasticism has had very different phases, and if it has always been shaped by its grappling with contemporary economic and political realities, then the recognition of this can bring a kind of freedom for monastics of today, challenging them to think anew and creatively about how they in turn must grapple with the realities of our own time.

And history – at least histories like this one – can inspire. In it we find drawn together the biographies of many women of the church down the centuries, women who have been holy, courageous, determined, original, radical, persevering ... To read of the lives and experience and struggles of the women described between these covers is to allow our imaginations to be opened to new possibilities, and our lives, perhaps, to be enriched.

If there is, as Robert Hale suggests and Sr Patricia concurs, a 'monastic dimension in every human being,' then we all, perhaps, have a stake in the well-being of the venture of the monasticism which is traced in this volume, and so we all have reason to be grateful to Sr Patricia Rumsey for the learning, passion and labour which have brought it into being.

Dr Karen Kilby
President, Catholic Theological Association of Great Britain
Head of Department of Theology and Religious Studies,
Nottingham University

Introduction

The central argument of this book is this: the way in which women religious are treated by and in the church is a product of history; their unique insight into their own way of life by monastic women is largely ignored, as it has always been, and therefore they are not treated by ecclesiastical authorities as if they can organise their own lives in the same way as monastic men. Historically, women in nearly all traditional societies have been oppressed and exploited by men. Consequently, even within Christianity, women have endured centuries of male domination and an ensuing lack of self esteem because of the blame attached to them for their assumed complicity in 'the sin of Eve'.[1] Within monasticism, this has reinforced a negative, world-denying spirituality which has owed much to Gnostic dualism, seeing 'the world' and the body as bad, while 'the spirit' was seen as good. This outlook which saw the body and all things of the flesh as bad led to practices such as excessive fasting, physical penances such as the discipline, emotional deprivation, a masochistic and unbalanced attraction to the Passion and the bizarre practices associated with enclosure. Medieval (and later) women accepted this as the religious *status quo* and even actively sought it (there is a parallel with women, who, having been daughters of abusive and alcoholic fathers go on to marry abusive and alcoholic husbands) because that was the recognised stereotype of female holiness passed on from generation to generation by hagiographers.

But Vatican II returned us to a positive model of holiness found in the gospels and in the letters of Paul, where all are

---

1. As a very small child, I remember my grandmother telling me in all sincerity: '"Woman" is called that because she brought woe to man.' It made a deep impression on my young mind.

'called to be saints'; women just as much as men. 'To all God's beloved in Rome who are called to be saints';[2] 'To the church of God that is in Corinth, to those who are sanctified in Christ Jesus, called to be saints ...';[3] 'To the saints who are in Ephesus and are faithful in Christ Jesus';[4] 'To all the saints in Christ Jesus who are in Philippi, with the bishops and deacons'.[5] Having been burdened for centuries with a world-denying spirituality that effectively denied the reality of the incarnation and was a legacy of Gnosticism, monastic life for women today is struggling with the task of re-inventing itself according to this positive and world-affirming spirituality that recognises that because of the incarnation the whole of the material creation is holy; there is nothing in this world that has not been touched by the Christ and therefore is sacred.[6] If women's religious life in its monastic form is to survive, it has to face some searching questions about the way it views this world and interacts with it. This book does not claim to have all the answers, but it offers a perspective on the lives of some women of the church where we might find some inspiration.

In order to study the way monastic life has evolved in the past and so gain some insights for its evolution into the future, this book sets out to examine the lives of monastic women at various eras in Christian history and put them into their own particular context. However, setting out on any exploration into the history of the lives and experiences of religious women, at any period in the long life of the church, as Elizabeth Castelli points out with particular regard to the early centuries, is fraught with difficulties:

> [I]t is to embark on a treacherous and often disappointing search for buried treasure. When the period of history is remote and evidence has had centuries to be lost, misfiled, unindexed, rewritten, suppressed, the task grows yet more

---

2. Rom 1:1.
3. 1 Cor 1:2.
4. Eph 1:1.
5. Phil 1:1.
6. P. M. Rumsey, 'All Praise be Yours, My Lord, for All Creation: Francis and Clare and Ecology', *The Cord*, Vol 61, No 1 Jan/March 2011.

frustrating. And when, finally, one turns to the history of women in Christianity in a remote period, the situation takes on Herculean contours. In attempting to understand a distant moment in the lives of Christian women, an historian faces not only the silence of misplaced information and absent texts, but the work of orthodoxy over the centuries.[7]

So researching material for this book, though a most enriching task which I have greatly enjoyed, has been rather like searching for the pieces of material in the rag-bag of time with which to make a patchwork quilt. Its development has been gradual and long drawn out and it has gone through many stages before appearing in its current dress. A much earlier version first saw the light of day, many years ago, as an MA dissertation on the place of women in early insular society. It was considerably revised and very much enlarged to become a module for an MA programme in women's monasticism. Since then, it has yet again been considerably revised and very much enlarged to reach its present still modest proportions. Its aim throughout, as well as arguing the above thesis, has been to fill a gap in the available literature by providing a reasonably popular introduction to the monastic life as *lived* specifically by women through the centuries.

However, I must make clear from the outset what it is not; it is not, and does not pretend to be, a fully comprehensive study of women's monasticism. Instead, by means of a series of historic 'snapshots' taken somewhat at random and focused on specific monastic women, and by situating these women within the setting of their own times, it demonstrates that female monasticism is an ongoing phenomenon in the history of the church right down to the present day. An obvious question, right at the start is 'why have I chosen these particular women and not others, when there are so many to choose from?' The answer is largely that of personal preference and the intention of making as wide a choice as possible within the limits allowed by the exigencies of publication. The various chapters do overlap, and so the same monastic woman may crop up in more than one

7. E. Castelli, 'Virginity and its Meaning for Women's Sexuality in Early Christianity', *Journal of Feminist Studies in Religion*, Vol 2, No 1 (Spring, 1986), pp 61-88, at pp 61-62.

chapter to illustrate a different aspect of religious life.

At a time when women's monasticism is at a critical stage of self-questioning and potential reinvention, this book shows that the monastic movement for women has struggled through the centuries to adapt itself (sometimes with difficulty) to the changing contexts of secular, political and economic history as well as that of the changing needs and evolving theology and spirituality of the church itself, and yet has survived, though sometimes in a different dress. As Bruce Venarde has rightly said: 'The importance of female monasticism lies precisely in its relationship to social, economic, and institutional organisation and development.'[8] As the following chapters will show in the studies of individual women religious, although the essential elements of monastic living have survived the centuries more or less unchanged and have remained fairly constant, the defining parameters of monasticism have been quite fluid down the ages, due to varying interpretations and changing historical, social and cultural conditions. It will soon become quite obvious that there have been varying 'fashions' in the concept of holiness and sanctity through the ages. The desert dwellers, both male and female, put great stress on asceticism, solitude and penitential living. The late-classical era set much store on the generous distribution of wealth and on learning. The Anglo-Saxons, if Bede, our main guide, is anything to go by, prized virginity and nobility, while the Irish were deeply impressed by the miraculous. The new mendicant Orders of the high Middle Ages impressed people by their practice of poverty, their simplicity of lifestyle, their ardent love of God. The mystics of the later Middle Ages caused wonder and admiration by their visions, ecstasies and their writings, while coming into more modern times, in assessing holiness we look for care of the less fortunate; we expect witness to 'gospel values', and we respect those who are prepared to sacrifice their lives for their ideals.

My specific aim is to show that women monastics have always had and still continue to have, their own unique and valuable contribution to make to monasticism and monastic theology and

---

8. B. Venarde, *Women's Monasticism and Medieval Society* (Ithaca and London: Cornell University Press, 1997), p 2.

spirituality as these have been lived and experienced down the centuries, and to this end there are frequent references to primary source material. I have tried as far as possible to let all these women speak of their religious experience for themselves and in their own words. Hence the number of quotations from women writers, both the few ancient ones accessible to us and then down through the centuries to the more prolific modern ones. In the course of this study, I will examine various aspects of monastic life and how these have developed and been lived in different ways or according to different interpretations through the centuries. The specific issues to be explored are the renunciation of property (or its appropriate administration, according to the understanding of the times); the renunciation of family ties and relationships, and the degree of seclusion from secular life and affairs which this entailed; and the appropriate expression, or renunciation, of status and independence. These are not the only practices which constitute the basic asceticism which underlies monastic life,[9] but they deal with those fundamentals which eventually came to be formulated canonically as the traditional religious vows of poverty, chastity and obedience (the so-called 'evangelical counsels'), with the possible addition of enclosure. (In the Benedictine tradition and its various reforms and offshoots, the vows taken by both monks and nuns are those of stability, conversion of manners and obedience.)

However, as this book also shows, women religious have always had and are still continuing to have, their own very specific problems and difficulties in endeavouring to have their independent way of life recognised and accepted by a male dominated church; women's monasticism and the spirituality it has engendered have always been closely allied to frequently controversial issues of gender and sexuality. When seen against the historical backdrop, the tremendous variations in different forms of

---

9. The ascetic life has also traditionally involved the practice of fasting, seclusion and silence, among other things, while prayer, both communal and individual, by night and by day, has always been the essence of monastic life. For a detailed examination of many of these practices in the lives of medieval women, see Caroline Walker Bynum, *Holy Feast and Holy Fast: The Religious Significance of Food to Medieval Women* (Berkeley: University of California Press, 1987).

women's monasticism both historically and across the different
Christian denominations become obvious; and it can be seen
that female monasticism is not a medieval phenomenon limited
to the Roman Church, but has been part of the wider monastic
movement from the beginning and has endured right across the
Christian world from the beginning and is still alive and well
today.[10]

The book begins with two main introductory chapters: the
first analyses early Christian attitudes to women and how these
attitudes have shaped the theological view of women which has
endured throughout the history of the church right down to the
present day; the second examines critically the historical development, analyses the specific character of monasticism and describes the foundation of prayer, specifically the Liturgy of the
Hours,[11] which has given the basic structure to monastic living
for both monks and nuns through the centuries. These two
chapters set the scene and provide an introduction for readers
less familiar with the monastic way of life. The following chapters provide studies of specific monastic women set against the
historical period in which they lived. While I have deliberately
avoided women who were unmistakably atypical (for instance,
Brigid of Kildare[12] and Hildegarde of Bingen,[13] both of whom
have already received substantial attention) the fact that others
were known by name and their lives recorded immediately raises
them out of the vast throng of faceless and unknown nuns who
have lived quiet, faithful and dedicated lives 'hidden with Christ
in God' through the ages. Castelli makes the point vividly:

10. For a fairly popular study of contemporary Anglican religious life
for women, see, for example, I. Losada, *New Habits: Today's Women who
Choose to Become Nuns* (London, Hodder and Stoughton: 1999).
11. This is the prayer, composed mainly of psalms, hymns and readings
from scripture, which is said or sung at regular times during the course
of the day, to consecrate those various times, or 'Hours' to God. It is
also known as the Divine Office, the *Opus Dei*, the Prayer of the Hours
and the Prayer of the Church. See Chapter 2.
12. For a recent study of Brigid, see K. Ritari, 'Saints and Sinners in
Early Christian Ireland: Moral Theology in the Lives of Saints Brigid
and Columba', *Studia Traditionis Theologiae* 3 (Turnhout: Brepols, 2009).
13. For a study of Hildegarde, see F. Beer, *Women and Mystical
Experience in the Middle Ages* (Woodbridge: The Boydell Press, 1992), pp
15-55.

How many women lost their places in the written record of the church because no one chose to write their biographies and because the men whose lives they influenced omitted any record of them? How many exceptional women may have been only mentioned and been otherwise lost without a trace? How many 'ordinary' virgins are absent from the record altogether?[14]

In her paper, she had already commented by way of example that Macrina, the sister of Basil of Caesarea and Gregory of Nyssa, had 'single-handedly converted her worldly brother Basil to asceticism' but that in the whole of Basil's writings 'which comprise four volumes of Migne's *Patrologi* and includes 366 letters' Macrina gets not a single mention.[15]

The second part of the book is more biographical in character. Chapter three focuses on the beginnings of desert monasticism for women and examines the lives of Amma Syncletica, Amma Sarah, Amma Theodora and Mary of Egypt. Their lives demonstrate that, although more secluded and less obviously visible than their male contemporaries, women were not slow to adopt the new way of living the Christian challenge in the deserts of Egypt, Palestine and Syria. However, because they were women, their contribution was regarded with suspicion by the more numerous male monastics. These brief biographical sketches also demonstrate the predilection for the theme of the penitent and converted harlot; another instance of female sexuality needing to be controlled by male ecclesiastical figures and its popular presentation in legend and hagiography.

In chapter four the scene jumps to Rome, and then Asia Minor, and Palestine while looking at Marcellina, the two Melanias, Macrina, Paula and her daughter Eustochium and the late classical world in which they lived. This world and its social and economic upheavals gave inspiration and birth to a very different type of monasticism undertaken by a very different type of woman with a very different type of male influence.

14. E. Castelli, 'Virginity and its Meaning for Women's Sexuality in Early Christianity', *Journal of Feminist Studies in Religion*, Vol 2, No 1 (Spring, 1986), pp 61-88 at p 63.
15. Ibid., p 63. See also S. Elm, *'Virgins of God' The Making of Asceticism in Late Antiquity* (Oxford: Clarendon Press, 1994), pp 82, 83.

Chapter five presents the various social strata from which
women's monasticism was drawn in England, Ireland and Gaul
in the early medieval world – high-born queens such as
Etheldreda and Radegund and right down the social scale to
slave-women too lowly to have their names recorded, and how
monastic life adapted to suit their particular situation.

The colourful society of medieval Europe and the feudal
world, which was being threatened by the rising merchant class,
provide the scenic backdrop for chapter six, while concentrating
on the lives of Clare of Assisi, her own sister Agnes and the
other spirited Agnes, princess of Bohemia, and again shows
how the historical and the social milieux affected the understanding and living of religious life for and by women.

Then in chapters seven and eight the focus is slightly different
in that these chapters concentrate on aspects of the religious life
where women come into their own and can – and have – figured
as largely as men have done – prayer and martyrdom. There is
no male monopoly on either of these areas and women are
found among the ranks of the mystics and the martyrs just as
much as men (probably more of the former). However, in spite
of this, for a woman to be publically recognised in the church as
a mystic or as a martyr, her life had to be validated by the male
hierarchy before she could proceed to either beatification or
canonisation; so the fate of these women – both in this world
and the next – lay in male hands, either those men involved in
the canonisation process or those of the Inquisition.

Chapter seven examines a specific, and sometimes suspect,
way of prayer and looks at the women visionaries and mystics
of the later Middle Ages and the way they wrote about their
spiritual experiences. Many of them were connected with the
Béguines, which was a movement for women who had made no
formal commitment of their lives to God, and thus, strictly
speaking, are outside the parameters of this study. However, as
their visionary experiences had such a widespread and enduring influence on women religious and their spirituality, they
have been included here. This phenomenon of mystical writing
by women is closely allied to changing sociological patterns for
women; Bindoff comments perceptively in his book on Tudor
England:

[I]ndispensable as was their labour in house or field, at the treadle or the spinning wheel, and capable as they might here and there prove in a business career, women were wholly ineligible for public office and for the professions, while those who took religious vows did so as almost the sole alternative to the more customary task of reproducing the species.[16]

However, he goes on to point out that this historical period was a turning point for women, offering opportunities for at least some women which were not to be seen again for another four hundred or so years:

[T]he Renaissance was to stimulate an interest in women's education which was to have no parallel until the nineteenth century.[17]

Although this education was not forthcoming for all women, it did mean that at least some had access to learning which had not been theirs previously, and this consequently had an effect on their way of living the religious life and of passing that life on to those who were to follow them. They were now able to articulate and express their own spiritual experiences, desires and aspirations much more effectively than before.

Chapter eight examines the pattern of martyrdom throughout the history of the church and then comes into more modern times and explores the willingness women monastics have had in recent centuries to become involved with social and political issues and so ultimately lay down their lives for the Christ and his teaching, focusing on two Orthodox nuns, the New Martyr Elisabeth, and Maria Skobtsova.

Then in conclusion, chapter nine departs entirely from the biographical approach and brings the picture right up to date by discussing one major area regarding the evolution of women's monasticism in the present day: that of enclosure, which is an issue fraught with strong feelings, varying theologies and multiple practical interpretations. By tracing the history of the concept of enclosure within the church, this chapter also provides a résumé of the findings of the book up to this point. In almost

---

16. S. T. Bindoff, *Tudor England* (London: Penguin, 1976), p 28.
17. Bindoff, *Tudor England*, p 28.

every one of these chapters, the women involved have had to
struggle to have their way of life approved or even acknowledged by the institutional church. And yet, in spite of this, these
women have seen themselves very firmly as 'women of the
church' even if at times the institution has been slow or unwilling to own them, and has regarded them with suspicion and
(not always without reason) as dangerous, rebellious, innovative, sometimes subversive and – the ongoing problem with
women in the church – a temptation to male virtue. This was no-
ticed by a young woman visiting Rome in the late nineteenth
century; she commented on her experiences as a pilgrim in the
Eternal City thus:

> I still can't understand why it's so easy for a woman to get
> excommunicated in Italy! All the time people seemed to be
> saying: 'No, you mustn't go here, you mustn't go there;
> you'll be excommunicated.' There's no respect for us poor
> wretched women anywhere. And yet you'll find the love of
> God much commoner among women than among men, and
> the women at the Crucifixion showed much more courage
> than the apostles, exposing themselves to insult, and wiping
> our Lord's face. I suppose he lets us share the neglect he him-
> self chose for his lot on earth ...[18]

The young woman expressing herself so forcefully was
Thérèse Martin, the future St Thérèse of Lisieux; she too experienced in her own day the misogynist attitude of clerics in the
church and made her feelings known along with the conclusions she drew about the fidelity of women to the Christ.

The textual material on which this work concentrates is
hagiographical, and focuses on the significance and interpretation in the life of the church of the lives of women saints and
holy women religious down through the ages. And here a warning is necessary: the lives of the saints are not always what they
seem to be. Again it is Castelli who rightly remarks: '[T]o act
under the assumption that these texts portray history as twentieth century scholars understand that concept would be naive.'[19]

18. Thérèse of Lisieux, *Autobiography of a Saint*, trs R. Knox (London:
Harvill Press, 1958), p 176.
19. E. Castelli, 'Virginity and its Meaning for Women's Sexuality in

Put simply, the chief exegetical principle of the student of hagiography is that the lives of the saints tell us far more about the time in which they were written, its mentality, expectations, and conditions, than they do about the time they purport to represent. This is a fundamental principle of hagiography and it is impossible to overstress its importance. George Demacopoulos sums it up neatly when he says: 'Our knowledge of these women is limited by the fact that the *uitae* are the literary constructions of male authors (after the death of their subjects). Though the texts reveal much about what the authors want us to believe, they are unreliable as historical witnesses.'[20] There is a parallel between the hagiographical process and that of the illuminated manuscripts of the Middle Ages, where the artist tells us a great deal about medieval daily life, methods of farming, etc but nothing about the biblical scenes he is actually intending to illustrate. However, bearing this *caveat* in mind, the *Vitae* of these women have been constantly referred to, though used with due care and discretion.

The Roman Breviary as it was in use until the revision of the late 1960s, following Vatican II, contained many of these exaggerated accounts of saints' lives in the lessons for Matins, used quite uncritically. Surely the first prize in the miracle stakes must go to the infant St Nicholas of Myra (celebrated liturgically on 6 December) who was reported to have fasted on Fridays even while still at his mother's breast.[21] Many of these saints were described (predictably) as '*piis parentibus natus*',[22] and to have practised poverty and penance to such an extent that they

---

Early Christianity', *Journal of Feminist Studies in Religion*, Vol 2, No 1 (Spring, 1986), pp 61-88 at p 65.

20. George E. Demacopoulos, *Five Models of Spiritual Direction in the Early Church* (Notre Dame, Indiana: University of Notre Dame Press, 2007), pp 198-199, note 179.

21. '*Nam infans, cum reliquos dies lac nutricis frequens sugeret, quarta et sexta feria semel dumtaxat, idque vesperi sugebat: quam jejunii consuetudinem in reliqua vita simper tenuit*', *Breviarium Romano-Seraphicum, Ex Decreto S. Concilii Tridentini Restitutum (Augustae Taurinorum, MCMXXVI)*, p 972.

22. See, for instance, Blessed Peter of Treja, feastday Feb 20th. *Breviarium Romano-Seraphicum*, p 1153.

only possessed '*unica tunica*'.[23] When the Roman Breviary was renewed in 1974 after the Vatican Council, the choice of hagiographical readings for the Office of Readings was revised according to the following principles:

> In composing the special Propers of the Saints, emphasis should be given to historical truth and to the spiritual benefit of those who read or hear the hagiographical reading. Writings which merely seek to impress should be scrupulously avoided.[24]

This was in accord with the prescriptions of *Sacrosanctum concilium*, the *Constitution on the Sacred Liturgy*, which dictated:

> The accounts of the martyrdom or lives of the saints are to be made historically accurate.[25]

So, again with due care, the hagiographical readings from the Breviary have been a source of information and inspiration, thus illustrating the original purpose of these Lives of holy people, which is to motivate and challenge us as we follow in their footsteps in our Christian living:

> May all that splendid company,
> Whom Christ in glory came to meet,
> Help us on our uneven road
> Made smoother by their passing feet.[26]

It is in this spirit that Christians down the ages have looked to, prayed to and honoured their brothers and sisters in Christ who have gone before them into eternal life as helpers and examples on the road to heaven.[27]

---

23. See, for instance, Blessed Nicholas Factor, feastday Dec. 23rd. *Breviarium Romano-Seraphicum*, p 1020.

24. *The General Instruction to the Liturgy of the Hours, The Divine Office* (London: Collins, 1974), para 167, p lxx.

25. *Vatican, Second Ecumenical Council of the*, A. Flannery ed, (Dublin: Dominican Publications, 1975, 1977), *Sacrosanctum concilium*, para 92 (c), p 26.

26. Hymn, 'The Father's holy ones', © Stanbrook Abbey, *Hymns for Prayer and Praise* (Norwich, The Canterbury Press: 1996), p 504. I owe this reference to a monastic colleague, Mary Paul Clarke.

27. For an early example of the most enthusiastic devotion to the saints and the strong desire to have them as heavenly patrons, see Óengus

In the earliest Christian centuries, the accounts of the sufferings, trials and deaths of the martyrs were written down in
order to be circulated among neighbouring churches.[28] This was
the first hagiographical material. When martyrdom became a
less likely option after the Edict of Constantine in 313 other
ways of attaining holiness had to be sought and another genre of
hagiographical literature became enormously popular: the *passiones* of the martyrs were still treasured but now the *uitae* of the
non-martyred saints were read along with them as other models
of holiness began to be acknowledged.[29] These *uitae* also had
their own strict canons of compilation and interpretation.[30] The
aim was the same in both literary genres: to present the holy
person according to an accepted and stereotyped image, often
with scriptural referents, in order to excite the admiration and
emulation of the readers / hearers, and also to enhance the standing and reputation of the monastery / church / diocese which the
saint had traditionally founded or where the saint was buried
and revered, or which claimed to possess his or her relics.[31]

Many of these saints' *uitae* were originally composed with
the express purpose of being used as readings at Matins (or
Vigils) at the Divine Office (now the Office of Readings) on the
feast of the saint in question. They were written to honour the
saint, to contribute to his or her reputation as a worker of miracles
in answer to prayer and to encourage the listeners to have devo-

mac Óengobann, *Félire Óengusso (The Martyrology of Óengus the Culdee)*,
W. Stokes ed, (London: Henry Bradshaw Society 29, 1905; repr. Dublin:
DIAS, 1984).

28. For martyrdom see E. Ferguson, 'Martyr, Martyrdom' in E.
Ferguson (ed), *Encyclopedia of Early Christianity* (Chicago: St James
Press, 1990), pp 575-580. Also the *Acts* of the various early martyrs,
Ibid., pp 11-12.

29. See P. Brown, *The Cult of the Saints: Its Rise and Function in Latin
Christianity* (Chicago: University of Chicago Press, 1981).

30. The classical study is H. Delehaye, *The Legends of the Saints* (Sociéte
des Bollandistes, 1955, repr. Dublin: Four Courts Press, 1998). This is required reading for anyone with an interest in the *uitae* of the saints.

31. This is a very brief description of what was often a long and com-
plex process; for a more detailed account of this process at work see: T.
O'Loughlin, *Discovering St Patrick* (New York: Paulist Press, 2005); also
K. Jankulak, *The Medieval Cult of St Petroc* (Woodbridge: The Boydell
Press, 2000).

tion to the saint and to pray to him or her. Saints' lives were
written to inspire, to edify, to be imitated, not to provide detailed, critical and historically accurate and verifiable material
about the saint as we understand it today. The reaction of St
Ignatius of Loyola (1491-1556), convalescent after breaking his
leg at the battle of Pampluna, to the lives of the saints which he
had been given to read in lieu of more entertaining material, the
'aimless and exaggerated books about the illustrious deeds of
the famous' to which he was 'very addicted', according to his
biographer, Luis Gonzales, was that intended by the hagiographer: 'What if I were to do what blessed Francis did or what
blessed Dominic did?' And by thus turning these questions over
in his mind, eventually the Society of Jesus was born. Reading
the lives of the saints had changed his whole mentality and his
whole way of life, which was what it was supposed to do.

In the expectations of the medieval mind, saints behaved in
certain very special and quite distinctive ways which had pre-
dictable results. The readers or listeners knew what to expect
from their hagiography. When they read or listened to the lives
of the saints, they wanted to be edified, inspired, impressed, and
challenged to deeds of virtue themselves by the example of the
holy ones. They expected the founders and holy men of their
monasteries to work miracles, to have heavenly visions, to converse with angels, in other words, to be 'different'.[32] In fact, they
took this kind of behaviour for granted. It was what made a
saint a saint.[33] If the relics of the friends of God were still present

---

32. See P. Hunter Blair, *Northumbria in the Days of Bede* (London: 1976,
repr. Felinfach: Llanerch Publishers, 1996), pp 144-145: 'Angels were
sometimes the means by which souls were conveyed to heaven.
Cuthbert, in a setting reminiscent of the shepherds in Palestine, was
watching his master's flocks by night in the hills above the Leader
Water when he saw an angel carrying a souls to heaven 'as if in a globe
of fire' – Aidan's soul as it proved. St Columba was frequently seen in
the presence of angels, whose attendance might on occasion be accompanied by unpleasant consequences if their advice was not promptly
heeded. Columba himself was scarred for the rest of his days by an
angelic scourge, brought upon him by his refusal to obey a command
contained in a book which an angel had given him'.
33. See, for example: J. Bruce, *Prophecy, Miracles, Angels and Heavenly
Lights? The Eschatology, Pneumatology and Missiology of Adomnán's Life of
St Columba* (Carlisle: Paternoster Press, 2004).

among them, they expected that these relics would work miracles, the greater and more impressive the better, in order to prove their superiority over the saints and founders of neighbouring monasteries or towns or cities. And today if we are reading these lives to obtain information about the saint, this is where we have to be very careful. It is one of the axioms of medieval history that works of hagiography are not particularly useful as factual history because that was not what they were written to provide, but they can be extremely valuable as giving us a picture of ideas and ideals, or what the people who lived then were expecting of their saints and holy people. Regarding our own focus, Castelli again remarks: 'The question then is how to use these texts to understand and interpret the experience and meaning of asceticism and virginity for women, and for the culture as a whole.'[34]

So this is simply one of the 'many books on the cult of saints' which Peter Brown declared have 'yet to be written'.[35] With Brown, but with far more truth, I can say: 'Being an essay in interpretation, it does not attempt to replicate the encyclopaedic erudition on which it has drawn with admiration and gratitude.'[36] Although this book remains only a comparatively brief introduction to a vast and complex subject, it has a very full bibliography to enable readers to follow up the material presented and so carry out research further into these various aspects of monastic life as lived by women through the centuries. In this, the present work endeavours to be both a readable introduction for the interested non-specialist and a research tool for the serious student. I am aware that I have left many loose ends, many gaps in the history, many monastic women saints not even mentioned and many questions unanswered and this is not entirely accidental. I hope the reader, and even more so the serious student, will be inspired to fill in those gaps, research the missing saints and find answers to those unanswered ques-

34. E. Castelli, 'Virginity and its Meaning for Women's Sexuality in Early Christianity', *Journal of Feminist Studies in Religion*, Vol 2, No 1 (Spring, 1986), pp 61-88 at p 65.
35. P. Brown, *The Cult of the Saints: Its Rise and Function in Latin Christianity* (Chicago: University of Chicago Press, 1981), p xv.
36. Brown, *The Cult of the Saints*, p xiv.

tions by their own labours. Most of the works referred to have
their own very extensive bibliographies and so they open up the
whole vast subject area of monasticism in the church and the
even vaster area of women's studies.

An explanatory word about the focus of this book: 'monasticism' in the title is to be understood in its very widest sense, and
even then, I am sure, there will be those who take issue with the
inclusion of some of the women who appear in the following
pages, not seeing their lives, or even their own intentions in the
ordering of those lives, to have been 'monastic' in the strict
sense of the term. The nearest I can find to an 'official' definition
of 'monastic life' comes within the document *Verbi sponsa*:

> Monasteries of nuns belong [...] to the venerable monastic
> tradition, expressed in the various forms of the contempla-
> tive life, when they are entirely devoted to divine worship
> and live a hidden life within the walls of the monastery,
> [and] observe papal enclosure.[37]

However, although this is the traditional legalistic and
canonical interpretation of 'monastic life', in this study I understand 'monastic' in the broader, more anthropologically aware
sense used by Robert Hale when he speaks of 'the monastic dimension in every human being, that deepest level at which one
seeks "blessed simplicity", the "one thing necessary". And
hence the insistence that at the heart of the charism of every religious order – whether Franciscan or Dominican or Jesuit or any
other – is the monastic'.[38] All the women in these pages were
seeking this 'one thing necessary',[39] in company with their
prototypes, Mary the mother of the Lord, who 'treasured all
these things and pondered them in her heart',[40] and Mary of
Bethany who chose the better part by sitting at his feet and lis-

---

37. *Verbi sponsa: Instruction on the Contemplative Life and on the Enclosure
of Nuns* (Vatican City: 1999), para 13.
38. R. Hale, 'Monasticism' in P. Sheldrake (ed), *The New SCM Dictionary
of Christian Spirituality* (London: SCM Press, 2005), p 445.
39. For a deeper study, see M. Casey, 'Thoughts on Monasticism's
Possible Futures' in P. Hart (ed), *A Monastic Vision for the 21st Century:
Where Do We Go From Here?* (Michigan, Kalamazoo: Cistercian
Publications, 2006), pp 23-42, esp pp 24, 25.
40. Luke 2:19.

tening to his words,[41] and so I have included them under the monastic 'umbrella', whether they were 'monastic' in the juridical, canonical sense, or not.[42] Perhaps a better definition than the one found in *Verbi sponsa* would be that given by Joan Chittister:

> To live a religious life takes all the life we have. To live a religious life takes the heart of a hermit, the soul of a mountain climber, the eyes of a lover, the hands of a healer, and the mind of a rabbi. It requires total immersion in the life of Christ and complete concentration on the meaning of the gospel life today. It presumes a searing presence.[43]

So religious life is not a life of negativity, of limitation, boundaries to be observed, rules to be kept, but a life of giving with total generosity until it hurts : 'costing not less than everything'.[44] That is how it has been understood and lived by the women in these pages. Sandra Schneiders has her own definition:

> It is a life-movement at the heart of the church which has taken very diverse forms at different periods in church history and is undergoing massive change in our own times.[45]

She goes on to insist, very rightly, that the significance of religious life lies in what it is in its essence because it is a distinctive state of life within the church, and not in what individual religious may actually do in and for the church, however valuable that work may be in itself.

---

41. Luke 10:38-42.
42. See also S. Schneiders, *Religious Life In a New Millennium, Volume 1: Finding the Treasure* (New York: Paulist Press: 2000), p 29: 'Aloneness is the inner structure of the life of the religious just as faithful and fruitful mutuality is the inner structure of matrimony. In this sense all religious life is monastic. This does not imply that ministerial religious life involves lifestyle elements of monastic orders such as cloister, habit or choral recitation of the Divine Office. But all religious life is organised around the single-minded God-quest, the affective concentration of the whole of one's life on the "one thing necessary" which is union with God.'
43. J. Chittister, *The Fire in These Ashes: A Spirituality of Contemporary Religious Life* (Kansas City: Sheed and Ward, 1995), pp 92-93.
44. This is the title of a book by John Dalrymple, published by Darton, Longman and Todd, 1991.
45. S. Schneiders, 'Religious Life: The Dialectic Between Marginality and Transformation', *Spirituality Today*, Winter 1988 Supplement, Vol 40, pp 59-79.

It is a fact of the greatest significance, but one not sufficiently recognised that in the past monasticism, whether for men or for women, has all too often been confused with 'Benedictinism' whereas in fact it is a very much broader phenomenon, and in the long years of its history it has included very many quite disparate ways of living, from that of the total seclusion and extreme penance and asceticism of the eremitical life in the early centuries, to that of highly organised communal living in a large and settled monastic community with a fair degree of security, to that of the pilgrim-monk travelling his lonely road either in order to spread the gospel or in self-imposed exile or to visit far away shrines and holy places, to that of the scholarly academic teaching in the medieval schools, or the later universities. Monastic life for women has had to be more circumscribed because of the imposed requirements of enclosure, but even so, as this book will show, there is still a very broad spectrum of monastic experience witnessed to by women through the centuries.

When teaching on an MA course, I became aware of a gap in the material available: there are vast numbers of academic monographs on many aspects of monasticism and also on the place of women in various historic eras, some of which are included in the bibliographies in the present work, but there was no readily available general introduction for the serious reader or the student. I have been assured by my students that there is a great need for a book such as this, which combines history, theology and spirituality with monastic studies and all from a feminist perspective. My purpose throughout has been both to inform on the situation of women monastics through the centuries and specifically in our own day, and also to stimulate and encourage further research in key areas of monastic life through the Church's history, while introducing the reader to some of the most attractive and inspiring, yet little known, women in the history of the church by giving brief biographies.

My main debt of gratitude to the many religious women who have been an inspiration to me down the years is apparent in the dedication, but I also owe thanks to many friends who have assisted and contributed in ways both large and small. Professor Tom O'Loughlin read an early draft of the book and his trenchant comments produced a much more focused and critical final text. Hilary Bonser also read the early draft and her comments, though kinder, also produced improvements. Frances Teresa Downing read and commented on the chapter on Clare and her wide knowledge of all things clarian saved me from more than a few inaccuracies. My brother, as always a perceptive but gentle critic, added his own observations which I have greatly appreciated and sometimes (after much discussion) used to improve the text. I have found inspiration from conversations with Dr Juliette Day about Melania and other early Roman women. Katy and Bethany Parkin read an early version of the text and made many useful comments. Members of my own community have listened to my theories (usually patiently and sympathetically), looked up obscure references which were escaping me and have been supportive, interested and encouraging at all times. However, whatever mistakes and misinterpretations remain are all my own work and are not to be attributed to these kind friends.

I hope all of these, and other readers, will enjoy reading the finished article as much as I have enjoyed writing it. I hope it reveals the changing, yet ever constant, face of monasticism as lived by women who were ever faithful, but not always submissive, meek or compliant 'women of the church'.

P.M.R.

Feast of St Junia, May 17, 2011

I have chosen Junia's feast on which to date this Introduction, partly for the obvious reason that this is the day on which it was completed, and partly because, although not a monastic woman, Junia stands as a symbol and type of all the religious women who have had their gender ignored and exploited by men down the centuries.

CHAPTER ONE

Early Christian Attitudes to Women – History and Theology[1]

The attitude of Christianity towards women has been ambivalent almost from the time of its inception, and this apparently in contradistinction to the approach of Jesus himself.[2] The new faith brought with it a paradoxical situation in which, because of the importance of the individual in Christian thought, and because of the attitude of Jesus himself towards women, in which he was not typical of the attitudes of his time and people, Christian women began to receive a new respect and a certain independence. We see this in Paul's letters, where he warmly mentions women such as Phoebe (the deaconess of the church in Cenchreae), Prisca, Mary, Junia ('outstanding among the apostles'[3]), Tryphaena and Tryphosa, Julia, the sister of Nereus and Olympas,[4] all of whom have 'worked hard for the Lord'.[5] Yet

---

1. Essential background reading for this chapter is P. Brown, *The Body and Sexuality: Men, Women and Sexual Renunciation in Early Christianity* (New York: Columbia University Press, 1988); also W. A. Meeks, *The Origins of Christian Morality: The First Two Centuries* (New Haven: Yale University Press, 1993).
2. For a study of Jesus' relationship with women, see J. Collicutt McGrath, *Jesus and the Gospel Women* (London, SPCK, 2009).
3. For recent research on this woman, see: E. J. Epp, *Junia: The First Woman Apostle* (Augsburg Fortress Publishers: 2005). Junia has become a focus for gender issues since her name (originally understood to be that of a woman and understood as such by early Christian writers such as Origen and John Chrysostom) was changed to the masculine form 'Junias' in the Middle Ages because it was deemed impossible that a woman should be addressed as 'outstanding among the apostles' by Paul himself. Only in the last thirty years has her name been restored to its original feminine form. See E. J. Epp, 'Junia' in Daniel Patte (ed) *The Cambridge History of Christianity* (Cambridge: CUP, 2010), p 668.
4. See Rom 16: 1-16; also Phil 4: 2-3: 'I appeal to Evodia and I appeal to Syntyche to come to an agreement with each other, in the Lord; and I ask you, Syzygus, to be truly a 'companion' and to help them in this. These women were a help to me when I was fighting to defend the Good News ...'.
5. For a description of the eastern Mediterranean world at the time of

the paradox occurs because, at the same time, the mentality of most of the male thinkers and teachers in the early church retained the patriarchal attitudes of the larger societies to which they belonged. Our familiarity with the gospels lessens our sensitivity to the way in which Jesus is presented as disregarding the laws and customs of his time in order to treat women as equals; in the accounts of his activities women occupied, if not a privileged position, then at the very least a position of equality with the male followers of the Lord. From the gospel texts it appears that he himself had a great respect for women, related to them with freedom, and in this way transcended the narrow prejudices that were current in his immediate society. Both the Synoptic and the Johannine traditions present him as numbering women among his close friends and followers, while Luke presents him as being particularly sympathetic towards women. Some of the best known and most well loved gospel passages and stories are those involving women: Mary and Elizabeth in the nativity stories;[6] the Samaritan woman;[7] the Canaanite woman and her little daughter;[8] Jairus' daughter; the woman with the issue of blood;[9] the woman 'who was a sinner';[10] the women who followed him and 'provided for them out of their own resources';[11] Martha and Mary;[12] the widow of Nain;[13] the widow who gave her last mite;[14] Mary of Magdala and the other women who stood at the foot of the cross with his mother, when the men had fled.[15] Even though they were not believed by men who heard them, women were the first witnesses of the resur-

Paul, particularly the women who worked with him, see J. Taylor, 'St Paul's Missionfield: the World of Acts 13-28' in *Proceedings of the Irish Biblical Association* 21 (Dublin, 1998), pp 9-24. For a fuller study, see W. A. Meeks, *The First Urban Christians: The Social World of the Apostle Paul* (New Haven, Yale University Press, 2nd ed, 2003).

6. Luke 1-2.
7. John 4:1-42.
8. Matthew 15:21-28.
9. Mark 5:21-43.
10. Luke 7:36-50.
11. Luke 8:1-3.
12. Luke 10:38-42; John 11:1-44.
13. Luke 7:11-17.
14. Luke 21:1-4.
15. John 19:25-27.

rection[16] and were present in the Upper room with the apostles and the 'brothers of Jesus'.[17] Women were active with men in the spreading of the gospel throughout Asia Minor, and were addressed by Paul in his letters, by name as his fellow workers. We see from these letters and from the *Didache*,[18] another text which is roughly contemporaneous, that women were actively involved in ministry and had positions of responsibility. They functioned as apostles, prophets and deacons and there is some archaeological evidence from the catacombs that they presided at the Eucharist.[19] Thus, Suzanne Wemple could write:

> Christianity initiated a new era not only in the history of monasticism but also in the history of feminism. Accepted as fully equal to men in their spiritual potential, Christian women could transcend biological and sexual roles and seek fulfilment in religious life.[20]

This infers that Christianity had brought with it a whole new *Sitz-im-Leben* for women and an overturning of gender roles in the society of the day and yet, in spite of this potential, it remained unfulfiled and women were still subject to the current prejudices of that society.[21]

Some of the attitudes of Hellenistic society towards women can be gauged from the opinions of the Greek thinkers they praised as their philosophers and 'men of wisdom'. Aristotle (384-322), for instance, had seen the female state as 'a deformity': in his view woman was a mutilated or imperfect male; while the view of Plato (428/427-348/347) was that 'Woman is the source

---

16. Luke 23:55-24:11; John 20:1-18.
17. Acts 1:12-14.
18. For the most recent study of the *Didache*, see T. O'Loughlin, *The Didache: A Window on the Earliest Christians* (London: SPCK, 2010).
19. See the fresco '*Fractio panis*' in the Greek Chapel in the Catacomb of St Priscilla. D. Irvin, 'The ministry of women in the early church: the archaeological evidence', *Duke Divinity School Review* 45. 2 (1980), pp 76-86.
20. S. Wemple, *Women in Frankish Society: Marriage and the Cloister 500-900* (Philadelphia: University of Pennsylvania Press, 1981), p 149.
21. Essential reading on gender roles, sexuality, virginity, continence and asceticism is P. Brown, *The Body and Society: Men, Women, and Sexual Renunciation in Early Christianity* (New York: Columbia University Press, 1988).

of all evil; her love is to be dreaded more than the hatred of men.'[22] Porphyry of Tyre (234-c. 305?), the Neo-Platonist philosopher, writing to his wife, Marcella, counsels her thus:

> Do not preoccupy yourself with the body, do not see yourself as a woman, since I no longer hold you as such. Flee in the spirit everything feminine as if you had a male body which enveloped [you].[23]

This heavily patriarchal and ambivalent attitude towards women, who were seen to be a source of evil in the world, were regarded with distrust and suspicion, seen as 'unclean',[24] and considered to be a temptation to men, was adopted generally by the fathers of the church. Among these, Tertullian was one of the most condemnatory of women:

> Do you not realise that you are each an Eve? The curse of God on this sex of yours lives on even in our times. Guilty, you must bear its hardships. You are the gateway of the devil; you desecrated the fatal tree; you were the first to betray the law of God; you softened up with your cajoling words the one against whom the devil could not prevail by force. All too easily you destroyed the image of God, Adam. You are the one who deserved death; because of you the son of God had to die.[25]

And John Chrysostom, Archbishop of Constantinople and

22. F. Beer, *Women and Mystical Experience in the Middle Ages* (Woodbridge: The Boydell Press, 1992), p 3.

23. Porphyry, *Ad Marcellam*, quoted in E. Castelli, 'Virginity and its Meaning for Women's Sexuality in Early Christianity', *Journal of Feminist Studies in Religion*, Vol 2, No 1 (Spring, 1986), pp 61-88 at p 74.

24. See U. Ranke-Heinemann, *Eunuchs for the Kingdom of Heaven: Women, Sexuality and the Catholic Church* (London: Penguin Books, 1990), pp 21-27: 'The Ancient Taboo Against Menstrual Blood and its Christian Consequences'. See also C. T. Wood, 'The Doctor's Dilemma: Sin, Salvation, and the Menstrual Cycle in Medieval Thought', *Speculum*, Vol 56, No 4 (Oct, 1981), pp.710-727. Also M. Douglas, *Purity and Danger* (London, Routledge and Kegan Paul: 1966). For Jewish attitudes, see: T. J. Horner, 'Jewish Aspects of the Protoevangelium of James', *Journal of Early Christian Studies*, Vol 12, No 3, Fall 2004, pp 313-335.

25. Tertullian, *De cultu feminarum, Corpus Christianorum, Series Latina*, vol 1, 343.

famous preacher of his day, expressed the problems caused to men by women thus:

> There are in the world a great many situations that weaken the conscientiousness of the soul. First and foremost of these is dealings with women. In his concern for the male sex, the superior may not forget the females, who need greater care precisely because of their ready inclination to sin. In this situation the evil enemy can find many ways to creep in secretly. For the eye of woman touches and disturbs our soul, and not only the eye of the unbridled woman, but that of the decent one as well.[26]

This lack of coherence between the teaching and example of Jesus as presented in the gospels, and that of the church fathers can also be seen in the writings of Jerome, who among others, typified this patriarchal attitude:

> It is not the harlot, or the adulteress who is spoken of; but woman's love in general is accused of being insatiable; put it out, it bursts into flame; give it plenty, it is again in need, it enervates a man's mind, and engrosses all thought except for the passion which it feeds.[27]

These passages from the church fathers and the attitude they reveal, show not only what a threat women's sexuality was seen to be but also show how these writers themselves understood this threat: it interfered with a man's thought processes and thus distracted him from the rational world of the mind which they saw as defining him as a superior 'spiritual' being.[28]

The apogee of this attitude, however, is artistic rather than textual. In Michelangelo's depiction of the Fall on the ceiling of the Sistine Chapel: 'the identification of Eve, or Woman, with evil became so natural in Christian thought that the serpent

26. Quoted in Ranke-Heinemann, *Eunuchs for the Kingdom of Heaven*, p 121. See Chapter VIII: Celibates' Fear of Women, pp 119-125 and Chapter IX: The Suppression of Women by Celibates, pp 125-136 for further examples.
27. Jerome, 'Against Jovinian', quoted in Salisbury, *Church Fathers, Independent Virgins*, p 23.
28. J. Salisbury, *Church Fathers, Independent Virgins* (London: Verso, 1991), p 23.

acquired female features'[29] and in this fresco is clearly depicted as a woman; probably one of the most insulting pieces of art work ever produced.

One of the results of the above-mentioned male assumption that only men are capable of rational thought and thus are superior 'spiritual beings' is the masculinisation of not only religious thought, but also of religious experience.[30] Throughout the centuries of Christian spirituality nearly all theologians have been men, also all confessors, spiritual guides and directors and (until recent times) counsellors. Much spiritual writing has been authored by men. The result of this overwhelmingly masculine influence on the spiritual lives of women has been to inculcate a masculine approach to, and way of living out, the life of the spirit that has all but negated the experience of the women themselves. Sandra Schneiders comments:

Men have taught women to beware of specifically male vices: pride, aggression, disobedience to lawful hierarchical authority, homosexuality, lust and the like. Women have rarely been alerted to those vices to which their socialization prompts them, for example, weak submissiveness, fear, self-hatred, jealousy, timidity, self-absorption, small-mindedness, submersion of personal identity, and manipulation.[31]

That this attitude of male, and especially clerical, superiority was still alive and well in the late twentieth century can be seen from the following passage in which the author was instructing the clergy in their preaching duties:

One must use simple language for the women. Substantives and those difficult compound words which commonly encumber our language should be avoided as much as possible. Technical terms and foreign words must be explained if they cannot be avoided. They are indispensable and self-explanatory for the priest, who is steeped in the classics, but women often do not understand them at all or only imper-

29. M. Warner, *Alone of all her Sex: The Myth and the Cult of the Virgin Mary* (Picador: 1990), fig 8, see p x.
30. S. Schneiders, 'The Effects of Women's Experience on their Spirituality', *Spirituality Today*, Summer 1983, vol 35, No 2, pp 100-116.
31. Ibid.

fectly. They are patient listeners but they are easily intimidated by bombastic expressions. It is unfortunate that women can hardly read the papal encyclicals or learn from them on account of their classical style, or perhaps more so on account of the defective and clumsy translations. Here the priest would have ample material for talks, but he would have to explain and translate everything.[32]

Although giving some recognition to the positive contribution women have made in the history of the church, the general tone of this work is that the place of women is *'Kinder, Küche, Kirche'*.[33] Women are seen as a danger to priestly virtue throughout the book:

He may possibly be ill at ease in the presence of women and girls because women are still a problem for him. He may refuse to associate with women, not because they deserve such treatment, but because he cannot cope with them.[34]

Though published originally in Germany in 1958, this book was translated into English and published in 1964, thus providing evidence that such misogyny was still to be encountered in Catholic life and writing in comparatively recent times; almost unbelievably, it was written by a woman.

So we can see from all this that from the time of influential early Christian writers, often honoured with the title 'fathers of the church', right down to the present day, women have been seen as a danger and a distraction to male virtue and rational thought. The fathers of the church saw it as necessary that they be strictly controlled, and yet on the other hand, women could be praised, as were the scriptural heroines Judith, Ruth and Esther, for saving their people by the sometimes dubious exercise of their sexual attraction. These two strands are inextricably

---

32. O. Mosshamer, *The Priest and Womanhood* (Cork: Mercier Press, 1964), p 250.
33. '... Augustine was the brilliant inventor of what Germans call the three K's (*Kinder, Küche, Kirche* – children, kitchen, church), an idea that still has life in it, in fact it continues to be the Catholic hierarchy's primary theological position on women.' Ranke-Heinemann, *Eunuchs for the Kingdom of Heaven*, p 88.
34. Mosshamer, *The Priest and Womanhood*, p 274.

entangled, even appearing in the same passage, by the same author, showing how complex the scriptural attitude to women is.
For instance, Paul's well-known passage in 1 Cor 11 is very
male-oriented, but after the infamous verse that 'woman was
created for the sake of man', becomes remarkably inclusive:

> A man should not cover his head, since he is the image of God
> and reflects God's glory; but the woman is the reflection of
> man's glory. For man did not come from woman; no, woman
> came from man; and man was not created for the sake of
> woman, but woman was created for the sake of man ...
> However, though woman cannot do without man, neither
> can man do without woman, in the Lord; woman may come
> from man, but man is born of woman, both come from God.[35]

And Paul seems to have practised what he preached in this
passage, as in other letters of his (and his letters are the earliest
New Testament texts we have), we see women actively working
as equals alongside men in Christian mission situations,[36] although the main reason that these powerful women could be so
influential in the church was because they were already women
of means and social status, like Chloe.[37] Some of the houses in
which the first generation of Christians met and worshipped
were owned by women, and out of the twenty-eight people he
greets by name in Romans 16, nine are women.[38] But Paul's
thought on the place of women both in the wider society and in
the more circumscribed structure of domestic life is ambivalent,
and this same ambivalence can also be seen in 1 Peter:

> Wives should be obedient to their husbands ... do not dress
> up for show ... all this should be inside ... the ornament of a
> sweet and gentle disposition, this is what is precious in the

35. 1 Cor 11:7-9, 11, 12.

36. There is a vast bibliography on the place of women in the writing
and thinking of Paul. See, for instance, K. Ehrensperger, *That we may be
Mutually Encouraged: Feminism and the New Perspective in Pauline Studies*
(London: T & T Clark, 2004).

37. 1 Cor 1:11.

38. See E. Clark, 'Women', in E. Ferguson ed, *Encyclopedia of Early
Christianity* (Chicago, St James Press: 1990), pp 940-943. See also entries:
'Deaconess', 'Mary', 'Virgins, 'Widows'.

sight of God ... like Sarah, who was obedient to Abraham and called him 'Lord'.[39]

However, this subservient attitude is immediately super-seded by a much more theologically balanced approach:

> In the same way, husbands must treat their wives with con-sideration in their lives together, respecting a woman as one who, though she may be the weaker partner, is equally an heir to the life of grace.[40]

So there are two contradictory avenues of thought regarding women in those early documents valued by Christians. One sees woman as man's equal, formed to be his complement and his helpmate, equal heir with man to the grace of God and the possibility of salvation; the other sees her as the cause of man's downfall, a perpetual source of temptation and sin, subject to man as her master and lord.[41] Clement even went as far as to say that 'every woman should be overwhelmed with shame at the thought that she is a woman.'[42]

In the early churches, as we see from Paul's letters, the situa-tion seems to have been as follows: there was an initial stage in which women assumed public missionary activity, which is characteristic of enthusiastic new sects throughout the ages. The ministry of hospitality, regarded as eminently appropriate for women, especially widows,[43] was also an opportunity for spreading the good news,[44] and wealthy women opened their houses to the local Christian communities for worship and fel-lowship. Although Paul depicts women as active in the mission and work of the early church in various ways, as time passed,

39. 1 Pet 3.
40. 1 Pet 3.
41. cf 'It was not Adam who was seduced but the woman who was seduced and fell into sin,' 1 Tim 2:14.
42. Quoted in Beer, *Women and Mystical Experience*, p 3.
43. See 1 Tim 5:10: 'She must be a woman known for her good works and for the way in which she has brought up her children, shown hos-pitality to strangers and washed the saints' feet, helped people who are in trouble and been active in all kinds of good works.'
44. See D. Wayne Riddle, 'Early Christian Hospitality: A Factor in the Gospel Tradition', *Journal of Biblical Literature*, Vol 57, 2 (June, 1938), pp 141-154.

their roles were increasingly regulated and curtailed. The ministry of the church was becoming increasingly more formalised with regard to the celebration of the Eucharist and more hierarchic in structure. Also, some early heretical groups gave greater prominence to the role of women and permitted them higher positions of leadership which included teaching and some ritual activity (for example, the Montanist sect[45] hailed two women, Priscilla and Maxima among its founders,[46] and both Montanist and Gnostic groups may have regularly allowed women to baptise and preside at the eucharist[47]). In reaction to this, mainstream Christian women were not allowed to seek such offices. This is seen in a Christian letter from the late first or early second century that claimed Paul as its author:

> Similarly, I direct that women are to wear suitable clothes and to be dressed quietly and modestly, without braided hair or gold and jewellery or expensive clothes; their adornment is to do the sort of good works that are proper for women who profess to be religious. During instruction, a woman should be quiet and respectful. I am not giving per-

---

45. For the Montanist movement, see D. E. Groh, 'Montanism' in E. Ferguson (ed), *Encyclopedia of Early Christianity*, pp 622, 623. See also R. S. Kraemer, *Her Share of the Blessings: Women's Religions Among Pagans, Jews and Christians in the Greco-Roman World* (New York: Oxford University Press, 1992), pp 157-173.

46. For a study of the role of women in Montanism, see F. C. Klawiter, 'The Role of Martyrdom and Persecution in Developing the Priestly Authority of Women in Early Christianity: A Case Study of Montanism', *Church History*, Vol 49, No 3 (Sept 1980), pp 251-261.

47. See E. Clark and H. Richardson, *Women and Religion: The Original Sourcebook of Women in Christian Thought* (San Francisco, HarperCollins; rev ed, 1996), p 23: 'One example of the church fathers' horror at female leadership among the Gnostics is Tertullian's famous outcry: "How bold these heretical women are! They have no modesty; they are bold enough to teach, to argue, to perform exorcisms, to undertake cures and maybe even to baptise!"; also T. Churton, *The Gnostics* (London: Weidenfeld and Nicolson: 1987), p 59: 'As Kurt Rudolph writes in *Gnosis*: The percentage of women was evidently very high and reveals that gnosis held out prospects otherwise barred to them, especially in the official church. They frequently occupied leading positions either as teachers, prophetesses, missionaries or played a leading role in cultic ceremonies (baptism, eucharist) and magical practices (exorcisms).'

mission for a woman to teach or to tell a man what to do. A woman ought not to speak, because Adam was formed first and Eve afterwards, and it was not Adam who was led astray but the woman who was led astray and fell into sin.[48]

Although in almost every other respect seen as inferior to men and subject to their husbands, the one claim which women had to salvation was their function as life-givers and the church saw woman's maternal role as crucial, both for society and for her own eternal salvation. In the later New Testament books, domestic order is encouraged[49] and women were counselled to remain in their traditional submissive roles of wife and mother: 'Nevertheless, she will be saved by childbearing, provided she lives a modest life and is constant in faith and love and holiness.'[50] This childbearing was paralleled with the motherhood of Mary, so women were seen and honoured as givers of life. Mary was held up as a model for all women; as virgin she was an example for unmarried girls; as wife and mother for the married; as widow for the many women whose husbands had been killed in battle and warfare. But this parallel could only go so far, especially for women living in the rough and semi-barbaric world of the early Middle Ages. The church teachers and writers put Mary on the loftiest of pedestals, immaculate from the first moment of her existence, they understood her to have been a virgin before and after the birth of Jesus,[51] assumed into heaven without experiencing the decay of the grave; thus she was set up as a model of behaviour with which no mortal woman could

---

48. 1 Tim 2:9-10.
49. See Titus 2: 3-5: '[T]ell the older women to be reverent in behaviour, not to be slanderers or slaves to drink; they are to teach what is good, so that they may encourage the young women to love their husbands, to love their children, to be self-controlled, chaste, good managers of the household, kind, being submissive to their husbands, so that the word of God may not be discredited.'
50. 1 Tim 2:15.
51. See, for example, St Ambrose: 'Non enim virilis coitus vulvae virginalis secreta reseravit, sed immaculatum semen inviolabili utero spiritus sanctus infudit,' Expos. Luc. 2.56, p. 55: 1654C. Quoted in P. Brown, The Body and Sexuality: Men, Women and Sexual Renunciation in Early Christianity (New York: Columbia University Press, 1988), p 354.

identify, and as an ideal unattainable by any other earthly woman.[52] By definition she was unique.

> [S]ometimes the Mother of God is celebrated as so special, so different, that we lose a sense of her solidarity with us and that is an appalling loss ...The application of Mariology has led, tragically, to certain kinds of encultured trouble. It has seemed at times to promote a particular image of woman which has certain beauties and may provide an idealised image of how men would sometimes like women to be, but assuredly does not carry the total reality of women's lives and their way to God.[53]

Theoretically, Mary was acknowledged by all men as the most perfect expression of womanhood, and yet in practice this did nothing to improve the way in which women in general were regarded and treated. By social custom and in the writings of both laymen and ecclesiastics, the lesser daughters of Eve were condemned to inferior status. Athanasius, Bishop of Alexandria from 328-373, wrote instructions to the virgins under his care, taking Mary as an example, in phrases that would probably elicit amusement rather than edification today:

> Mary was a holy virgin, having the disposition of her soul balanced and doubly increasing. For she desired good works, doing what is proper, having true thoughts in faith and purity. And she did not desire to be seen by people; rather she prayed that God would be her judge. Nor did she have an eagerness to leave her house, nor was she at all acquainted with the streets; rather, she remained in her house being calm, imitating the fly in honey. She virtuously spent

52. Studies of Mary and her place in scripture, theology, legend, poetry, art and the life of the church are innumerable. See M. Warner, *Alone of all her Sex: The Myth and the Cult of the Virgin Mary* (Picador: 1990); E. A. Johnson, *Truly our Sister: A Theology of Mary in the Communion of Saints* (New York; London: Continuum: 2003); M. O'Carroll, *Theotokos: A Theological Encyclopedia of the Blessed Virgin Mary* (Wilmington: Michael Glazier, 1982, 1983), but the list is endless.
53. W. Robinson, 'Mary: The Flower and Fruit of Worship', in J. Behr, A. Louth and D. Conomos (eds), *Abba: The Tradition of Orthodoxy in the West, Festschrift for Bishop Kallistos (Ware) of Diokleia* (Crestwood, New York: St Vladimir's Seminary Press, 2003),pp 193-205, at p 198.

the excess of her manual labour on the poor. And she did not acquire eagerness to look out the windows, but rather to look at the scriptures. And she would pray to God privately, taking care about these two things: that she not let evil thoughts dwell in her heart, and also that she not acquire curiosity or learn hardness of heart. And she did not allow anyone near her body unless it was covered, and she controlled her anger and extinguished the wrath in her inmost thoughts.[54]

So Athanasius saw Mary as humble, piously devout, meek, submissive, pure in body and mind, and controlling her curiosity. According to this understanding of what constituted holiness for a young unmarried woman, he endeavoured to encourage these virtues in the girls under his care, but one wonders how successful he actually was.

In the sermons and various writings of other church fathers, women were also expected to imitate Mary's meekness, her obedience, her humility – all of which, if anything, encouraged the repression and subjection which were their lot. Schneiders remarks:

> The only feminine model who has been invoked with real fervour and consistency in the male church has been Mary, the mother of Jesus, and that invocation has been badly misused in many periods of church history to reinforce and sacralise the subordination and passivity of women.[55]

For example, one of the great marian writers of the church, the Cistercian Bernard of Clairvaux, who is quoted as having said 'De Mariam numquam satis', in his Homilies of the Glories of the Virgin Mother wrote as follows:

> For God this kind of birth was fitting: that he should be born of none other than a Virgin; and such a childbirth was fitting for the Virgin: to bring forth none but God. Man's maker, then, when about to be born of man in order to become man,

---

54. Athanasius, *First Letter to Virgins* [*Epistula virginibus I*], trs in D. Brakke, *Athanasius and Politics of Asceticism* (Oxford: Clarendon Press, 1995), pp 274-291.
55. S. Schneiders, 'The Effects of Women's Experience on their Spirituality', *Spirituality Today*, Summer 1983, vol 35, No 2, pp.100-116.

had to choose, indeed create, a mother for himself from among all such as he knew befitted himself and would be pleasing to him. He therefore willed a virgin to exist without stain, from whom he himself would come without stain, to cleanse away the stains of all. He willed her humble, from whom he was to come forth meek and humble of heart, to show in himself the example of these virtues that for all men was necessary and most healthful. So he granted childbirth to the Virgin when he had already inspired in her the vow of virginity, and had granted her the merit of humility.[56]

Many other theologians also delighted in extolling the glories of Mary's childbearing, and indicated that in this she is a model and example for all women, yet Mary's traditionally virginal bearing of Christ was light years away from the pain, hardship, squalor and real danger experienced by women giving birth in the early Middle Ages. Some actual statistics from Frankish society tell it all: the average age of women at death was about thirty six. More women than men died between the ages of fifteen and thirty nine – 48% of women, compared to 31% of men. Only 39% of women lived to be 40 or over, compared to 57% of men. The highest proportion of men died between 40 and 54; the highest proportion of women between 25 and 39. So obviously, this had a lot to do with women's biological function and the dangers of childbearing.[57] The female ideal emerges, in imitation of Mary as she was seen from the late classical era and the early middle ages onwards, as complete and entire obedience to her father or other close male relative before marriage and in the matter of marriage, and then obedience to her husband once married, when motherhood was the function expected of her. This traditional interpretation of the role of Mary in the plan of salvation and the consequent influence it has had on the place of women in society and in the church is being strongly critiqued today by feminist theologians and a new picture is emerging.[58] At the same time, current New Testament

---

56. Bernard of Clairvaux, *Homilies on the Glories of Mary, Hom 2*, 1-2. 4: *Opera omnia*, Edit. Cisterc. 4 [1966].

57. See Wemple, *Women in Frankish Society*, p 101.

58. See for instance, E. A. Johnson, *Truly Our Sister: A Theology of Mary in the Communion of Saints* (New York: Continuum, 2003).

scholarship, such as the work of American Catholic priest John P. Meier, is more inclined to emphasise Mary's links with our common humanity rather than to denigrate these and place her on an unattainable pedestal, and so takes the 'brothers' of Jesus at their face value rather than resorting to linguistic gymnastics in order to argue that they were his cousins, and consequently sees Mary as having given birth to at least six other children besides Jesus.[59] If traditional Catholic piety, with its belief in Mary's perpetual virginity (*in partu and post partum*) finds this offensive, it should be pointed out that Meier's magisterial work has been granted an Imprimatur (by the Most Rev Patrick Sheridan, VG) – in itself most unusual today – indicating that it contains nothing contrary to Catholic faith and moral teaching, and has even been strongly recommended by the highest authority in the Catholic Church, Pope Benedict XVI himself, in his own work *Jesus of Nazareth*: 'Excellent studies are already available ... [such as] the exhaustive study by John P. Meier, *A Marginal Jew* (4 vols, New York, 1991, 1994, 2001, 2009).[60] Meier's work receives another accolade in the bibliography where Benedict XVI refers to it as 'a model of historical-critical exegesis'.[61]

But this is to look ahead into the far distant future. We can sum up the attitude of the early church to women, and the position of women within that church, by saying that it was complex and anomalous. There were at least two distinct traditions within Christian thinking regarding the place and function of women. One was the tradition of the church as an organised and organising body with strict canons emanating from Synods and Councils, and the influential writings of the church fathers,

---

59. J. P. Meier, *A Marginal Jew: Rethinking the Historical Jesus*, Vol. 1: The *Roots of the Problem and the Person* (New York, Doubleday: 1991), 'Family, Status and Status as a Layman', pp 316-371. See also Johnson's discussion of the three main positions on this issue: Johnson, *Truly Our Sister*, pp.195-199. For the significance of this in a liturgical setting, see T. O'Loughlin, *Liturgical Resources for Advent and Christmastide, Years A, B, and C* (Dublin, The Columba Press: 2006), pp 207-210.

60. J. Ratzinger, *Jesus of Nazareth*, Part Two, *Holy Week: From the Entrance into Jerusalem to the Resurrection* (trs P. J. Whitmore), (London: Catholic Truth Society, 2011), p xv.

61. Ibid, p 296. See also p 302.

which reflected the patriarchal prejudices of the masculine-dominated societies of the Middle Eastern world where Christianity was born and first began to grow. The other was the more prophetic and contemplative tradition, which although it at times got lost in the proliferation of heretical sects and movements condemned by the Councils, still managed to keep alive in mainline Christianity the principle of equality set forth in the gospel.

Olivier Clément claims that the church writers of the Christian East were not as dismissive of women as were those of the West, particularly, as we have seen, Tertullian, Augustine, Ambrose and Jerome. To support this view, he quotes Origen, Gregory of Nyssa and Clement of Alexandria. He refers to the latter as saying:

> Woman has the same spiritual dignity as man. Both of them have the same God, the same Teacher, the same Church. They breathe, see, hear, know, hope and love in the same way. Beings who have the same life, grace and salvation are called ... to the same manner of being.[62]

However, he falls back, unconvincingly, into the classic argument regarding the place of Mary in the plan of salvation being the greatest glory of womankind (and dismisses this in one short paragraph)[63] and so nullifies any possible credibility for his viewpoint. Once again, we have to admit that the position regarding the theological position of women in the writings of the fathers is ambiguous. Regarding the position of the Orthodox Church, which Clément sees as more sympathetic towards women than the West, another Orthodox writer, Elizabeth Behr-Sigel, 'laments the exclusion of women from the development of marian theology'.[64]

For most women, Christianity had little to offer them in the way of greater freedom and progress. The church did not approve of divorce, and second marriages were not sanctioned;

---

62. Clement of Alexandria, *Tutor*, 1, 4 (PG 8,260) quoted in O. Clément, *The Roots of Christian Mysticism* (London: New City, 1993), p 292.
63. Ibid., p 293.
64. E. Behr-Sigel, 'Mary and Women', *Sobornost: Eastern Churches Review* 23 (2001), p 25, quoted in E. A. Johnson, *Truly Our Sister*, p 10.

contraception and abortion were totally rejected. Wives were constantly urged to be obedient and submissive even if husbands were brutal or abusive. We can see that the possibility of a certain qualified emancipation might be present for some Christian women in the choice of religious life, but society was very grudging in the freedom which it gave to its women folk to make this choice. Certain classes of that society, especially the highest and the lowest, had particular difficulty in obtaining this freedom. It was particularly hard for women from the nobility and aristocracy because they were too precious a commodity in terms of their potential for dynastic marriages and bearing sons as future rulers, and for women from the lower social strata of society because they counted for nothing. Men still had almost total control of which women were granted the freedom to gain access to monastic life, and even when the fortunate ones had attained it, their agenda was set in masculine terms. The possibility of holiness and sanctity was not completely denied them but, in accordance with tradition dating from the earliest days of monasticism, this holiness was defined in masculine terms, and in order to attain it, women had to renounce their feminine gender and become 'manly women'. Even within the monastic tradition, where women were accepted, though grudgingly, they were seen as a danger, and one of the earliest monastic writers, Palladius, when he wishes to incarnate diabolical temptation, does it in female form:

> The demon took on the form of an Ethiopian maiden whom I had once seen in my youth gathering papyrus, and sat on my knees. Filled with anger, I gave her a box on the ear and she disappeared. Then for two years I could not bear the evil smell of my hand.[65]

This passage illustrates both the antifeminist and the apparently racist views of early monastic writers and demonstrates the background against which the earliest attempts of women to live the monastic life have to be seen. Another example comes from sixth- or seventh-century Egypt, where, in a fresco in the

---

65. Palladius, *Historia Lausiaca*, trs Robert T. Meyer (London: Longmans, Green and Co, 1965), p 82.

monastery of St Apollo in Bawit, St Sisinnios on horseback transfixes with his lance, a demon in the form of a woman.[66] The attitudes this antifeminism has engendered have persisted throughout the history of the church, as witness the struggles of women religious down to the present day with regard to the (male-authored) legislation by which their lives are still largely governed. Sandra Schneiders states the situation:

> Canon law regarding religious, of whom three out of every four in the church are women, has been formulated by men without the input of the women whose lives it governs, and, in most respects, it is also enforced by men.[67]

There is a fundamental idea of hierarchy present here which is so deeply imbedded in our notion of the sacred that we do not realise how profoundly it influences our theological attitudes and judgements:

GOD

MAN – Adam

WOMAN – Eve

ANIMALS

MATTER

In this context, Schneiders comments: 'God, to women, is man "writ large". Men are God "writ small". God and man belong to the same order of things and from that order, women are excluded.'[68]

66. P. Brown, *The World of Late Antiquity AD 150-750* (London: Thames and Hudson, 1971, 1991), p 100.
67. S. Schneiders, 'The Effects of Women's Experience on their Spirituality', *Spirituality Today*, Summer 1983, vol 35, No 2, pp 100-116,
68. Ibid.

This attitude can be identified in theological writing throughout the history of the church, and still exists today, in spite of the lip service paid to feminine emancipation and the renewed place of women in documents issuing from the Vatican. Bindoff, in his work on the Tudor period, comments on the position of women both at that period and later:

> In Tudor England, as in England down to very recent times, the inequality which affected the largest number of people was not a social, but a sexual one. The woman of the time, whatever her rank in society, was treated as an inferior being, and her freedom of action was restricted at every turn. Prior to marriage she was an infant, to be watched over by parent or guardian. Her marriage, which was normally a business arrangement in which she had no say whatever, converted her into a *feme covert* and submerged her legal personality in that of her husband. Only as a widow could she hope to enjoy something approaching equality with man in the disposal of her person and property.[69]

We shall see all the above situations, in which women figure at a disadvantage, at work in the following pages.

Perhaps one of the most potent causes of the inferior status attributed to women through the centuries is the way the scriptures have been interpreted. Schneiders comments:

> A [...] particularly lamentable effect of male dominance in the area of spirituality has been the partial eclipse of the feminine experience and feminine models in scripture and in the history of spirituality. Women have rarely been encouraged to imitate the great women of salvation history. Rarely is a Eucharistic president, even at a liturgy celebrated by a preponderantly female community, sufficiently sensitive to modify the Eucharistic Prayer's retracing of salvation history in order to call to mind not only Adam but Eve, not only Abraham and Isaac and Jacob but also Sara and Rebeccah and Rachel, not only Moses but Miriam, not only David but Ruth, not only Peter but Mary Magdalene.[70]

69. Bindoff, *Tudor England* , p 28.
70. S. Schneiders, 'The Effects of Women's Experience on their Spirituality', *Spirituality Today*, Summer 1983, vol 35, No 2, pp 100-116.

In scriptural studies the women mentioned in the genealogy in Mt1 have traditionally been seen as sinful, weak and fallen, thus demonstrating how truly the Lord became 'one of us' in that he also had skeletons in his family cupboard. But these women can also be seen as women who had been wronged, or somehow let down or otherwise abandoned by men in a time of great need, and who were strong and feisty – determined to fight with great conviction for what they believed to be theirs by right and so get their lives back 'on track'. Thus Tamar showed up her guilty father-in-law when he ordered her out to be burned; Rahab claimed safety for herself and her family when the city in which she lived was to be razed and its inhabitants slaughtered; Ruth, the young Gentile woman from the land of Moab, set about making a new life for herself and her mother-in-law after they had been left as widows (perhaps the most disadvantaged position for a woman in the ancient world[71]) after the death of both their husbands; and Bathsheba claimed security and their just rights for both herself and her son Solomon. These were strong and decisive women, very different from weak, fragile and sinful creatures as they have traditionally been portrayed. Raymond Brown comments that the first four women in the genealogy: 'had a marital history that contained elements of human scandal or scorn' and yet 'they were enterprising instruments, however, of God's spirit in continuing the sacred line of the Messiah'.[72] As new studies in theology present themselves with a female face perhaps these women from the Old Testament can show the way to a new understanding of what it means to be a faithful, and loyal, but also enterprising, original and fearless, woman of the church.[73]

---

71. See S. Orr, 'Women and Livelihoods in 1st Century Palestine: Exploring Possibilities', *The Expository Times*, 121 (11), 2010, pp 539-547, at p.546: '[The widows] are poor (Mk 12:42) and in distress (Jas 1:27), generally alone and older (1 Tim 5:5,9) and they are exploited by wealthier classes (Mt 23:14, Mk 12:40). These were women at the bottom of the pile socially and economically.'
72. R. Brown, 'The Genealogy of Jesus Christ' (Matthew 1:1-17), *Worship* 60 (November 1986), pp 482-490.
73. See E. A. Johnson, *Truly Our Sister*, pp 221-226.

CHAPTER TWO

The Origins and Significance of Monastic Life

The life of withdrawal from the affairs of everyday society and family life into greater or lesser solitude, including a celibate lifestyle, for religious reasons, which we have traditionally called 'monasticism' already had a long history before Christianity came into being. There have been, since time immemorial, men and women whom we could designate with the terms (Christian in origin) of 'monks' and 'nuns' both before and outside Christianity. David Knowles says: 'What we may agree to call the monastic life has appeared in several of the major religions of civilised man, and is therefore a common human response to deep moral and spiritual aspirations'.[1] It is a phenomenon which has existed throughout the centuries and in many different cultures and religions and has usually involved such ascetic practices as voluntary celibacy, fasting and abstinence from meat and other animal products and strong alcoholic drink, solitude, contemplation, shortened and/or broken hours of sleep for the sake of greater prayer, manual labour and a generally simplified, austere and disciplined way of living. The first specific reference to a monk in the Christian tradition dates to 324 in an Egyptian papyrus document, although Antony of Egypt (c. 251-356) is credited by Athanasius in his *Vita Antonii* with being the first monk. Athanasius depicts Antony as seeking advice from an 'elder' and also from others who were living ascetic lives in the neighbourhood of their own villages and as placing his younger sister in a community of virgins to be cared for when he set off for the desert, so these details in his *Vita* (if

---

1. D. Knowles, *Christian Monasticism* (London: Weidenfeld and Nicolson,1969), p 9. Essential background reading for this chapter are: P. Brown, *The World of Late Antiquity AD 150-750* (London: Thames and Hudson, 1971, 1991); P. Brown, *The Cult of the Saints: Its Rise and Function in Latin Christianity* (Chicago: University of Chicago Press, 1981); P. Brown, *The Body and Sexuality: Men, Women and Sexual Renunciation in Early Christianity* (New York: Columbia University Press, 1988).

plausible) show that there were already both monastic communities, male and female, and solitaries in existence before
Antony.

'*Monachos*' – 'monk' comes from the Greek word '*monos*' –
'alone' and while it sometimes was the equivalent of 'hermit' or
'solitary' it also referred to the monk's single-minded focus on
God and the consequent marginality required in relation to 'the
world', as well as the state of celibacy which has nearly always
been linked to the monastic way. A monk lived 'alone' in every
sense. These men and women deserted the towns and villages in
such numbers that one commentator has remarked: 'Many have
wondered at the explosion of Egyptian monasticism during the
fourth century.'[2] Athanasius himself in his *Vita Antonii* says that
'the desert became a city', from which Derwas Chitty took the
title of his classic work on early monasticism.

The traditional explanation of the origin of Christian monasticism is as follows: two main influences in its inspiration were
the delay in the second coming of Christ, and the increasing success and spread of Christianity.[3] In the second and third centuries, before Christianity became a *religio licita* under Constantine,
martyrdom was seen as the ultimate expression of Christian
commitment. The martyr chose death rather than conform to the
Roman and pagan way of life. With the peace that ensued in the
fourth century and the cessation of persecution, there was a
great influx of new members into the church – it became fash-
ionable to be a Christian – and there was a lowering of standards, which was seen by some as a compromise with and a con-
forming to the ways of the world. Contemporary society witnessed 'the swift transformation of the Christian church from a
persecuted and fervent sect into a ruling and rapidly increasing

2. George E. Demacopoulos, *Five Models of Spiritual Direction in the Early
Church* (Notre Dame, Indiana: University of Notre Dame Press, 2007), p 46.
3. For the received version, see D. J. Chitty, *The Desert a City: An Introduction
to the Study of Egyptian and Palestinian Monasticism under the Christian
Empire* (New York: St Vladimir's Seminary Press: 1999); C. Marmion, *Christ
the Ideal of the Monk: Spiritual Conferences on the Monastic and Religious Life*
(Herder: 1926), also J. Ryan, *Irish Monasticism, Origins and Early
Development* (Dublin: Talbot Press, 1931, repr. Dublin: Four Courts Press,
1992); D. Knowles, *Christian Monasticism* (London: Weidenfeld and Nicolson,1969).

body, favoured and directed by the emperor',[4] and saw the great material and social advantages which were obtained by adhering to this body. In this new environment, the monastic life developed partly as a statement against society's growing compromise with the ways and standards of 'the world'. According to this view, the monastic replaced the martyr as the Christian hero, he/she was the one who chose to die to a secular lifestyle by his/her commitment to a life of austerity, sexual renunciation and solitude. This is the view expressed by Sebastian Brock:

> [T]he ascetic is in many ways the successor of the martyr. To the early church the martyr represented an ideal, and after the end of the persecutions, when this ideal was no longer attainable, it was replaced by that of the ascetic, whose whole life was in fact, often regarded in terms of a martyrdom ...[5]

So these men and women became the earthly embodiment of the heavenly communion of saints, especially those who had been martyred and thus shed their blood for Christ. In fact for some, their status even exceeded that of the martyrs, because the martyr suffered only once and for a short, sharp moment, but for the ascetic, the battle was long drawn out and lifelong. This parallelism goes a long way to explaining the high regard the early church had for the relics both of the ascetics and of the martyrs. As in the attitude of the ascetics, the body is the site of Christian warfare; combat and athletic endeavour are frequently used images, but this time the bodies of the combatants – the martyrs – are holy and sacred and contact with their remains – their relics – brings an increase in holiness to the devotee.[6]

The respect paid to the ascetics as holy men and women of God gave them a certain authority in popular eyes – among the ordinary people – and this became a source of concern to the ecclesiastical authorities, who wanted to bring them under their

---

4. Knowles, *Christian Monasticism*, p 12.

5. S. P. Brock, 'Early Syrian Asceticism,' *Numen* 20 (1973), p 3. See Castelli, 'Virginity and its Meaning for Women's Sexuality in Early Christianity', p 67 for further references.

6. See W. A. Meeks, *The Origins of Christian Morality: The First Two Centuries* (New Haven: Yale University Press, 1993), p 145.

own control. Initially these men and women who sought a more austere way of life in contrast to the 'softening up' (as they saw it) of the Christian ideals, lived their chosen way of life within their own homes or on the outskirts of their villages. But more radical forms of asceticism became popular and these seekers after God left the comparative comfort and the security of the towns and the cities and sought God under the direction of a chosen spiritual father or mother in the desert. This frequently involved living a life of often extreme hardship: many of these ascetics were quite eccentric, and some even seem to have been psychologically unbalanced.[7] Men and women went out into the desert for a twofold purpose: to seek the face of God in the place made sacred by memories of the journeyings of the Children of Israel and their encounters with God. They believed they had been called out of the luxury and idolatry of Egypt and their religious traditions said he was to be found in the desert wilderness. And, apparently in contradiction to this, but in actual fact a very real connection was soon discovered, to do battle with the devil in the waste and empty place that tradition said belonged in a special way to the power of evil, where the devil could be found and fought with nothing to distract the spiritual warrior – the Athlete of God. Elm describes the motivation of these desert warriors graphically:

> The world inhabited by the Desert Fathers is unique in its starkness. It was a world of constant, relentless battle, of ceaseless resistance against the sheer overwhelming force of the environment, as well as the equally ceaseless resistance against the demons that assailed the 'inner man'. The desert was the ultimate arena, where the true athletes fought to achieve the *'imitatio Christi'*.[8]

This is the standard explanation for the phenomenon of monasticism and the view of traditionalist writers such as David

---

7. J. E. Goehring, 'Monasticism' in E. Ferguson (ed), *Encyclopedia of Early Christianity* (Chicago, St James Press: 1990), pp 612-619. Also J. M. Wooding, 'Monasticism' in C. Snyder (ed), *Early Peoples of Britain and Ireland, An Encyclopedia* (Oxford: Greenwood World Publishing, 2008), pp 395-402.
8. Elm, *'Virgins of God' The Making of Asceticism in Late Antiquity* (Oxford: Clarendon Press, 1994, p 256.

Knowles,[9] and also even of recent feminist writers such as Elizabeth Castelli and Ross Kraemer. Their argument is that the exhortation to asceticism with its emphasis on celibacy and virginity are present in the Christian tradition from the very beginning. Castelli is unequivocal:

> The roots of asceticism lie at the very heart of the Christian tradition, in Jesus' more radical exhortations on the requirements of discipleship and in Paul's advice to early Christian communities to follow his example of the celibate life so as not to detract from preparation for the coming kingdom of God.[10]

However, this explanation of the origins of asceticism has to be seen in the context of the early Christian expectation of the immediate eschaton, as Castelli herself points out when she speaks of the 'eschatologically motivated words of Paul'.[11] Kraemer questions why 'sexual asceticism was so prominent an aspect of early Christianity' and agrees with Castelli in saying that Christian asceticism is 'a logical extension of earliest Christian belief in the imminent end of the universe as they knew it, which rendered normal social relationships, particularly marriage and childbearing, more or less irrelevant'.[12] They find the inspiration for monasticism and its attendant sexual asceticism in the teaching of Jesus as presented in the gospels and in the letters of Paul. However, other writers, such as John P. Meier, place Jesus in his context as a first-century Jew and argue that it would have been unjustifiable to find in his teaching an appro-

---

9. D. Knowles, *Christian Monasticism*, p 11: '[E]arly apologists of monasticism were justified in holding that the spiritual ideal was as old as Christianity, and was based upon the teaching of Christ. They could point to the call of Jesus to the young man ... and those other words in which he spoke of those who made themselves eunuchs for the kingdom of heaven.'
10. E. Castelli, 'Virginity and its Meaning for Women's Sexuality in Early Christianity', *Journal of Feminist Studies in Religion*, Vol 2, No 1 (Spring, 1986), pp 61-88, at p 65.
11. Castelli, 'Virginity and its Meaning for Women's Sexuality in Early Christianity' p 66.
12. R. S. Kraemer, *Her Share of the Blessings: Women's Religions Among Pagans, Jews and Christians in the Greco-Roman World* (New York, Oxford University Press: 1992), p 139.

bation of celibacy / virginity, which would have been completely contrary to Jewish thought and practice at the time.[13]

Because traditionally, specifically Christian monasticism and its attendant sexual asceticism have been seen as finding their inspiration in the words and example of Jesus (Mt 19:10-12), I will analyse this saying at greater length, using arguments put forward by Meier in his work *A Marginal Jew*. In Matthew 19:12 Jesus declares that there are 'eunuchs who have made themselves that way for the sake of the kingdom'. Meier discusses the whole question of Jesus' marital status at length,[14] and in the process, faces the possibility that 'this saying was created by the early church to justify a state of voluntary religious celibacy among some of its members'.[15] However, he concludes that:

> In fact, so striking, indeed shocking and violent – and so un-paralleled in 1st century Judaism or Christianity – is the imagery of a religious celibate as someone who "eunuchizes" himself for the kingdom of heaven that one might argue, by the criteria of embarrassment and discontinuity, that this offensively graphic metaphor for celibacy goes back to the unconventional and shocking Jesus.[16]

Meier suggests that the saying finds its context in slurs cast by his enemies and detractors on Jesus' own single way of life; his 'total, all consuming commitment to proclaiming and realising the kingdom of God'.[17] So what has traditionally been interpreted as a general exhortation by Jesus to a celibate way of life should more accurately be seen as his own self-defence against criticism levelled at his personal lifestyle. So although a celibate way of life was not ruled out in the earliest strata, nowhere is this ascetical practice promoted as some kind of 'ideal state' in some way superior to marriage and family life, which were seen as the accepted norm for the Christian.[18]

13. J. P. Meier, *A Marginal Jew: Rethinking the Historical Jesus*, Vol 1: *The Roots of the Problem and the Person* (New York, Doubleday: 1991).

14. Meier, *A Marginal Jew*, pp 332-345.

15. Meier, *A Marginal Jew*, pp 342-343.

16. Meier, *A Marginal Jew*, p 344.

17. Meier, *A Marginal Jew*, p 342

18. Mk 10:6-9.

The other classic New Testament passage used to justify celibacy is that of Paul in 1 Cor 7. However, Paul acknowledges that he has no teaching from the Lord on the matter of virginity, and says that what he gives is his own opinion. He writes that the unmarried man or woman has more opportunity to attend to the things of the spirit. He also wishes that 'all could be as he himself', i.e. celibate, but Paul's marital status, including his possible widower-hood, has been the object of much discussion.[19] His first letter to the Corinthians with its strictures on marriage has to be read with Paul's expectation of an immediate eschaton in mind; if the Parousia was imminent then marriage, procreation, child-rearing and their attendant cares and worries were irrelevant.[20] All the above mentioned texts have to be read against the early Christian expectation of the imminent return of Jesus and the end of this world order. Castelli poses the question to which we now wish to formulate a new answer: 'How did the eschatologically motivated words of Paul and the historical exigencies of the early centuries of the common era combine to produce an ascetic ideology and practice virtually unheard of in antiquity and certainly never before practised by such large numbers of people representing such a spectrum of society?'[21]

The classic explanation of the concept of monasticism in the sense outlined above, with its emphasis on severe asceticism and sexual renunciation to be found in the teaching of Jesus and Paul, is frequently portrayed as an inheritance from Judaism, and the Qumran community has often been cited as an example of quasi-monastic life in pre-Christian Judaism.[22] However, Qumran, rather than representing mainline Judaism, was an

---

19. See J. Murphy-O'Connor, *Paul: A Critical Life* (Oxford: OUP, 1996), pp 62-65.
20. Will Deming makes a full examination of the whole issue of Paul's attitude to marriage and celibacy against the Hellenistic background: W. Deming, *Paul on Marriage and Celibacy: The Hellenistic background of 1 Corinthians 7* (Cambridge, CUP, 1995).
21. E. Castelli, 'Virginity and its Meaning for Women's Sexuality in Early Christianity', p 66.
22. See P. Brown, *The Body and Sexuality: Men, Women and Sexual Renunciation in Early Christianity* (New York: Columbia University Press, 1988), pp 36-40.

isolated Jewish sect intent on maintaining its distance from the 'impure'. Wayne Meeks describes the separatist Essene attitude:

> The monastic, hierocratic community at Qumran used yet more rigorous practices to assure their purity and to reinforce their separation, already accomplished spatially by withdrawal into the wilderness, from the world of the Prince and the children of Darkness.[23]

For the Jews, the notion of sexual renunciation had no basis in Jewish thought and practice and to be unmarried or childless was to be under 'a reproach'[24] which was shameful and a disgrace, while marriage was God's greatest gift.[25] Having reviewed several passages in the Old Testament, Jerome Kodell remarks:

> The Talmud reflects the rabbinic doctrine that refusal to marry was considered a sin. 'One who does not marry is like a person who sheds blood': he refuses to transmit the life within him.[26]

Other writers, such as Maryanne Cline Horowitz, concur with this:

> [F]or the rabbis there was no dispute that marriage was the proper state of the human species ... The command to procreate was important, for it led to the perpetuation of beings in the image of God ... A Mishnah said, 'A man shall not abstain from the performance of the duty of procreation of the race unless he already has children.'[27]

She goes on to show that by the Middle Ages a Jewish man

23. W. A. Meeks, *The First Urban Christians: The Social World of the Apostle Paul* (New Haven, Yale University Press: 2nd ed 2003), p 97.
24. Luke 1:25.
25. See D. Cohn-Sherbok, *Judaism: History, Belief and Practice* (London: Routledge, 2003), pp 538-543.
26. J. Kodell, 'The Celibacy Logion in Matthew 19:12', *Biblical Theology Bulletin*, Feb 1978, vol 8, No 1, pp 19-23.
27. M. C. Horowitz, 'The Image of God in Man: Is Woman Included?' *The Harvard Theological Review*, Vol 72, No 3/4 (Jul-Oct, 1979), pp 175-206, at p 188.

was obliged to beget both a son and a daughter so that 'male and female he created them' might be repeated in every generation.[28]

So the Christian acceptance and development of monasticism with its insistence on celibacy can be said to be the unconscious and uncritical importation of an ideal of holiness that was Hellenistic rather than Jewish. There were various attitudes towards the body in early Christianity. Judaism had always had a high regard for marriage as sharing with God in the act of creation, and Christianity inherited this ideal. In the first century, mainstream Christians regarded those who rejected marriage as heretical. They maintained the Jewish notion that procreation was a participation in God's own act of creation and was therefore good and holy. Early Christian writers, too, rejected those who rejected marriage and regarded them as heretical.[29] In Jewish thought the day of a man's marriage was the greatest day of his life. This is reflected in the story of the marriage feast at Cana,[30] and other references to marriage and weddings in the gospels.

Hellenistic culture, on the other hand, supported an ideal of sexuality which was very different from that of Judaism:

> [T]he doctors hastened to add a significant note of caution for the male ... Frequent sexual activity was frowned upon. It decreased the fertility of the male seed and hence the father's chance of children ... The most virile man was the man who had kept most of his vital spirit – the one, that is, who lost little or no seed.[31]

Philosophers such as Plato and doctors such as Soranus and Galen taught that sexual activity was dangerous to health: 'Men who remain chaste are stronger and better than others and pass their lives in better health.'[32] The Stoics taught that the only

---

28. M. C. Horowitz, 'The Image of God in Man: Is Woman Included?' p 189.
29. 'They forbid marriage and prohibit foods which God created to be accepted with thanksgiving'. 1 Tim 4:3.
30. John 2:1-11.
31. Brown, *The Body and Sexuality: Men, Women and Sexual Renunciation in Early Christianity*, pp 18-19.
32. Brown, *The Body and Sexuality: Men, Women and Sexual Renunciation in Early Christianity*, p 19. See also Ranke-Heinemann, *Eunuchs for the Kingdom*, p 10. See the whole Chapter, pp 9-20.

valid reason for sexual intercourse was to produce offspring.[33]

The first century Christian critique of celibacy as heretical which we find in scripture[34] is the early suspicion of this Hellenistic ideal; the Gnostics in particular, having a dualistic concept of creation, saw celibacy and the rejection of the 'works of the flesh' as good and were therefore opposed by mainline Christians.[35] However, as awareness of the difference between Christianity and Greek culture subsided, so celibacy and virginity became gradually more and more acceptable, eventually becoming seen as a 'higher' state than that of marriage. The idea that marriage and sexuality are inferior states before God stems from writers such as Jerome and Augustine, who relegated married Christians to the rank of second class citizens in the kingdom of God. Thus 'the body', and specifically sexuality, came to be seen as dangerous to the life of the spirit; the Christian life was understood as waging war against 'the passions'. The arguments in favour of celibacy and virginity were undergirded by a body/spirit dualism which owed much to Gnosticism where the body was seen as 'bad' and the spirit opposed this as 'good'. Throughout the Hellenistic tradition, which encompassed both Gnosticism and Stoicism, there was a persistent suspicion of the body which was deeply influential in the Christian ascetic tradition of virginity and celibacy. Harriet Luckman comments:

> Celibacy was by no means a universally accepted lifestyle in the early Christian communities. Documents reveal the ongoing struggles within these communities concerning the practice which in the early Jewish/Christian world was seen as contrary to the commandment of God to go forth and multiply.[36]

These opposing views of marriage and virginity, Jewish and Greek, can be seen in the parallel myths of Jephthah's daughter

---

33. Brown, *The Body and Sexuality: Men, Women and Sexual Renunciation in Early Christianity*, p 21.

34. See 1 Tim 4:3.

35. For Gnosticism, see P. Perkins, 'Gnosticism' in E. Ferguson (ed), *Encyclopedia of Early Christianity* (Chicago: St James Press, 1990), pp 371-376; also T. O'Loughlin, 'Gnosticism' in P. Sheldrake (ed) *The New SCM Dictionary of Spirituality* (London, SCM Press: 2005), pp 323-325.

36. H. A. Luckman, 'Celibacy' in P. Sheldrake (ed) *The New SCM Dictionary of Spirituality* (London, SCM Press: 2005), pp 182-182.

and Agamemnon's daughter, Iphigenia. In the first story,[37] Jephthah had been victorious in battle over the Ammonites, and in thanksgiving, vowed to offer to God in sacrifice whatever or whoever came out of his house to greet him on his victorious return. He was met by his only daughter, and in fulfilment of his vow, he offered her to God as a sacrifice, her only request being that she should be allowed time to go into the mountains and 'bewail her virginity'. In this harsh story, virginity is seen as a temporary, unfulfilled state, and to die a virgin is a misfortune, to be 'bewailed' and mourned.[38] On the other hand, in Homer's story of Iphigenia, Agamemnon deliberately sacrifices his virgin daughter in order to appease the gods, asking them to grant him fair winds for his ships to sail for Troy and join in the Trojan war. When the blood of his virgin daughter is spilt and her body is burned on the funeral pyre, the rising smoke is seen to be blown by the wind – the gods are pleased with the virgin sacrifice and grant his request for favourable winds so that even nature approves of the virgin sacrifice. In this equally harsh epic, virginity is seen as pleasing to the gods and as necessary for obtaining their favour. It is this second interpretation which found its way into Christian thought via Jerome and his love for classical literature and has influenced Christian theology and spirituality ever since.

The whole phenomenon of the appearance of monasticism and its popularity since its inception through the centuries raises many questions. Can we derive monastic life from the teaching of Jesus, and/or from first century texts? Is monastic life, with its emphasis on asceticism and a world-denying spirituality, in accord with the nature of the incarnation, which declares everything created to be holy? Jewish scholars sometimes remark that they appreciate the sacredness of matter as created by God, whereas Christians by-pass matter in pursuit of the sacred. However, if the nature of the incarnation is the affirmation of the materiality of the creation and the affairs of this present world as the place of the revelation of the divine, then how can

---

37. Judges 11.
38. For a study of Jephthah's sacrifice see: E. Fuchs, 'Marginalization, Ambiguity, Silencing: The Story of Jephthah's Daughter', *Journal of Feminist Studies in Religion*, Vol 5, Pt 1, 1989, pp 35-45.

'leaving' that domain for the sake of greater holiness be justified? How can we justify monasticism as a system which was inspired largely by Greek rather than Christian philosophy? These are complex issues to which we do not have satisfactory or even fully adequate answers. Brown remarks: 'We know very little about the origins of the ascetic movement in its Near Eastern background, but enough to suspect any simple answer.'[39]

However, perhaps a partial answer with relevance for this present study of specifically female monastic life, is that until the twentieth century, apart from royal and aristocratic ladies, women were largely excluded from the affairs of 'the world', which was seen as the masculine domain, so in adopting a monastic way of life, women were simply living out in a more specifically religious way, the confined and circumscribed lifestyle that was already theirs. This would give a partial explanation to the paucity of female religious vocations in latter years, as women now take their place fully alongside men in all the social, economic, academic and professional aspects of life. So apart from the very few women who, by reason of birth, breeding or brains, left their mark on the pages of history, religious women lived the same obscure, secluded, hardworking lives in the cloister that they would have lived in their farms, villages or small towns had they not chosen the monastic life, the only difference being that they were freed from the constant child-bearing and rearing that has been the lot of most women through the centuries. Sheena Orr identifies 'a range of possible activities', which were open to Jewish women in biblical times that were probably typical of women's work in most traditional societies. They include 'bread-making, weaving, flax spinning, handicrafts, harvesting, fruit-picking and hairdressing' and also quasi-medical procedures such as assisting in childbirth, knowledge of plants and herbs and medicines.[40] Thus for the monastic women whose lives are examined in these pages, no matter how high-born they might have been in secular society, to take on manual labour, as well as being a practical necessity for earning

---

39. P. Brown, *The World of Late Antiquity AD 150-750* (London: Thames and Hudson, 1971, 1991), p 100.
40. See S. Orr, 'Women and Livelihoods in 1st Century Palestine: Exploring Possibilities', *The Expository Times*, 121 (11), 2010, pp 539-547, at p 541.

their living, became an expression of the new and lowly way of life they had adopted. So, for instance, Macrina took on the work of slave girls by baking bread. Elm describes the significance of this gesture thus:

> Macrina's life had taken a new turn: she began to bake her mother's bread with her own hands. By the mere quality of this work, even if its quantity may have been negligible, Macrina took a conscious step to humble herself considerably before those who were in a position to observe her, and perhaps most of all in her estimation of herself. By baking her mother's bread she engaged in work strictly reserved for slaves. This act of servitude, though it may appear small enough to us, must have had a significant impact on those who knew her.[41]

By this action, Macrina showed that in adopting the monastic life she had broken the rigid social structures of the time and had deliberately chosen to abandon her prestigious rank in order to identify herself with the lowliest strata of society.

We now have to look at that life in more detail: for those who chose the monastic way of life, or had it chosen for them – what did it entail?

Although in so many ways similar to that of their brothers and sisters who remained at home in their villages, there were two aspects of this way of life that marked it out as different: one was living according to a strictly organised rule of life, passed on from the holy man or woman who had founded the particular monastic house, and the other was that of regular prayer at specific and set times of the day and night. We will look at both of these in more detail, as they form the backbone of the religious life lived by all the women whose lives figure in the following pages.

The monastic rules that have come down to us from the early period are a very varied collection: they range in comprehensiveness from a few disconnected precepts to scrupulous directives covering many aspects of both individual and collective behaviour. The reasons for this variety can be traced back to the

---

41. S. Elm, *'Virgins of God' The Making of Asceticism in Late Antiquity* (Oxford: Clarendon Press, 1994), p 46.

basic function of the written rule – it was never meant to stand alone or to act as a substitute for the authority of the abbot or abbess to decide the norms of common life in the monastery. A religious Rule, such as that attributed to Benedict or Columbanus, upholds or prescribes an idealised situation: 'This is what you are required to do'. It sets out the ideal required of those who profess it according to the vision of the saint or holy person who is credited with having founded the Order.[42] Most rules deal with abstracts and generalities, in other words, 'the religious/monastic ideal'.

The earliest monastics did not order their lives according to specific written instructions; those who went out into the desert frequently went in order to find a 'spiritual father' who would guide them on their religious quest, and the wisdom they sought from these elders was passed on by word of mouth and by example from mentor to disciple. This oral teaching was eventually set down in compilations such as the *Apothegmata Patrum*.[43] With the development of the cenobitic monastic life,[44]

---

42. cf The beginning of the Regula of St Clare of Assisi: 'The form of life of the Order of Poor Sisters which the Blessed Francis founded is this: to observe the Holy Gospel of our Lord Jesus Christ, living in obedience, without anything of one's own, and in chastity', R. J. Armstrong, *Clare of Assisi, Early Documents*, (New York: Paulist Press, 1988), p 62.

43. 'Sayings of the Fathers': a collection of wisdom sayings and anecdotes dating from the late 5th century, but enshrining the traditional teaching of the early desert fathers on aspects of prayer, asceticism and virtue. The alphabetical collection presents approximately 1,000 sayings of 130 spiritual fathers and has been highly influential on later monasticism down to the present day. See Elm, *'Virgins of God' The Making of Asceticism in Late Antiquity*, pp 255, 256.

44. In a coenobium (from Greek *koinos bios*, 'common life') the monks lived in a single complex of monastic buildings and so in much closer proximity to each other than in a *laura* (a group of cells separate from and yet close to each other) or a hermitage (an isolated monastic dwelling), and their way of life was more strongly communal; the Office was said in common and meals were eaten together daily; a superior provided both spiritual and temporal guidance for the monks, and eventually clear directives evolved for entry into and then full admission to the community. See A. Donahue, 'Cenobites', in *New Catholic Encyclopaedia* 3 (Washington: 2003 [second ed]), p 334, and J. Gribomont, 'Cenobitism' in *New Catholic Encyclopaedia* 3, pp 334-5. Also Smith and Cheetham, *A Dictionary of Christian Antiquities*, pp 401-2.

where sometimes hundred of monks lived together in community, more specific and detailed regulations were found to be
necessary for the peaceful and smooth running of daily life.
Pachomius (c. 292-346) has been traditionally regarded as the
originator of cenobitic monastic life and has been credited with
compiling the first rule for communal monasticism.[45] Having
been born into a pagan family, he was conscripted into the army
in Egypt where he experienced a very harsh way of life as a
young soldier. He eventually became a Christian after experi-
encing the kindness of a Christian couple and was baptised in
the village of Chenoboskion where, sometime later he became a
hermit and lived the ascetic life under the direction of his spiritual guide, Apa Palamon. After some years, he built his first
monastery at Tabennesi, as he believed, in answer to a divine
command and after some initial difficulties it prospered, so that
eventually other communities sprang from this first one. By the
time Pachomius died, in 346, he was the head of a confederation
of nine men's monasteries and two houses for women.[46] In his
Rule, he demanded complete obedience to the abbot. Knowles
comments on the different understanding of obedience in the
eremitic and the communal forms of monastic life:

> While the hermit obeyed an elder as one more spiritually
> wise and experienced, the Pachomian monk obeyed his
> superiors as the disposers of his life and energies, and re-
> garded the consequent abandonment of personal choice as a
> spiritual gain of the first importance.[47]

However, although Pachomius put great emphasis on strict
obedience, his attitude to asceticism was not overly harsh.
Knowles again:

> In daily life the regime of the monastery was moderate in

---

45. See Elm, 'Virgins of God' The Making of Asceticism in Late Antiquity, pp
282-310. Also Dunn, The Emergence of Monasticism, pp 25-34.
46. For Egyptian monasticism see D. J. Chitty, The Desert a City: An
Introduction to the Study of Egyptian and Palestinian Monasticism under the
Christian Empire (New York: St Vladimir's Seminary Press: 1999), also D.
Knowles, Christian Monasticism (London: Weidenfeld and Nicolson, 1969),
pp 9-24.
47. Knowles, Christian Monasticism, p 14.

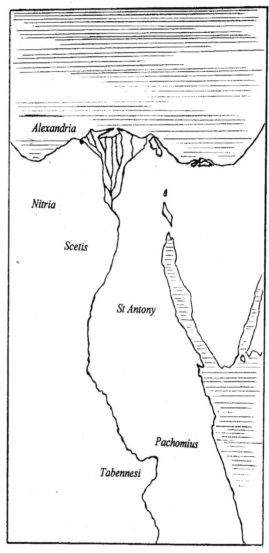

Early Monastic Egypt

comparison with that of the hermitage. Wine, meat and oil were banned, but fish, cheese, fruit and vegetables were allowed in addition to bread.[48]

According to his *Vita*, Pachomius was responsible for the founding of the women's houses at the instigation of his sister, Maria. Palladius in his *Lausiac History* describes the way of life of the monks in some detail and says quite specifically that the women observed the same rule of life. He describes it as follows:

> [T]hose appointed to serve for the day rise early and go to the kitchen or to the refectory. They are employed until mealtime in preparing and setting the tables, putting on each table loaves of bread, charlock, preserved olives, cheese made of cow's milk, and small vegetables. Some come in and eat at the sixth hour, others at the seventh, others at the eighth, others at the ninth, others at the eleventh, still others at late evening, some every other day, so that each group knows its proper hour.
>
> It is the same with regard to their work. One works the ground as husbandman, another works as gardener, another as smith, another as baker, another as fuller, another as weaver of large baskets, another as hoemaker, another as copyist, another as weaver of tender reeds. They all learn Holy Scripture by heart.[49]

This passage gives quite a graphic picture of life in a large monastic community, and as Palladius claimed the women lived in an identical manner to the men it probably illustrates fairly accurately the nuns' diet, work patterns and way of life also. For most peasant women, in its practical details, it would not have differed greatly from the lives of their married sisters who were living at home in their villages and farms.

However, whereas Pachomius' monasteries were – by the standards of the times – not excessively austere, a much harsher regime was put into practice in the houses founded by Pachomius' near-contemporary, Shenoute (388-c.450).[50] The sig-

---

48. Knowles, *Christian Monasticism*, p 14.
49. Palladius, *Historia Lausiaca*, pp 94-95.
50. See Elm, *'Virgins of God' The Making of Asceticism in Late Antiquity* pp 283-310.

nificance of Shenoute on future monastic generations in Egypt is summed up by Elm:

> At least as far as Coptic Christianity is concerned, there can be little doubt that Shenoute's importance, in clear contrast to his 'international' fate, far surpassed that of Pachomius.[51]

Shenoute's influence on the wider monastic world might have been greater had he written in Greek rather than Coptic. However, he introduced into monasticism two fundamental concepts which were to have the greatest impact on future monastic practice: to test the motivation and stability of aspirants, he enforced a period of probation, which he decreed had to last at least two or three months (which later developed into the novitiate) and he introduced the formal monastic vow: neophytes had to promise not to swear, not to steal or lie and not to defile their bodies.[52]

Shenoute took over the supervision of two women's monasteries and his legislation was for men and women alike: *'sive mas, sive femina'*.[53] In theory, he treated them equally, but this was not carried out in practice, and there seems to have been much resentment on the part of the women: 'In clear contradiction of all theoretical pronouncements, Shenoute demanded supreme authority over the female community and its leader.'[54] This is probably why his model for female monastic living did not long survive him.

Another major influence on monasticism through his life and even more through his writings was Basil of Caesarea (c.330-c.378).[55] Elm describes Basil as the one who 'in the eyes of his contemporaries and followers – became the founder of monasticism in Asia Minor'; his 'written precepts' were 'to set the standards for generations to come.'[56] However, Basil's monasticism was very different from the model lived in the Egyptian houses. Regarding these differing concepts of asceticism, Gerard Ladner cites Basil:

51. Elm, *'Virgins of God' The Making of Asceticism in Late Antiquity*, p 299.
52. Dunn, *The Emergence of Monasticism*, p 34.
53. Elm, *'Virgins of God' The Making of Asceticism in Late Antiquity*, p 300.
54. Elm, *'Virgins of God' The Making of Asceticism in Late Antiquity*, p 305.
55. Elm, *'Virgins of God' The Making of Asceticism in Late Antiquity*, pp 60-105.
56. Elm, *'Virgins of God' The Making of Asceticism in Late Antiquity*, p 61.

[T]he less strictly monastic origins of his asceticism make it more easily understandable that he linked his coenobitical idea to the primitive Christian community of Jerusalem, the church of the apostles. From St Basil onward the derivation of coenobitical monasticism from the community of the apostles was at any rate an important element of early Christian and medieval monastic ideology.[57]

Unlike the soldier Pachomius and the peasant Shenoute, Basil had studied widely in Caesarea, Constantinople and Athens; he was also well travelled and had visited the main sites of the monastic world in the East: Palestine, Syria, Mesopotamia (modern Iraq and Iran) and Egypt, and although he only lived the life of a monk for five years, after which he was made bishop, it was his intellectual genius and that of the two Gregorys which gave a theological content to the monastic movement. Basil was firmly cenobitic in his approach to the ascetic life.[58] He wrote:

> [B]ut if each of us should choose to live in solitude, we would not serve the common good in the ministry according to God's good pleasure, but would be satisfying our own passion for self-gratification. How could we, divided and separated, preserve the status and the mutual service of members or our subordinate relationship to our Head who is Christ? … Consider, further, that the Lord by reason of his excessive love for man was not content with merely teaching the word, but, so as to transmit to us clearly and exactly the example of humility in the perfection of charity, girded himself and washed the feet of the disciples. Whom, therefore, will you wash? To whom will you minister? In comparison with whom will you be the lowest, if you live alone?…[59]

He had been greatly influenced in his adoption of the ascetic life by his elder sister, Macrina,[60] and it is significant that, although all three of the monastic founders mentioned so far –

---

57. G. Ladner, *The Idea of Reform* (Cambridge: MA, 1959), pp 341-344, at p 343.

58. See Dunn, *The Emergence of Monasticism*, pp 34-41.

59. Basil, 'The Long Rules', in *Ascetical Works*, trs. M. Wagner (Washington: Catholic University of America Press, 1962), pp 249–252.

60. See Chapter 4.

Pachomius, Shenoute and Basil – had sisters who adopted a similar way of life, as far as we know, these women lived according to the Rules written for and by the men.

Our next influential male writer, roughly contemporary with Basil and the two Gregorys, also had a younger sister who followed him in the ascetic life: Jerome (Eusebius Hieronymus; c. 347-419/20). Jerome was born in Stridon in modern Croatia and studied in Rome, where he was baptised, Trier and Antioch. He lived a very varied life; for some time he was a hermit in the Syrian desert; he accompanied his bishop to the Second Ecumenical Council of Constantinople in 381, and eventually went on to Rome, where he became the secretary to Pope Damasus I. Although Jerome did not write a monastic rule himself, his contacts with the aristocratic women monastics of his day and the foundations that they made, the letters he wrote both to them and to others, and his biblical and patristic translations, commentaries and homilies were enormously influential on monastic life, both then and later.[61]

Augustine (354-430) had been profoundly influenced in his own conversion experience by Athanasius' *Vita Antonii* and eventually set up his own quasi-monastic establishment in response. He composed a Rule which Dunn describes as 'the first western monastic rule' and, although saying that it is debatable 'whether this rule was addressed to monks or to an episcopal clerical community', she concludes 'There seems no good reason not to regard it as a monastic rule.'[62] Ladner comments on the inspiration for Augustine's concept of religious life:

> St Augustine quotes at length and discusses fully the entire text from the fourth chapter of the Acts of the Apostles, in which the life of the primitive Christian community of Jerusalem is described. These sermons … are very interesting also because they show how the Bishop Augustine used the example of apostolic Jerusalem to impose the monastic way of life on the clergy of his church.[63]

---

61. For more on Jerome's life and his attitude to women, see Chapter Four.
62. Dunn, *The Emergence of Monasticism*, pp 64-66, at p 65; also Notes 18 and 19 where she gives a full bibliography of the discussion.
63. G. Ladner, *The Idea of Reform*, p 347.

There is further debate as to whether the adaptation specifically for women, of Augustine's original Rule, written in the
390s, is by Augustine himself, or by an 'anonymous adapter'[64]
but whichever, we now have a rule written for women.

   With John Cassian (c.365-c.433) we come to one of the major
figures of early monastic life. He was largely responsible for
bringing the spirituality of the deserts of the East to the church
in the West, so he stands as a witness to the undivided church.
Cassian was born probably in modern Romania about the year
365. With his friend Germanos, he visited the monks of Palestine
and Egypt, and spent about fifteen years living there, so he
knew Eastern monasticism from the inside. He eventually left
Egypt, as a result of the Origenist controversy and sought
refuge in Constantinople where he was welcomed by John
Chrysostom, who ordained him deacon. When Chrysostom fell
foul of the emperor he was sent into exile and Cassian and
Germanos were sent to Rome to plead his cause with the Pope.
In about 415 he came to Marseilles. Here he founded two
monasteries, one for men and one for women, and wrote for
them his *Institutes* and *Conlationes*, which embody the fruits of
his years living with the hermits and monks of the desert. These
were required reading for generations of monastics, and were
hugely influential throughout the Middle Ages right to our own
day.[65]

   Another major influence is anonymous. All we know about
the author is that he was an Italian abbot and lived in the mid-
sixth century. His work is known as the *Rule of the Master*, and
its influence was very great. It shows us a small community of
twelve monks and their abbot, carrying out a round of
psalmody, work and reading, with a common dormitory and refectory. David Knowles remarks: 'The life in such a house must
have been as simple and as unadorned as that in the early
Franciscan friaries. St Benedict, as we know, lived in and among
monasteries of this type at Subiaco, and such must have also
have been the primitive community of Monte Casino.'[66]

   The end of the eighth century and the beginning of the ninth

64. Dunn, *The Emergence of Monasticism*, p 57.
65. See Dunn, *The Emergence of Monasticism*, pp 73-81.
66. Knowles, *Christian Monasticism*, p 33.

was a significant time in monastic history in Europe. It was a time of change, begun by Pepin, Boniface and Chrodegang, and continued eventually by Charlemagne, a time when Roman liturgical usage and the *Regula Benedicti*,[67] attributed to Benedict of Nursia (c.480-547),[68] were being enforced throughout Europe. This was the time of the 'relentless drive for uniformity of practice in every aspect of religious life, from the design and layout of the standard monastery (reflected in the famous 'Plan of St Gall') to the regulation of its everyday activities'.[69] By the year 800 the Rule attributed to Benedict was emerging as the dominant monastic Rule in the West. It was championed by the Carolingians as part of the general campaign to reform the churches in the Frankish kingdoms and in Italy. This was one of the vast projects that occupied Charlemagne in the last decades of his life. He wanted to apply Benedict's Rule throughout his dominions, and although he died before he had achieved this aim, it was taken up by his son, Louis the Pious. A monastery was founded near the imperial court at Aachen where Benedict of Aniane, a famous reformer, was abbot. Two monks from every abbey were supposed to come there for 'refresher courses' in monastic life. Thus the Carolingians successfully imposed a single Rule on the Western church. This Rule was the Rule of Benedict; it was not the only one, but it was the dominant one.[70]

Benedict's Rule begins with a call to the individual monk – and nun, as the women who followed the Benedictine path observed the same Rule as the men – to hear and obey:

> Listen, O son, to the precepts of your master and incline the ear of your heart. Receive willingly and carry out effectively your loving father's advice, that by the labour of obedience you may return to him from whom you had departed by the sin of disobedience.[71]

---

67. Benedict, *Regula*, trs D. Ph. Schmitz (Maredsous, 1962 [3rd edition]).
68. See J. Ryan, *Irish Monasticism*, pp 409-413 for an analysis of this situation.
69. D. Ó Cróinín, 'A Tale of Two Rules: Benedict and Columbanus', in M. Browne and C. Ó Clabaigh eds, *The Irish Benedictines* (Dublin: The Columba Press, 2005), pp 11-24.
70. For a fuller treatment of the *Regula Benedicti*, see Chapter 6.
71. Benedict, *Regula*, trs Justin McCann (London: Sheed and Ward, 1976), Prologue 1.

But with the appearance of a carefully codified Rule, the emphasis shifted; it was no longer as it had been in the beginning – the spontaneous obedience freely given to a spiritual father or mother, but the obedience was now to a written Rule of which the superior was the interpreter and monitor and obedience to it was gradually and specifically required of all those who aspired to religious life. It was quite common for a founder or an abbot to combine two or more Rules. A very popular combination was that of the Rule of Benedict and the Rule of Columbanus of Luxeuil.[72] In seventh century Gaul, whenever the Rule of Benedict is mentioned it is always coupled with that of Columbanus.[73]

Caesarius of Arles (470-542) was one of the most important figures in the sixth century Gallic church, especially for his pastoral efforts. He wrote the first Rule specifically for women, the *Regula ad uirgines,* for the women's monastery he himself founded in the early years of the sixth century. He borrowed quite extensively from Augustine's Rule. And in its turn, Caesarius' Rule was adopted by several women's houses and so became the core of other women's Rules.[74] There was much borrowing and cross fertilisation of rules: Bede in his *Lives of the Holy Abbots of Wearmouth and Jarrow,* describes how Benedict Biscop, when he was dying, told the brethren that the Rule he had given to them was not his own composition, but the fruit of the visits he had paid to seventeen different monasteries.

By the twelfth and thirteenth centuries, the groups of pious women (and men) that were springing up all over Europe, were causing great anxiety to the church authorities both by their great number and by the unorthodox lifestyles they were adopting.[75] Many of them were determinedly independent and highly critical of ecclesiastical power, and often of dubious doctrinal soundness even to the point of heresy. One of the aims of the Fourth Lateran Council, convened by Pope Innocent III in 1215, which was one of the great reforming councils of the Middle

---

72. See Columbanus, *Regulae,* G. S. M. Walker (ed), *Sancti Columbani Opera* (Dublin: Institute for Advanced Studies, 1957, 1970, 1997), pp 122-181.
73. See Dunn, *The Emergence of Monasticism,* pp 191-193.
74. See Dunn, *The Emergence of Monasticism,* pp 98-107.
75. See Chapters 6 and 7.

Ages, was an attempt to limit and organise these religious groups. The influential Canon 13 stated:

> Lest too great a diversity of religious orders lead to grave confusion in the church of God, we strictly forbid anyone in the future to found a new order, but whoever should wish to enter an order, let him choose one already approved. Similarly, he who would wish to found a new monastery, must accept a rule already approved.

Since then, in theory at any rate, new religious families have had to adopt one of the existing Rules, usually either that of Augustine or Benedict or Francis. The first Rule to be written by a woman, for women, was the *Forma vitae* of Clare of Assisi in the thirteenth century.[76]

We will now look at the custom of praying at specific and regular times of the day, which was rather more complex in its development than that of the monastic *Regulae*. There were two different 'arrangements' for this daily prayer which had developed gradually over the first few centuries. The earliest Christians took with the utmost seriousness the New Testament command to 'pray without ceasing',[77] and the Lord himself, by word and example, gave the model for Christian prayer.[78] The aim of the early church regarding prayer is described by Duchesne:

> The ideal of the Christian life was that of a constant communion with God, maintained by as frequent prayer as possible. A Christian who did not pray every day, and even more frequently, would not have been considered a Christian at all.[79]

We know from one of the earliest texts we have that around AD 50[80] Christians were praying the Our Father three times

---

76. See Chapter Six.

77. 1 Thess 5:16-18; Col 4:2; Eph 6:18; Luke 18:1.

78. Matthew 6:9-13; Luke 11:2-4.

79. L. Duchesne, *Christian Worship: its Origin and Evolution*, (London: SPCK, 1904), p 446.

80. See T. O'Loughlin, 'The Didache as a Source for Picturing the Earliest Christian Communities', The Case of the Practice of Fasting' in *Christian Origins, Worship, Belief and Society*, The Milltown Institute and the Irish Biblical Association Millenium Conference, K. O'Mahoney ed, *Journal for the Study of the New Testament Supplement Series 241* (Sheffield: Sheffield

every day, and by this act of prayer, using a single formula, seeing themselves as united in a common moment of time, even
though physically separated.[81] In times of persecution, they
were unable to gather together for worship, but they understood that even if separated by distance, to pray together with
others at a specific time creates an especially significant spiritual
bond which renders that prayer more powerful.[82]

By the beginning of the fourth century, with the new-found
freedom the church experienced with regard to worship and all
public aspects of her life after the so-called Peace of Constantine
in 312, there was a vast increase of documentary evidence regarding liturgical worship. Eusebius of Caesarea bears witness
to the custom of the public celebration of Lauds and Vespers
with the people in secular churches. He writes of 'the hymns
sent up in the church throughout the world both morning and
evening'. Epiphanius of Salamis, John Chrysostom and the author of the *Apostolic Constitutions* all mention morning and
evening as times of public prayer, while Augustine offers the
graphic personal reminiscence: '(My mother) went twice a day,
morning and evening without fail, to Thy church, not to listen to

---

Academic Press, 2003), 83-112, for a discussion of the dating of the
Didache: '... today there is a broad consensus that the original form of this
document goes back to the middle of the first century, and that it draws on
the same strands of tradition – written or oral – that both Matthew and
Luke drew upon, and that it received the form in which we have it by the
end of the first century (if not earlier) ...'

81. See O'Loughlin, *'The Didache as a Source for Picturing the Earliest Christian
Communities'*, p 103: 'The *Didache* does not want Christians to pray at the
same time as 'the hypocrites' (*Didache* 8, 2), they are to pray using a special
formula (*Didache* 8, 2), and to do so three times each day (*Didache* 8, 3). This
implies that they viewed this thrice daily prayer as an act of collective worship, the prayer of the whole Christian community, rather than instructions to Christians on how to organise a personal prayer regime. Rather,
*three times a day, the whole church assembled and made an act of prayer using a
single formula and unified through a common moment of time.* (Emphasis mine).
82. That this principle existed even in Old Testament times can be seen by
such passages as 1 Kings 18:36: *'At the time when the offering is presented,*
Elijah the prophet stepped forward. "Yahweh, God of Abraham, Isaac and
Israel," he said, "let them know today that you are God in Israel, and that I
am your servant, that I have done all these things at your command";
Judith 9:1: *'At the same time in Jerusalem the evening sacrifice was being offered*

useless tales and old women's gossip, but to Thy words, and so that Thou wouldst hear her in her prayers'.[83] This office that Monica attended so faithfully was a popular service which used candles, incense, processions, vestments, chants, responses and hymns in which the people participated, and all the local clergy – bishop, priests, deacons, lectors, cantors – exercised their particular ministry. It was intended as a liturgy of praise and intercession, so only certain psalms appropriate to the time of day or season were used.[84]

This was the model of daily prayer which was used in parish churches throughout the early Christian world and to which has been given the name 'Cathedral' or 'People's Office'. Following the work of Anton Baumstark[85] it has become customary to contrast the 'Cathedral Office' with the 'Monastic' or 'Desert Office': the prayer of the monks, which is the other model for daily prayer and which concerns us more closely.

From the beginnings of the monastic movement in fourth century Egypt, the ideal of the early monks was to establish and maintain a life where the prayer of the monk in his heart[86] was

---

in the Temple of God, Judith said ....'; Dan 9:21; Tobit 3:17. In the first three of these references, even greater potency is accorded to prayer offered with others at the same time that sacrifice is being offered in the Temple (added emphasis).

83. Augustine, *Confessiones,* V.9.17.

84. For a more detailed treatment of the Office in the early Church, see P. Bradshaw, *The Origins of the Daily Office* (Alcuin Club Annual Reports, 1978); P. Bradshaw, *Daily Prayer in the Early Church,* Alcuin Club Connections 63 (London: SPCK, 1981); P. Bradshaw, P., *The Search for the Origins of Christian Worship: Sources and Methods for the Study of the Early Liturgy* (London: SPCK, 1992); P. Bradshaw, *Two Ways of Praying* (Nashville, Tennessee: Abingdon Press, 1995); P. Bradshaw, *Early Christian Worship: a basic introduction to ideas and practice* (London: SPCK, 1996).

85. A. Baumstark, *Comparative Liturgy,* B. Botte ed, trs. F. L. Cross (Westminster: Newman, 1958).

86. This led, especially in the East, to a vast literature; see Nikodimos of the Holy Mountain and Makarios of Corinth, *The Philokalia.* This work, which has always been regarded with the greatest respect amongst Orthodox monastics, has been translated into English from the Greek text in five volumes by Palmer, Sherrard and Kallistos Ware. There is also an abbreviated version, translated from the Slavonic text by Palmer and Kadloubovsky, *Writings from the Philokalia on Prayer of the Heart.*

as nearly ceaseless as possible, where even sleeping and eating occupied a minimal place so as not to interrupt this constant rhythm of prayer.[87] So their theology and practice of prayer was very different from that of the 'Cathedral Office'. However, monastic prayer only became a true liturgical action over the course of time. Originally, it was a prolonged personal meditation though usually in common, on the Word of God.[88] Thus the two forms of prayer, although taking place at approximately the same time – dawn and dusk – had each a very different purpose: the aim of the Cathedral Office was to celebrate in common the time of day as a symbol of Christ's redeeming death and burial (Vespers) or of his resurrection (Lauds), while the intention of the prayer of the monastics was to meditate on the psalms as the Word of God irrespective of the time of day so that each individual monk might grow closer to God through his own life of prayer and asceticism. So the monks were not praying in the name of the church, but meditating personally on the Word of God, as a prelude to turning to him in prayer.[89]

Cassian describes the practice of the monks of the Egyptian desert, the heartland of monastic life, in Books II and III of *De institutis*: 'In Egypt and Thebaid ... we see the prayers prescribed by the Law preserved in the evening assemblies and night vigils'.[90] So the ascetics, the monks and nuns in the desert, also prayed at dawn and dusk, these synaxes or meetings consisting of the recitation in common of psalms, the number of which was controversial and varied between twelve and thirty, but was eventually fixed at twelve psalms in the evening and twelve psalms at dawn;[91] both these offices concluded with readings

87. 'To these monks formal, organised times of prayer were less conducive to spiritual perfection than constant, non-verbal communication with God', J. Dyer, 'Monastic Psalmody of the Middle Ages', *Revue Bénédictine* 99 (1989), 41-74, at p 42.
88. See E. Dekkers, 'Were the Early Monks Liturgical?', *Collectanea Cisterciensia* 22 (1960), pp 120-137. See also for the fourth century Egyptian monastic office: R. Taft, *The Liturgy of the Hours in East and West: The Origins of the Divine Office and its Meaning for Today*, pp 57–73; for the urban monastic office: Taft, pp 75–91.
89. Taft, op. cit., p 364.
90. Cassian, *De institutis coenobiorum* II, 3, 1: CSEL 17, 18–19.
91. J. Mateos, 'The Origins of the Divine Office', *Worship* 41 (1967), pp 477-485, at p 481.

taken from the Old and New Testaments. Although there was no absolute uniformity, the accepted situation seems to have been: the hours of the Office, or at least morning and evening prayer, in the cell on the five week days, and the Office in common in the church on Saturday and Sunday, with a vigil on Saturday night. The rest of the time the monk was committed to prayer in his heart and meditation on the psalms while at work or in the silence and solitude of his cell.

Unlike the psalms used in the cathedral worship, those recited by the Egyptian monks in their office were not chosen because they were appropriate for the time of day or night or for the particular sentiments they expressed. They had no obvious connection either with the time or with the feelings of those reciting them, but were recited as they occurred numerically in order (*in cursu*) in the psalter, regardless of their meaning, as the primary reason for their recitation was to inspire the personal meditation and contemplation of the monks. These psalms seem to have been recited in a loud voice by one monk alone, while the others sat on low stools and listened, while they prayed in their hearts and meditated on the words of the psalms. At the end of each psalm they stood and prayed silently with raised hands, then they all prostrated. After a short time, the superior prayed aloud a concluding collect, 'collecting' the silent prayers of all the monks.

The very great importance given to the praying of the Divine Office in later monasticism is shown by the legislation of monastic Rules already mentioned. The Italian abbot whose work has come down to us under the title of the *Rule of the Master*, made the Liturgy of the Hours, organised as a fixed and regular daily cycle, the main priority for monks.[92] Columbanus devoted a whole chapter to the Divine Office in the Rule he composed for the Irish monks on the Continent.[93] The Rule attributed to St

92. J. Dyer, 'Monastic psalmody of the Middle Ages', *Revue Bénédictine* 99 (1989), pp 41-74, at 42.
93. G. S. M. Walker (ed), *Sancti Columbani Opera*, (Dublin: Institute for Advanced Studies, 1957, 1970,1997), pp 129–133; see also J. B. Stevenson, 'The Monastic Rules of Columbanus', in *Columbanus: Studies on the Latin Writings* (Woodbridge: The Boydell Press, 1997), pp 203-216.

Benedict emphasised the place of the *Opus Dei* in the life of the monk by prescribing:

> *Ad horam diuini officii mox auditum fuerit signum, relictis om-nibus quaelibet fuerint in manibus, summa cum festinatione cur-ratur, cum gravitate tamen, ut non scurrilitas inueniat fomitem. Ergo nihil operi Dei praeponatur.*[94]

> *Fratres qui omnino longe sunt in labore et non possunt occurrere hora competenti ad oratorium et abbas hoc perpendet, quia ita est, agant ibidem opus Dei ubi operantur, cum tremore diuino flectentes genua. Similiter qui in itinere directi sunt, non eos praetereant horae constitutae; sed ut possunt agant sibi et seruitutis pensum non negligent reddere.*[95]

This prescription that the hours of the Office must be ob-served by monks unable to be present in choir, goes back to the very beginnings of organised community living, being found in the writings of Pachomius. Basil is even more specific: 'If one cannot be present in person in the oratory, the duty of devotion should be carried out in whatever place one finds oneself.'[96] The monastics who lived in the cities and worshipped in their local churches (known as 'urban monastics') also joined in the regular Hours with the local clergy and people.

By the mid-fifth century, the monastic movement had spread from its beginnings in rural Egypt in the late third / early fourth centuries right across the Christian world and had arrived in Ireland.[97] Although its character and discipline differed in detail from one location to another, wherever monastic life existed it held as supreme and sacred the gospel command of the Lord to 'Pray always',[98] even though the way this prayer was carried out differed from country to country and even from monastery

---

94. *Benedicti Regula,* trs D. Ph. Schmitz, (Maredsous, 1962 [3rd edition]), Chapter 43, p 131.
95. Ibid., Chapter 50, p 147.
96. See T. G. Kardong, *Benedict's Rule, A Translation and Commentary* (Collegeville, Minnesota: The Liturgical Press, 1996), p 412.
97. 'And the Irish leaders' sons and daughters are seen to become the monks and virgins of Christ', T. O'Loughlin, *St Patrick, the Man and his Works* (London, SPCK, 1999), p 77.
98. Lk 18:1.

to monastery.[99] Because of the locations of its beginnings, Eastern influence remained strong in the monastic tradition, especially in Ireland, which had received her monastic legacy from Britain and Gaul, and where Cassian was the acknowledged authority.[100]

In the West, the recitation in common of the canonical Hours was assuming the primacy. Columbanus bears witness to the early Western tradition when he says:

> Sed quia orationum canonicarum noscendus est modus, in quo omnes simul orantes horis conueniunt statutis, quibus absolutis unusquisque in cubiculo suo orare debet.[101]

So by the beginning of the seventh century at least, the ideal was that the monks should celebrate the Hours of the Office together in the church and then return to their own individual cells to pray in solitude, and Columbanus takes his inspiration for this practice from the gospel: Tu autem cum orabis intra in cubiculum tuum et cluso ostio tuo ora Patrem tuum in abscondito et Pater tuus qui uidet in abscondito reddet tibi.[102]

The anonymous author of the Vita sanctissimi Ceolfridi abbatis gives us a graphic insight into the importance of the Office for monks of his time in Northumbria when he tells of the following incident:

> ... in the monastery which Ceolfrith ruled, all those who could read or preach or were able to sing the antiphons and responsories were carried off by the plague except the abbot himself and one small boy, who has been brought up and taught by him and who until the present day holds the rank of a priest in the same monastery and commends the abbot's laudable actions in words and writings to all who wish to

---

99. 'Cassian found to his disappointment that the different customs in Egypt and the Orient were almost as numerous as the monasteries and cells.' J. Ryan, *Irish Monasticism, Origins and Early Development* (Dublin: Talbot Press,1931, repr. Dublin: Four Courts Press, 1992), p 334.

100. For the teaching and legacy of Cassian, see Dunn, op. cit., pp 73-81. For Cassian's influence in Ireland, see Ryan, *Irish Monasticism*, pp 328-334; also Dunn, op. cit., p 145.

101. Walker, *Sancti Columbani Opera*, p 130.

102. Matthew 6:6.

know them. Because of the plague the abbot was very sorrowful and ordered the previous custom to be interrupted and that the whole psalter except at Lauds and Vespers should be recited without antiphons. But when this was done for the space of only one week with many tears and laments, he felt unable to bear it any longer so he decided that the psalms with antiphons should be resumed as before. With everyone trying their best, he completed this by himself but with the help of the boy mentioned above, with no small labour, until he trained sufficient companions in the work of God, or else obtained them from elsewhere.[103]

It is clear from this passage that the recitation of the psalms with antiphons and responsories was central to the monks' life and was a skilled work, which needed to be taught by someone competent. Hence Benedict[104] was at pains to bring back from Rome 'teachers who would establish in the church he had just founded the order of chant and ceremonies according to the usage of the Roman rite', and he and Ceolfrith 'learnt in Rome many of the church's laws and they brought back with them to England John, the arch-cantor of the Roman Church and abbot of St Martin's monastery, who generously taught [...] the order of chanting both by word of mouth and by his writings'.[105]

In eighth century Ireland, the description of the prayer life of the hermit of Clonard illustrates that, even those living the solitary life observed the full round of canonical hours:

He used to make two hundred genuflections at lauds, a hundred at each of the canonical hours, and a hundred at matins. Seven hundred genuflections in all did he make in the twenty four hours.[106]

---

103. Plummer, *Ven. Bed. opera historia* I, pp 388-404. This can be found in translation in D. F. Farmer, ed, 'The Anonymous History of Abbot Ceolfrith', *The Age of Bede* (London: Penguin, 1965, repr. 1983, 1988, 1998), p 218. See fn to above: 'The boy described has often and probably rightly been identified as Bede himself.'

104. Who with Ceolfrith was responsible for the founding of the monasteries at Jarrow and Wearmouth.

105. Farmer, ed and trs, 'The Anonymous History of Abbot Ceolfrith', p 216.

106. *Teaching of Máel Rúain*, n 103.

In another early medieval Irish text, the *Rule of Carthage*, under the section 'The duties of the Céli Dé',[107] we find the following admonition:

> If we are living the monastic life, a noble calling, let us frequent the holy church for each canonical hour.[108]

Here, the recitation in the church of the full Divine Office by all the monks together is seen as an integral part of the communal monastic vocation in the far West of the Christian world. This is the pattern set out in another Irish text, the *Rule of Ailbe*:

> He should be constant in prayer, never forgetting his canonical hours.[109]

Constancy (*foss*) was the great Céli Dé virtue, and of all the opportunities when it could be put into practice, constancy in prayer was the greatest. So from these passages, it seems that the canonical hours were said in common in the church, and then the monks went to their own individual cells to pray in silence and meditate.[110]

In the eighth century, a so-called reform of the church's liturgy took place on the Continent under Pepin, Boniface and Chrodegang. This was continued by Charlemagne, who was determined to produce liturgical uniformity in the regions where he ruled, and used the Roman Office as the basis of this uniformity.[111] One aspect of this so-called reform was the monasticisation of the clergy. The clergy had to live together and pray the office together, and whoever could not be in choir for the office had to say it privately. This was already the monastic practice but by the tenth century it became obligatory for all the clergy in the Western church. By the eighth/ninth century, the Cathedral Office had virtually disappeared (due at least in part to the clericalising and monasticising tendencies of Charlemagne's re-

---

107. 'Servants of God': for the Céli Dé monks and the nuns associated with them, see Chapter 5.

108. *Rule of Carthage; Duties of the Céli Dé*, n 1.

109. *Rule of Ailbe*, n 16.

110. For the Divine Office in early Ireland, see P. M. Rumsey, *Sacred Time in Early Christian Ireland* (London, T & T Clark, 2007).

111. See Taft, op. cit., 297-300.

forms), and the people's office had been taken over by the monastic office, with its seven hours of prayer during the day and vigils during the night, and the whole psalter sung every week.[112]

This very brief introduction to the origins and early history and development of the daily monastic prayer routine which has endured, though in different forms, right through the centuries, along with an account of the formation of the early monastic Rules, which ordered the lives of both monks and nuns, along with an analysis of the practice of monastic asceticism, together form the backdrop to all the following chapters. The monastic women in the subsequent pages, wherever in the Christian world their monasteries were situated, and whatever the century in which they lived, were all formed according to the above principles, although, as we shall see in the following chapters, the practical living out of these time honoured principles took vastly different forms.

---

112. For the later development of the Divine Office, see S. J. P. Van Dijk, and J. Hazelden Walker, *The Origins of the Modern Roman Liturgy* (London: Darton, Longman and Todd, 1960); also J. D. Crichton, H. E. Winstone, and J. R. Ainslie, eds, *English Catholic Worship* (London: Geoffrey Chapman, 1979); J. D. Crichton, *Christian Celebration* (London: Geoffrey Chapman, 1981, 1985); J. D. Crichton, *Understanding the Prayer of the Church* (London: Geoffrey Chapman, 1976, 1993).

CHAPTER THREE

Harlots and Holy Women –
Women's Monasticism in the Desert[1]

As we have seen in the previous chapter, in the first century, those who rejected marriage were regarded as heretical by mainstream Christians, who maintained the Jewish notion that marriage and procreation were a sharing in God's own act of creation and were therefore good and holy. Hellenistic culture, on the other hand, supported an ideal of sexuality which was very different from that of Judaism. Greek writers saw sexual activity as 'dangerous, hard to control, harmful to health and draining.'[2] The first century critique of celibacy as heretical is the early suspicion of this Hellenistic ideal;[3] however, as awareness of the difference between Christianity and Greek culture subsided, so celibacy and virginity became gradually more and more acceptable, eventually becoming seen as a 'higher' state than that of marriage.

So, by the fourth century, we find in the writings of the fathers of the church – Athanasius (c.293-373),[4] Ambrose (340-397), Jerome (c.345-419) – mention of women who chose to live a life of virginity, originally secluded in their own homes, later on, either as solitary ascetics in the desert, or in communities of like-minded women. They were told by these church teachers they should dress in black, wear a veil of the same colour, placed upon their head solemnly by the bishop at their consecration to God, cover their arms to the fingers, keep their hair cropped close to their head, have only one meal a day after the hour of

1. See P. Brown, *The Body and Sexuality: Men, Women and Sexual Renunciation in Early Christianity* (New York: Columbia University Press, 1988), especially pp 213-258. Also S. Elm, *'Virgins of God' The Making of Asceticism in Late Antiquity* (Oxford: Clarendon Press, 1994), pp 253-282, pp 311-330.
2. Ranke-Heinemann, *Eunuchs for the Kingdom*, p 10. See the whole Chapter, pp 9-20.
3. 'They forbid marriage and prohibit foods which God created to be accepted with thanksgiving', 1 Tim 4:3.
4. For his pastoral care of the young female ascetics in Alexandria, see Demacopoulos, *Five Models of Spiritual Direction*, pp 39-42.

None, consisting of bread and vegetables, which, if possible they should share with some poor woman. Athanasius gave the following instructions:

> Do not let the material of your clothes be expensive. Your cloak should be black – not dyed but naturally so – or onyx-coloured. The scarf should be the same colour, without tassels. The sleeves should be woollen, covering the arms to the fingers; the hair cut short, with a woollen headband tied round the head, and a hood, and a shoulder covering without tassels. If you meet a person, let your face be veiled and downcast: do not raise your face to a human being, but only to God.[5]

This passage shows the view prevalent among teachers of the church at the time: women were dangerous, even those dedicated to God were to be kept at a distance and were to make their appearance as unattractive as possible. The instructions on social behaviour are reminiscent of the later medieval prescriptions for those with the greatly feared disease of leprosy who were shunned by everyone and pushed to the margins of society.

One of the earliest monastic texts, the *Historia Lausiaca* of Palladius, tells both of women living in seclusion in their own homes,[6] women living the solitary life and also of several early monasteries of women in the Egyptian desert[7] and gives a vivid picture of early monastic life both for men and for women, and the world in which they lived. The *Historia Lausiaca* is described by Robert Meyer as one of the two most important source documents for the history of early monasticism in Egypt, and he places it on a level with Athanasius' *Vita* of St Antony.[8] It was written about 419 or 420,[9] and the author had been a monk since

---

5. Athanasius, 'On Virginity', PG 28. 264, quoted in G. Clark, *Women in Late Antiquity*,
6. See Palladius, *Historia Lausiaca*, pp 90-91; 108, 109.
7. See Palladius, *Historia Lausiaca*, pp 95-98. In these anecdotes, Palladius states clearly that the women followed the same way of life as the men in Pachomian monasteries, see p 95.
8. Meyer, *Palladius: Historia Lausiaca*, 3. See also Elm, *'Virgins of God' The Making of Asceticism in Late Antiquity*, pp 311-330.
9. Ibid, 7.

he was twenty three, living the monastic life in Palestine, Egypt and Asia Minor.[10] Although the writer claims to be an eyewitness of much he describes: 'today the *Historia Lausiaca* is accepted as a true account, but with due recognition given the fact that there are some passages marked by hyperbole and that Palladius accepted some stories from others (including possibly in some cases stories in written form) which are dubious.'[11] However, these stories and so many others like them were of value because they were intended to be read or heard by other people and to fire them with the desire to imitate these 'athletes of God', so that the grace in their lives might continue to be active in those of their hearers. An example of this genre is a story in which Palladius held up the practice of fasting of a female ascetic for admiration and emulation and described her dietary practices thus:

> She abstained completely from anything warm-blooded or animate, but she partook of fish and vegetables with oil on feast days, and otherwise satisfied herself with a little sour wine and dry bread.[12]

Women who wished to adopt this way of life were instructed by their male mentors to study the scriptures, rise during the night to pray, and gather together in church to chant the psalms at the traditional hours. They were to live secluded lives, not venturing out into the streets unless it was to go to church, and not taking any part in useless gossip or news mongering. Ambrose puts the ideal before them thus:

> She who seeks Christ should not be seen with the common mob, should not be found in the marketplace or on the streets, should not be loud-voiced, or unguarded in deportment, or ready to hear everything and be seen everywhere.[13]

In was in a community such as this that Antony, the 'Father of monks' placed his younger sister after the death of their parents, before he went to live as an ascetic himself, and thus, tradi-

10. Ibid, 3-7.
11. Ibid, 8.
12. Palladius, *Historia Lausiaca*, p 138.
13. Ambrose, *De uirginitate*, 83.

tionally, began the monastic life. According to the *Longer Rules* of Basil,[14] it was customary for monastic communities to accept young children who had been orphaned; in the social setting of the time it was possibly the only way a young man could provide for the upbringing and education of an orphaned younger sister, though Basil does hint at less worthy motives:

> Parents, and brothers and other relatives bring forward many girls before the proper age, not because the girls have an inner urge towards continence, but in order that their relatives may gain some material advantage from so doing.[15]

Under these circumstances it is, perhaps, not surprising that instructions such as those given by Ambrose and Jerome to young women, who actually experienced no attraction for the monastic way of life, were necessary.

However, the information which we have in these stories about the early women monastics, is ambiguous and complex. It has been filtered down to us by male authors such as Palladius, Jerome and Ambrose from a world in which the majority of saints and monastics were male, and the church hierarchy was male. The model for holiness was male – as witness the description given above of the way of life prescribed for the early consecrated virgins – it comes to us in the writings of the (male) fathers of the church – the women themselves seem to have had little or no say in the ordering of their lives. Jo Ann McNamara writers:

> Like most of their contemporaries, the fathers were infused with age-old prejudices which were heightened in this age by an atmosphere of sexual confusion and uncertainty. They were struggling against their own predispositions in a society that was producing heretical teachers preaching strange and disturbing trans-sexual images of the spiritual world.[16]

Jerome instructed Paula, Eustochium and their companions

---

14. See S. Elm, *'Virgins of God', The Making of Asceticism in Late Antiquity* (Oxford: Clarendon Press, 1994), p 71.
15. Basil, *Letter* 119.18, quoted in Brown, *The Body and Sexuality*, p 261
16. J. A. McNamara, 'Sexual Equality and the Cult of Virginity in Early Christian Thought', *Feminist Studies*, Vol 3, No 3/4 (Spring-Summer, 1976), pp 145-158.

as to how they were to live, but in the world they inhabited, the model of holiness was male, and by adhering to this model, and sharing in masculine virtues – and only by sharing in masculine virtues, women could become holy. To be more a saint was to be less a woman. The concept of the 'divine man' which Christianity inherited from the classical pagan world did not include women:

> The limitations of this concept are evident also: it is elitist and anti-democratic, since only the few chosen people could claim this status, giving them a position apart from the masses; it is also clearly a male concept, because the structures of society did not allow women to withdraw from the regular pursuits of life to the same degree as men. The elitist and male oriented nature of the concept has continued to be basic even in its modern version.[17]

This was powerful philosophy in the late classical world and the world of the early middle ages, and it seems to be the wisdom behind the phenomenon of what have been called the 'transvestite saints': the stories of women such as Thecla, Pelagia, Hilaria and others, who, in slightly differing circumstances are said to have donned the male monastic habit and lived as monks, sometimes achieving recognition for their holiness, and only discovered to have been female after their death.[18] The implication was that being female, they could only gain holiness by putting on the clothes of the male. It was a no-win situation for the women – if they were to become holy, they had to renounce their sexuality and become men. We have already mentioned the *Historia Lausiaca* by Palladius; he has the typical mentality of his time towards women:

> I must also commemorate in this book the courageous women [in Greek this is *gynaikon andreion* – that is 'manly women'] to whom God granted struggles equal to those of

17. H. Koester, 'The Divine Human Being', *Harvard Theological Review*, Vol 78, No 3/4 (Jul-Oct, 1985), pp 243-252.
18. See J. Anson, 'The Female Transvestite in Early Monasticism: the Origin and Development of a Motif', *Viator* 5, (1969), pp 1-32. Also V. L. Bullough, 'Transvestites in the Middle Ages', *American Journal of Sociology* 79, (1974), pp 1381-1394.

men, so that no one could plead as an excuse that women are too weak to practice virtue successfully.[19]

And Origen wrote to 'my most modest and manly (*andreio-tate*) Tatiana, from whom I am sure woman-like things have passed away in the same way they did from Sarah.' Although McNamara tries to prove that 'it was certainly not the object of the fathers to turn women into men through the virgin life',[20] passages such as the above from Origen and Palladius seem to indicate that the fathers expected the practice of the ascetic life to remove physical evidence of femininity from the lives of these women. Patristic writers, particularly Jerome and Ambrose, thought that virgins living the ascetic life could transcend their female sexuality and be transformed into men.[21] Asceticism and spirituality were sometimes associated specifically with masculinity, but even if women attained to this supposedly 'higher' state, their maleness was incomplete – they were still expected to be subordinate to men. Meeks comments that: 'The exposure of female infants provides perhaps the most chilling indicator of the lack of value placed on the female body.'[22] However, he does qualify this by adding: 'Examples abound of fathers who cherished their daughters and made provision for them.'[23]

Turning more specifically to the women who chose to live in the desert, we have few biographical details of which we can be certain regarding the lives of either the male or female desert dwellers. The names of many of the men who went out into the desert to follow Antony and Pachomius have come down to us in the extensive collections of their wise sayings.[24] Although

19. Palladius, *Historia Lausiaca*, p 117. It is significant that the very word 'virtue' comes from the Latin for 'man': *vir*. The implication is that to be 'virtuous' is synonymous with 'manliness'.

20. J. A. McNamara, 'Sexual Equality and the Cult of Virginity in Early Christian Thought', p 153.

21. See D. Hunter, 'Resistance to the Virginal Ideal in Late-Fourth Century Rome: The Case of Jovinian', *Theological Studies* 48 (1987), pp 45-64.

22. W. A. Meeks, *The Origins of Christian Morality: The First Two Centuries* (New Haven: Yale University Press, 1993), p 141.

23. Ibid, p 141

24. Such as the *Philokalia*; the writings of Cassian; the *Apothegmata patrum*.

they were not nearly as numerous, there were women living lives of asceticism in the desert too, but we have only a bare handful of names and very few of their sayings were thought worthy of being recorded. Amma ('Mother' – the female equivalent of 'Abba', 'Father', which in time became 'abbot') Syncletica probably lived in the fourth century in Alexandria. Born into a privileged Macedonian family, her beauty and wealth presupposed that she would make a good marriage, but she refused this because of her commitment to God. Her story is similar to that of Antony; on the death of her parents, who had moved with Syncletica and her two brothers and younger sister from Macedonia to Alexandria, she gave away her inheritance and went with her sister, who was blind, to live in an empty tomb on a family estate. Here, Syncletica cut off her hair, to symbolise her break with secular society and renewed the vow of virginity she had previously made. Tradition has it that she died c.400, aged over eighty, after much suffering from the cancer which attacked her throat and mouth.

All that is known of the details of Amma Sarah's life is that she lived in the fifth century as a solitary in a hut near a river, which presumably was the Nile. She is famous for her long battles with her sexuality, described in the *uitae* according to the understanding of the time as the 'demon of fornication'. 'She never prayed that the warfare should cease but she said, O God, give me strength.'[25] Tradition has it that she died near Scetis in the time of the Emperor Theodosius II (who became Emperor in 408 aged 7; his sister Pulcheria, acted as regent from 408-416; he then ruled from 416-480).

Even less is known of the life of Amma Theodora, but she is recorded as living in the desert somewhere near Alexandria, possibly in the nearby monastic enclaves of Nitria, Kellia or Scetis. Sayings attributed to her discuss the problems caused by the demon of *accedia*, the spirit of restlessness and boredom which so troubled the male desert monastics. There is evidence that she maintained contact with Theophilus, (Bishop of Alexandria from 385-412), thus emphasising her status as a spir-

---

25. Quoted in Benedicta Ward, *Harlots of the Desert: A Study of Repentance in Early Monastic Sources* (Kalamazoo: Cistercian Publications, 1987), p 6.

itual guide, and this would place her dates in the late fourth/ early fifth century. Elm describes her as 'a true desert 'mother', a formidable figure.'[26] The few sayings of all these women are recorded as 'add-ons' in the otherwise masculine collection of the sayings of the fathers of the desert known as the *Apothegmata Patrum.*

So Amma Sarah, Amma Syncletica, Amma Theodora and those women who came to follow them saw themselves, like the fathers of the desert, as seeking a new kind of martyrdom – that of giving their lives in self-imposed asceticism and sacrifice, the twin object of which was to find and contemplate God and to engage in spiritual battle with the devil, who they believed to be present in a particular way in the wilderness, and also the 'demons' or 'vices' within themselves which they fought so unceasingly by prayer and by physical penance. These two aims, of seeking God and fighting the devil, they saw to be interdependent. This identification of martyrdom with monasticism has been expressed thus:

> In his separation from the world, the monk is heir not only to the virgin, but also to the martyr. One of the most interesting aspects of the early treatises on martyrdom is their use of themes and images which would later become associated with the monastic vocation.[27]

Thus one of the classic texts on monasticism cherished by Orthodox Christians is entitled *The Arena,*[28] recalling the location where so many of the early martyrs gave their lives for Christ. This connection in the Christian tradition between the monastic calling and martyrdom can be seen in references to monasticism as 'white martyrdom' – a total offering and sacrifice of one's life to God, but without the shedding of blood.[29] However, it can, and frequently has in the course of history, provided opportunities for 'red martyrdom'.

26. Elm, *'Virgins of God' The Making of Asceticism in Late Antiquity'*, p 263.
27. M. D. Totah, 'The History of Enclosure' in J. Prou and the Benedictine Nuns of the Solesmes Congregation (Eng. ed trs and ed David Hayes), *Walled About with God* (Gracewing: 2005), p 38.
28. I. Brianchaninov, *The Arena: An Offering to Contemporary Monasticism* (Madras: Diocesan Press, 1970).
29. An idea first formulated in Athanasius' *Vita* of Antony.

One form of Christianity in the early church was that of 'martyrdom'; although many found this too difficult to accept, it was accepted as 'heroic'. Categories of holiness were later expanded to include holy men and women whose virtue had been recognised in other ways than martyrdom, and this was reflected in the lists of saints drawn up in the church's martyrologies.[30] Monks saw themselves as successors to the martyrs by their lives of solitude, asceticism and self denial.

> By totally rejecting ordinary human structures and almost provocatively renouncing worldly institutions, they paradoxically came to represent another kind of power. Their advice was sought in matters of spirituality, salvation, doctrine even social life and political action.[31]

And this new way of attaining holiness was not the sole prerogative of men, though women were only recognised very grudgingly. Sometimes certain women with the reputation for exceptional holiness, were allowed to share in masculine virtues. One of the sayings attributed to Amma Sarah bears out both her reputation for holiness and the male attitude towards this:

> Two old men, great anchorites, came to the district of Pelusium to visit her. When they arrived, one said to the other, 'Let us humiliate this old woman.' So they said to her, 'Be careful not to become conceited thinking to yourself: Look how anchorites are coming to see me, a mere woman.' But Amma Sarah said to them, 'According to nature I am a woman but not according to my thoughts'.[32]

This saying is illuminating in that it provides evidence that men long experienced in the monastic way of life and famed for

---

30. See E. Bickersteth Birks, 'Martyrology' in W. Smith and S. Cheetham eds, *A Dictionary of Christian Antiquities* (London: John Murray, 1908), 1132-1139.

31. J. Chryssavgis, 'From Egypt to Palestine: Discerning a Thread of Spiritual Direction', in John Behr, Andrew Louth and Dimitri Conomos (eds), *Abba: The Tradition of Orthodoxy in the West, Festschrift for Bishop Kallistos (Ware) of Diokleia* (Crestwood, New York: St Vladimir's Seminary Press, 2003), pp 299-315, p.- 299.

32. *Apothegmata Patrum*, quoted in M. Dunn, *The Emergence of Monasticism* (Oxford: Blackwell, 2000), p 46.

their observance of it would come some distance to visit 'a mere woman', suggesting either curiosity or maybe a qualified respect, and yet in spite of her reputation for holiness would still see it as their duty to 'humiliate' this old woman by their criticism of her sex and use this as a reason to denigrate her ascetic achievements. To be a holy person, she had to abandon her female identity: her 'thoughts'.

The asceticism of the desert fathers and mothers was based on a negative view of contemporary society which they saw as corrupt and 'moribund';[33] it thus had to be rejected. Their view of human nature was similarly pessimistic: it was incurably sinful and had to be overcome and tamed by severe asceticism. And their view of the world in general was that it was coming to an imminent end:

> Who cannot see that the world is already in its decline and no longer has the strength and vigour of former times? ... The world tells its own tale and its general decadence bears adequate witness that it is approaching its end ... everything in these days is rushing to its doom and is affected by the general debility.[34]

This was the reason for their flight from society into the desert and their harsh penances and asceticism; they wanted to be ready and waiting for the Christ when he came at the end of time, and where better to wait for him than the wilderness where he had called Israel to be his own people in a special way? Elm describes their view of their surroundings thus:

> The conception of the desert, as reflected in the *Apothegmata*, is primarily that of a place of sterility and death, the dwelling place of savage animals and equally savage demons. It is, however, also a place of supreme purity, where 'the air is more pure, the sky more open, and God more familiar'. It is the place where Jesus fought temptations, and where his follower, the ascetic, battles against his internal demons, his

33. The judgement of J. Lacarrière, *The God-possessed* (London: George Allen & Unwin, 1963), p 27.
34. Letter of Cyprian of Carthage to Dimitrianus, quoted in Lacarrière, *The God-possessed*, p 26.

temptations and afflictions. If successful, it is here that he might also find God, that is to say redemption, through *hesychia*, tranquillity and solitude.[35]

According to the *Vitae* of these desert saints, there were various models or patterns of holiness recognised and held up for imitation by their authors. For men, one model was that of the repentant robber, such as Abba Moses, who after his freeing from slavery took up the life of a brigand in the desert before he was converted to Christianity and a life of repentance as a monk.[36] A favourite character in the literature of the desert mothers is that of the repentant prostitute.[37] These women were seen as a temptation to the virtue of their male counterparts (as were all women, but particularly women of loose virtue), and their sinful condition was inevitably linked to their bodily state as females until they were rescued from this by the authority or influence of a male religious figure. Probably the best and most popular example of this literary type is the story of Mary of Egypt, which had enormous appeal for Christians of both East and West right into the later Middle Ages and beyond.[38] As we have it in its various forms it includes details from other saints' *uitae*, both male and female: Thaïs, Anastasia, and Paul of Thebes. The life of Mary of Egypt is legendary but it was extremely popular throughout the early church, both East and West, and remained so well into the Middle Ages. The legend of Mary, the converted harlot, illustrates the belief current in ancient societies that there were only two ways in which a woman could serve the gods and be accepted by them: by expending her sexual energy (consecrated prostitution) or by preserving it (sacred virginity).[39]

Although Derwas Chitty dismisses the tale as 'hardly hist-

35. Elm, *'Virgins of God' The Making of Asceticism in Late Antiquity* (Oxford: Clarendon Press, 1994), p 260.

36. See D. Keller, *Oasis of Wisdom: The Worlds of the Desert Fathers and Mothers* (Collegeville, Minnesota: Liturgical Press, 2005), pp 138-144.

37. See, for example, the *Life of St Mary the Harlot, Niece of the Hermit Abraham*, Helen Waddell (trs), *The Desert Fathers* (London: Constable, 1936), pp 215-224.

38. See Benedicta Ward, *Harlots of the Desert: A Study of Repentance in Early Monastic Sources* (London: 1987), especially pp 26-56.

39. See Warner, *Alone of All her Sex*, The Penitent Whore, pp 224-235.

ory',[40] it is of particular value in this study, precisely because it is not historical. In this piece of hagiography, we have a theological interpretation of Mary's life, in that it illustrates a favourite theme in early saints' lives of the repentant harlot converted to a better way of life by a male ecclesiastical figure. According to the story, which appears in several slightly differing forms, when she was twelve years old Mary ran away from home to become a prostitute in the city of Alexandria, which is presented as infamous because of its immorality.[41] After seventeen years of this life she went to Jerusalem on pilgrimage, though more out of curiosity than devotion. When the other pilgrims in her party entered the Church of the Holy Sepulchre an invisible force prevented Mary from doing so. She realised her sinful life was preventing her from following them, and, touched suddenly by divine grace, turning to an icon of the Blessed Virgin Mary, she expressed her repentance and her desire to amend her ways. Thus freed from the obstacle, she went in and prostrated before the cross where she vowed to begin a new life. In accordance, as she believed, with divine guidance, she set out for the desert east of the Jordan, where she lived an extraordinarily penitential life for many years in total solitude. These were years of intense struggle as memories of her former way of life came back to tempt her vividly, but she remained true to her conversion experience to the end of her life. In her extreme old age, the priest Zosimas discovered her in the desert, and heard her story. A year later he took her communion and on returning a year later again, found her dead body, which according to the legend, a lion helped him to bury. She died as she had lived, alone, in solitude and penitence in the desert, but it was necessary for her to have the validation of a male ecclesiastical figure for that life to be recognised as holy (by other men ...). According to one commentator, the story of Mary's sudden conversion from prostitu-

---

40. Derwas J. Chitty, *The Desert a City* (New York, St Vladimir's Seminary Press, 1999), p 153.
41. However, it was Corinth that was the recognised seat of immorality in the ancient world; Alexandria was given a bad name by extension because it was a great port and trading city; this bad reputation eclipsed the reality of its being a centre of scholarship with its famous library.

tion in Jerusalem, shows a movement from the pagan understanding of sexuality to that of Christianity.[42] Another commentator, Marina Warner remarks thus:

> The church venerates two ideals of the feminine – consecrated
> chastity in the Virgin Mary and regenerate sexuality in the
> Magdalene. Populous as the Catholic pantheon is, it is never-
> theless so impoverished that it cannot conceive of a single
> female saint independently of her relations (or lack of rela-
> tions) with men.[43]

So, claims Warner: 'there is no place in the conceptual archi-
tecture of Christian society for a single woman who is neither a
virgin nor a whore.'[44] Strong words, and yet a trawl through the
Common Offices of Saints in the Roman Breviary reveals that in
the stakes for sanctity men can be 'apostles' or 'martyrs' or 'pas-
tors' or 'doctors' or just plain 'holy men', whereas women have
only the options of 'virgin' or 'holy woman' – with a sidelong
glance at 'doctors of the church' since Teresa of Avila, Catherine
of Siena and Thérèse of Lisieux were elevated to that status.
However, even this, grim as it may be, is an improvement on the
Breviarium Romanum in use prior to Vatican II where the sanctity
options for women were unapologetically explicit: '*Commune
Unius Virginis*' or '*Commune Unius Non Virginis*'. Male saints
have never been thus categorised according to their sexual status. In passing, it is worth noting that in the course of the whole
liturgical year of the R. C. Church (as presented in *The Divine
Office*, The Liturgy of the Hours according to the Roman Rite)
only four married women are commemorated: Elizabeth of
Portugal on 4 July; Monica, the mother of Augustine, on 27
August; Margaret of Scotland, on 16 November and Elizabeth of
Hungary on 17 November. However, there were some married
women who, after they had been widowed redeemed their status by entering religious life. These were saints such as Bridget
of Sweden (23 July), Jane Frances de Chantal (12 August), and
Hedwig (16 October). (While counting halos of saints, it is worth

---

42. Lacarrière, The *God-possessed*, pp 146-149.
43. Warner, *Alone of All her Sex*, p 235.
44. Warner, *Alone of All her Sex*, p 235.

putting on record that, as presented in the Breviary, male saints number 146 [minimum, as several of these are listed as 'St N and Companions'] while female saints total less than a quarter of that number, at just 30).

According to the accounts we have of them, Mary of Egypt and these other early women ascetics lived in what seem to us to be conditions of almost unimaginable poverty and squalor in the desert; their fasting practices were extreme; they lived in tiny huts, caves or unused tombs and any suggestion of comfort-seeking or care for personal hygiene or cleanliness was regarded as an unacceptable weakness. Even to wash the tips of one's fingers was hardly allowable. The following story, illustrating the ascetics' attitude to all forms of bodily ease and comfort, is told, probably of Melania the Elder (who herself had been a woman of culture, wealth and the highest social standing), by Palladius:

> The weather was terribly hot for us, and when we arrived at Pelusium, Jovinus took a basin and gave his hands and feet a thorough washing in very cold water. Afterwards he lay down to rest on a leather cushion thrown on the ground. Melania approached him like a wise mother approaching her own son, and she scoffed at his weakness, saying: 'How can a warm-blooded young man like you dare to pamper your flesh in that way? Do you not know that this is the source of much harm? Look, I am sixty years old and neither my feet nor my face, not any of my members, except for the tips of my fingers, has touched water, although I am afflicted with many ailments and my doctors urge me. I have not yet made concessions to my bodily desires, nor have I used a couch for resting, nor have I ever made a journey on a litter.[45]

There is an explicit rejection of physicality in this story. It illustrates the attitude to the body that was current among the desert ascetics (and their admirers) but it does not sit happily with the gospel, where Jesus is presented as caring for both his own physical needs and those of others.

There are other vivid accounts of this way of life which these

45. Palladius, *Historia Lausiaca*, pp 136.

ascetics took upon themselves elsewhere in the *Historia Lausiaca*. Describing 'a maidservant named Alexandra who left the city and immured herself in a tomb', Palladius reveals the attitude towards women current in his day:

> She received the necessities of life through a window and for ten years never looked a woman or man in the face ... Melania, the thrice blessed, of whom I shall speak later, also told us about her: 'I never beheld her face to face, but I stood near the window and asked her to tell why she had immured herself in a tomb. She then told me through the window: "A man was distracted in mind because of me, and rather than scandalise a soul made in the image of God, I betook myself alive to a tomb, lest I seem to cause him suffering or reject him."'[46]

According to Palladius, she relied on others for her meagre sustenance ('she received the necessities of life through a window ... '); and the reason for her choice of this life of such strict solitude and asceticism was because 'a man was distracted in mind' because of her. Alexandra lived in such strict seclusion that she never looked another human being in the face, but in spite of her apparent concern for the spiritual welfare of the man whom she had 'distracted', this illustrates a rejection of the human being made in the image and likeness of God as found in Genesis. In accord with the ideas of her time, as a woman, she believed herself to be the guilty party in causing temptation to this man and therefore felt the obligation to remove herself from society.[47] Male monastics regarded women with a suspicion and mistrust amounting almost to fear which was mitigated slightly as the women grew older, thus losing the physical beauty which was regarded as such a snare and danger to male virtue, and

---

46. Palladius, *Historia Lausiaca*, pp 36-37.
47. This is a recurring theme in hagiography; see G. Clark, *Women in Late Antiquity*; A. Fortini, *Francis of Assisi* (trs H. Moak) (New York, Crossroads: 1981), 129-130, esp: 'The admirable Susan was the acknowledged leader of a double community of Monophysite monks and nuns. She had taken a vow always to veil her head and look downwards: she was afraid of the effect she might have on men, or they on her, if she looked them in the face', p 130.

were no longer menstruating and so rendered 'unclean'. Apparently, once a woman was past the menopause she did not constitute such a threat to the male of the species.

As far as we can judge from the sources, the number of women solitaries was far smaller than that of their male counterparts, possibly because of the potential physical danger to a woman living alone in the desert. However, women's monastic communities seem to have been large and thriving. Palladius describes one numbering 'some four hundred women'. He says they 'had the same sort of management and the same way of life' as the corresponding house for monks, which was on the opposite bank of the river, at Panopolis, which Palladius said he himself had visited. Both these monastic houses had been founded by Pachomius himself.

His picture of the women's monastery in Antinoë is particularly vivid. He describes Amma Talis, who he claims is 'eighty years old in the ascetic life'[48] who was held in such affection by the young women who lived with her that 'no lock was placed in the hall of the monastery, as in others, but they were held in check by their love for her.'[49] Palladius claims that Talis 'had such a high degree of self-control' that when he was invited into the monastery she welcomed him by sitting next to him and placing her hands on his shoulders (however, it has to be remembered that Talis was an extremely old woman by this time).

By the side of their masculine counterparts these women seem to be indistinct and shadowy figures, but still something of their strong personalities, their commitment to the life of prayer and asceticism and their indomitable spirit in spite of the hardships they had to endure, shines through in the few anecdotes told about them, and the sayings attributed to them. That only these few sayings and anecdotes were recorded bears testimony to the prejudice held against these women in their own day. The following are some sample sayings of the desert mothers which somehow got recorded in spite of this prejudice and were passed down in the tradition of desert wisdom.

Many who live on the mountains behave as those who are in

48. Palladius, *Historia Lausiaca*, p 140.
49. Ibid.

the town and they are lost. It is possible, in the midst of so many people, to remain alone in thought, as also, living alone, one can have one's thoughts amongst the crowd. (Amma Syncletica)

Fight to enter by the narrow gate. Just as the trees, in fact, if they do not suffer from the winter and the rain, cannot bear fruit, so also for us, this earthly life is similar to winter and we will not be able to become heirs of the kingdom of Heaven except through anguish and suffering. (Amma Theodora)

Once the monks of Scete went to Amma Sarah, who offered to them a basket of fruit. They rejected the good ones and ate those which were rotten 'It is true that you are from Scete,' the woman remarked.

These sayings do not seem to us to be particularly impressive for their spiritual wisdom, but they do illustrate the down-to-earth knowledge of human nature of these women ascetics, and also show their wry humour. Their importance lies in the fact that they were recorded at all, given that they are attributed to women.

Nearer home, in the insular world of Britain and Ireland, both the holy women Brigid and Moninna are described as having 'masculine souls'. But even then, when women were recognised as holy and as having the ability to perform miracles, these virtues and these miracles were not quite as 'positive' as men's miracles – they were more down to earth and less spectacular. An angel is supposed to have appeared to Ailbe and said 'Leave little miracles to women and do not even consider them. They are alright for women ...'[50] Even in the monastic world, although it did grant them a certain amount of autonomy, and the opportunity to order their own lives up to a point and to attain some spiritual wisdom, women were only 'second class citizens' and still needed to rely on men for their liturgical and sacramental lives, and also for some of the heavier practical work of

50. L. Bitel, 'Women's Monastic Enclosures in Early Ireland: a Study of Female Spirituality and Male Monastic mentalities', *Journal of Medieval History* 12, (1986), pp 28-30.

everyday. The pattern of holiness which was held up to them by their male mentors and which they were striving to attain was also masculine in its characteristics; if they were to attain sanctity, they had to renounce their feminine gender and become men. This was the only hope of salvation for the women desert dwellers. The few details we have about them in their *Vitae* and their collected sayings present them as having such a negative view of human nature generally and their own sexuality in particular that one could write them off as unbalanced and not worth taking seriously. As mentioned above, their sayings are not particularly memorable for their wisdom or spiritual value but their significance lies rather in the fact that they were recorded at all. The low view of the value of women resulted in their being given a very minor place in the tradition of monastic texts.

CHAPTER FOUR

'Virgin Widows' and 'Virgin Wives' – The Late-Classical Model for Holy Women.[1]

Castelli begins her perceptive paper on the significance of virginity in early Christianity with the comment: 'The fervour with which large numbers of early Christian women pursued lives of asceticism and renunciation is a curious fact in the history of women in late antiquity.'[2] It is this 'curious fact' and its significance for future generations that we are now exploring. While Palladius wrote with admiration of former slave women, peasants and serving women who adopted a life of extreme asceticism in the desert for love of Christ, he also wrote about the women from the other end of the social scale who devoted their talents, their lives and their almost legendary wealth to the same cause, but in a rather different environment. There were aristocratic women of great means and education, of power and position in the Roman world of the third, fourth and fifth centuries. In secular society there were women such as Pulcheria, the sister of the Emperor Theodosius II. Theodosius became Emperor in 408 when aged only 7, but until he became old enough to rule in his own right in 416, Pulcheria acted as regent.

In ecclesiastical society, there were women such as Marcella, Paula and her daughter Eustochium, Melania the elder and her granddaughter, Melania the younger, the women of the *gens Anicii*: Proba, Juliana and Demetrias, and further afield, in Asia Minor, Macrina, the sister of Basil of Caesarea. In this chapter, we will focus on the lives of these women in greater detail; let us

---

1. See G. Clark, *Women in Late Antiquity: Pagan and Christian Lifestyles* (Oxford,Clarendon Press, 1993) for useful background information. Also P. Brown, *The Body and Sexuality: Men, Women and Sexual Renunciation in Early Christianity* (New York: Columbia University Press, 1988), especially chapter 13, 'Daughters of Jerusalem': The Ascetic Life of Women in the Fourth Century, pp 259-284.
2. E. Castelli, 'Virginity and its Meaning for Women's Sexuality in Early Christianity', *Journal of Feminist Studies in Religion*, Vol 2, No 1 (Spring, 1986), pp 61-88 at p 61.

begin with Marcellina, the elder sister of St Ambrose of Milan
(c.340-397). Their father was the prefect of Trier and she was
probably born there about 330. Sometime later, the family moved
to Rome, and the pope, Liberius, witnessed her consecration to
God in St Peter's Basilica in the year 353. She received her veil
from his hands and her brother, Ambrose, reported the pope's
sermon on the occasion. As Ambrose's elder sister, she had been
largely responsible for his early education and even when he
was Bishop of Milan she went to see him and gave him advice
about his episcopal affairs. However, even a woman as highly
placed in society and in the church and as well educated as
Marcellina had to turn to a male cleric for advice and inspiration
and it was at her request that Ambrose wrote out some of his
sermons on the consecrated life, which were highly praised by
Jerome and recommended by him to Eustochium:

> [T]here are the little pamphlets our own Ambrose recently
> wrote for his sister [de virginibus]. In these he has expressed
> himself very fully; in fact he has looked up, arranged and
> written out everything relevant to the praise of virginity.[3]

Marcellina was expected to follow the advice she had been
given by her male mentors; she lived a life of great austerity and
fasting in her own home rather than in a monastic community,
so much so that towards the end of her life, Ambrose urged her
to moderate her penances and fasting. In Ambrose's funeral ora-
tion for Satyrus, their younger brother, he referred to Marcellina
as 'worshipful for her innocence, equally so for her uprightness,
and no less so for her kindness to others.' Ambrose predeceased
his sister in 397; she died shortly afterwards and was buried in
the basilica of St Ambrose in Milan near to her brother.

Whereas the desert ascetics saw the established society of
their day as corrupt and fled from it, the high born women like
Marcellina who are the subject of this chapter, witnessed the actual
collapse of that society and that of the whole of the late classical
world as they had known it taking place around them under the
onslaught of the Vandals and the Visigoths.[4] After laying siege

---

3. Jerome, EP 22.
4. See P. Brown, *The World of Late Antiquity AD 150-750* (London:
Thames and Hudson, 1971, 1991).

repeatedly to the city, the Visigoths under Alaric sacked Rome in August, 410 and the Vandals invaded North Africa in 427.[5] It was the first time Rome had been conquered in 800 years and must have seemed like the end of the world to those who lived through such enormous social, economic and cultural upheavals. Palladius describes the cataclysmic event of the fall of Rome to Alaric thus:

> [A] barbarian deluge, mentioned long before in prophecy, fell upon Rome. Even the bronze statues in the Forum did not escape, for everything was plundered and destroyed with barbarian fury. Thus Rome, beautifully adorned for twelve hundred years, became a ruin.[6]

It was believed that this destruction of Rome had been foretold by the Sybelline Oracle, but Christian writers too, seeing the deterioration of moral standards and the licentiousness of society, had also foretold the end of the world as they knew it. Cyprian of Carthage (c.208-258) wrote:

> Who cannot see that the world is already in its decline and no longer has the strength and vigour of former times? ... The world tells its own tale and its general decadence bears adequate witness that it is approaching its end ... everything in these days is rushing to its doom and is affected by the general debility.[7]

The historian, Ammianus Marcellinus (c.330-395), wrote graphic descriptions of the decadence, licentiousness and corruption of Roman society. Chapter XIV of his *History* is entitled 'The Luxury of the Rich in Rome' and gives a vivid picture of the shallowness of society at this time:

---

5. It was in the aftermath of the sack of Rome and the consequent devastation and social upheavals that Augustine wrote one of his major works: the *City of God*, where he developed the idea of the heavenly City of God, with the church at its heart, in opposition to the material earthly city. This work was enormously influential throughout the Middle Ages and was instrumental in shaping Western society.
6. Palladius, *Historia Lausiaca*, p 135.
7. Letter of Cyprian of Carthage to Dimitrianus, quoted in Lacarrière, *The God-possessed*, p 26.

Others place the summit of glory in having a couch higher than usual, or splendid apparel; and so toil and sweat under a vast burden of cloaks which are fastened to their necks by many clasps, and blow about by the excessive fineness of the material, showing a desire by the continual wriggling of their bodies, and especially by the waving of the left hand, to make more conspicuous their long fringes and tunics, which are embroidered in multiform figures of animals with threads of diverse colours.

Others again, put on a feigned severity of countenance, and extol their patrimonial estates in a boundless degree, exaggerating the yearly produce of their fruitful fields, which they boast of possessing in numbers, from east and west, being forsooth ignorant that their ancestors, who won greatness for Rome, were not eminent in riches; but through many a direful war overpowered their foes by valor, though little above the common privates in riches, or luxury, or costliness of garments.[8]

And it was not only the rich and wealthy who came in for Ammianus' censure: he also criticised the common folk of Rome, who got drunk by night, 'spending the whole night in wine shops' and then lying 'concealed in the shady arcades of the theatres'. By day they stood around idly, having nothing better to do 'from sunrise to evening, through sunshine or rain, they stay gaping and examining the charioteers and their horses; and their good and bad qualities'.[9] The city that had once been so great, powerful and prosperous, was ripe for conquest through its degenerate corruption and immorality. This was the situation in society at the time in which these women lived.

Jerome, living in Bethlehem at the time, described how he heard of the siege and sack of Rome thus:

---

8. See W. Stearns Davis (ed), *Readings in Ancient History: Illustrative Extracts from the Sources* (Boston: Allyn and Bacon, 1912-13), Vol II: *Rome and the West*. http://www.fordham.edu/halsall/ancient/ammianus-history14.html.
9. See W. Stearns Davis (ed), *Readings in Ancient History: Illustrative Extracts from the Sources* (Boston: Allyn and Bacon, 1912-13), Vol II: *Rome and the West*. http://www.fordham.edu/halsall/ancient/ammianus-history14.html.

[A] terrible rumour arrived from the west. We heard that Rome was under siege and that the citizens were having to hand over their gold in exchange for their safety, and even after they had been robbed they were being rounded up again so that they finished by losing their lives as well as their possessions. My voice sticks in my throat and sobs interrupt my dictation of these words. The city which captured the whole world has itself been captured. In fact more people died of famine than by the sword and only a few citizens were left to be captured. People were driven mad by hunger and forced to eat things that are taboo: they ripped apart each others' limbs, while the mother did not spare her suckling baby, taking into her belly the child she had recently brought forth from it.[10]

Just before the Visigoths sacked the city, realising what was about to happen, Melania the younger (daughter of the elder Melania's son Valerius Publicola and his wife Albina, therefore granddaughter to the elder Melania)[11] together with her husband Pinianus, managed – though with some difficulty – to dispose of some of their vast estates, which were scattered throughout the Empire, some even as far away as Gaul and Britain, and fled from Rome, crossing the Mediterranean to North Africa. This disposal of such almost untold wealth and property, especially at such a critical time, threatened to destabilise the whole social system and the economy, especially for the senatorial classes at the apex of this society, because the basis of their security and status was the property they owned, and the responsibility this brought with it. The vast numbers of servants and slaves needed to run these estates throughout the Empire depended on the land-owning upper classes for their support and livelihood, and the city of Rome itself relied on the imported grain and other crops they produced in their far flung estates to feed its hungry citizens. The almost untold wealth of the Roman nobility is evident from the following:

10. C. White, *Lives of Roman Christian Women* (London: Penguin Classics, 2010), p 68.
11. E. A. Clark (ed and trs), *The Life of Melania the Younger; Studies in Women and Religion* (Edwin Mellen Press, 1984).

In AD 404 Melania freed 8000 slaves out of a total of 24,000
on sixty farms, villas or hamlets which she owned in the
vicinity of Rome. Her other landholdings included estates
elsewhere in Italy and in Sicily, Africa, Spain and Britain. She
may have had well over 100,000 slaves working on her lands,
maybe a quarter of a million. Unfortunately the names of her
villas in Britain are not known, but her rentals show her income to have been on a scale comparable to the imperial rev-
enues. As a comparison, the taxes of Numidia and Mauret-
ania in North Africa in the early fifth century were 10 and 6
centenaria of gold respectively; the medium range of income
for the senatorial aristocracy at that time – when there was
such a class in Britain too – was around 15 *centenaria* from
land rents; and Melania's biographer estimates her rents to
have been about that.[12]

So Melania enjoyed not only enormous wealth, privilege and
magnificent estates and villas, but also the honour and prestige
that went with them. When she and Pinianus reached North
Africa the bishops there, including Augustine (354-430), advised
this wealthy couple to use their money to found and endow
monastic houses, which they did. Palladius describes Melania's
disposal of her property:

> She divided up the rest of her silks and made various church
> decorations. Her silver and gold she entrusted to Paul, a cer-
> tain priest, a Dalmatian monk. She sent across the sea to the
> East ten thousand pieces of money to Egypt and the Thebaid,
> ten thousand to Antioch and the vicinity thereof, fifteen
> thousand to Palestine, ten thousand to the churches in the
> Islands and beyond; she likewise made donations to the
> churches in the West.
>
> All this and four times as much in addition did she rescue
> *from the mouth of the lion*[13] – I mean Alaric, if God will forgive
> the expression. Her own faith led her to set free eight thou-
> sand slaves who desired freedom ... She sold off everything
> she had in Spain, Aquitania, Taraconia, and Gaul, keeping

12. M. Wood, *Domesday: A Search for the Roots of England* (London: BBC
Publications, 1986), p 50. I owe this reference to Alan Parish.
13. Ps 22:21.

for endowment of the monasteries only her holdings in Sicily, Campania, and Africa.[14]

This passage gives some idea of the fabulous wealth and the vast estates owned by aristocratic Roman families at this time and also of the destabilising influence on society of suddenly freeing 'eight thousand slaves' at such an economically precarious time.

Edward Gibbon, writing in the style and from the viewpoint of an eighteenth century historian, describes eloquently in his *The Decline and Fall of the Roman Empire* the wealth and sumptuous splendour of Rome at this time:

The accurate description of the city, which was composed in the Theodosian age, enumerates one thousand seven hundred and eighty houses, the residence of wealthy and honourable citizens. Many of these stately mansions might almost excuse the exaggeration of the poet – that Rome contained a multitude of palaces, and that each palace was equal to a city, since it included within its own precincts everything which could be subservient either to use or luxury: markets, hippodromes, temples, fountains, baths, porticoes, shady groves, and artificial aviaries. The historian Olympiodorus, who represents the state of Rome when it was besieged by the Goths, continues to observe that several of the richest senators received from their estates an annual income of four thousand pounds of gold, above one hundred and sixty thousand pounds sterling, without computing the stated provision of corn and wine, which, had they been sold, might have equalled in value one-third of the money. Compared to this immoderate wealth, an ordinary revenue of a thousand or fifteen hundred pounds of gold might be considered as no more than adequate to the dignity of the senatorian rank, which required many expenses of a public and ostentatious kind. Several examples are recorded in the age of Honorius of vain and popular nobles who celebrated the year of their praetorship by a festival that lasted seven days and cost above one hundred pounds sterling.

---

14. Palladius, *Historia Lausiaca*, pp 142-143.

The families of Paula, Marcella, Melania the Elder and Melania the Younger

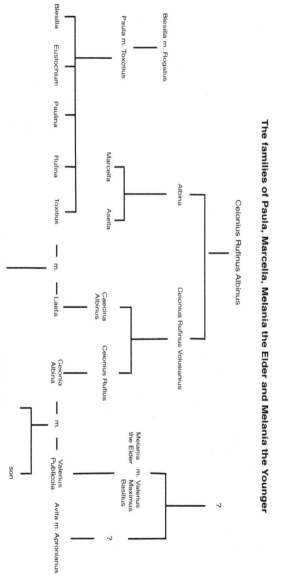

The estates of the Roman senators, which so far exceeded the proportion of modern wealth, were not confined to the limits of Italy. Their possessions extended far beyond the Ionian and Aegean seas to the most distant provinces: the city of Nicopolis, which Augustus had founded as an eternal monument of the Actian victory, was the property of the devout Paula; and it is observed by Seneca that the rivers which had divided hostile nations now flowed through the land of private citizens.[15]

Against this opulence and magnificence the ascetic fervour of these Roman matrons stands in stark contrast. Palladius described Melania's ascetic practices thus:

> She ate every other day, but in the beginning of her ascetical life at intervals of more than five days, and she arranged to do herself some of the daily work of her slave women, whom she made her associates in her ascetic practices.[16]

Even bearing in mind that Palladius was inclined to be very impressed by such ascetic exploits and that they will not have diminished in the telling, this demonstrates a very austere attitude to the spiritual life on the part of Melania.

Other female ascetics of the highest rank of society who fled from Rome in the wake of the sack by Alaric were Proba, Juliana and Demetrias, women of the Anicii family, and their companions. Demetrias' grandfather, Sextus Petronius Probus, who was a deathbed convert to Christianity, had served as proconsul of Africa, as praetorian prefect four times, as consul in 371 and as regent for the Emperor Valentinian II. Although the Anicii were one of the richest families in Rome, controlling 'virtually all the city's wealth'[17] the sources of their own vast estates were open to question, and Jerome suggests they had been acquired by the

---

15. E. Gibbon, *The Decline and Fall of the Roman Empire* (London, Penguin Classics: 1985), pp 590-591.

16. Palladius, *Historia Lausiaca*, p 143.

17. Quoted in B. Neil, 'On True Humility: An Anonymous Letter on Poverty and the Female Ascetic' in W. Mayer, P. Allen and L. Cross (eds.), *Prayer and Spirituality in the Early Church*, Vol 4: *The Spiritual Life* (Strathfield, NSW: St Paul's Publications, 2006), p 240.

unfair means of 'excessive taxation'.[18] Probus and his wife Proba had three sons, the eldest of whom, Olybrius, married Anicia Juliana and they were the parents of Demetrias. By the time of the siege of Rome by the Visigoths, Olybrius, who had shared the consulship with his brother Probinus, had died and Juliana was a widow, like her mother-in-law.

The widowed Proba had used some of her husband's wealth to found a religious community in Rome, but after Alaric's attack in 410 and the consequent pillaging, some of its members were abducted by the invaders. The three Anician women, Proba, Juliana and Demetrias, fled from Rome, Proba having rapidly liquidated her assets, to be criticised for this 'unsenatorial' behaviour by others of her social class. Palladius describes Melania the elder in an identical situation as 'actually fighting wild beasts – I mean the members of the Senate and their wives, who would have stood in the way of their renunciation.'[19]

Even when they had escaped the ravages of Alaric's warriors, these women still faced grave dangers and had to pay out large sums of money to ransom themselves in order to escape the clutches of Syrian slave-traders in Africa. Demetrias was young and marriageable and during their years of exile on their estates in North Africa, a match was arranged with another aristocratic refugee. She herself had other ideas, however, and became the first woman of her illustrious family to dedicate herself to a life of virginity. She accepted the veil from the Bishop of Carthage in either 413 or 414.[20]

These women, and others like them, had a very different conception of the ascetic life from that of the desert mothers in the previous chapter. Whereas for the women in the desert, the breaking of family and all social ties was understood to be of paramount importance, and to live unknown and in the total solitude and harshness of the desert was of the essence of the life they had chosen, for the aristocratic women, married, unmarried and widows of the late classical world, family ties were all-important and they frequently adopted a monastic style of life

---

18. B. Neil, 'On True Humility' , p 240.
19. Palladius, *Historia Lausiaca*, p 135.
20. See B. Neil, 'On True Humility', pp 233-246.

on a family estate, and in company with close relations and other members of their own family. In the words of Geoffrey Dunn, they 'were not other-worldly ascetics who fled the world into the desert in order to control themselves'.[21] This was how Macrina ('the younger' to distinguish her from her grandmother), the elder sister of Basil, Peter (of Sebaste), and Gregory (of Nyssa) and six other brothers and sisters, set up monastic life for herself and her relations.[22] She and her siblings were the grand-children of Macrina the elder, and their grandmother was re-sponsible for their upbringing and education. (She and her husband were exiled from their home during the persecution of the emperors Galerius and Maximinus (c.303-311) and took refuge in the hills and forests of Pontus, on the southern coast of the Black Sea in present day northern Turkey, to escape the particu-larly savage torture and punishments meted out to captured Christians.) Their parents were Basil the elder and Emmelia and the family was very wealthy and of important social standing.[23] Their daughter, Macrina, was born about 330 at Caesarea in Cappadocia and was betrothed to be married when she was twelve years old. However, her fiancé died suddenly and she made up her mind not to marry and, declaring herself to be a 'vir-gin widow', vowed herself to a life of virginity and stayed at home to help with the education of her younger brothers. Macrina had great influence over these younger siblings; when Basil returned to Caesarea after completing his studies at Constantinople and Athens (where he formed a lifelong friend-ship with another Gregory, from Nazianzus, where *his* father was bishop) she persuaded him to abandon his intended worldly career in law and rhetoric and to concentrate on monasticism in-stead. Macrina lived a communal life with her mother and other women who came to join them on a family estate at Annesi in

21. See G. Dunn, 'The Elements of Ascetical Widowhood: Augustine's *De bono viduitatis* and *Epistula* 130' in Mayer, Allen and Cross (eds), *Prayer and Spirituality in the Early Church*, Vol 4: *The Spiritual Life* (Strathfield, NSW: St Paul's Publications, 2006), p 250.
22. For the *Life of Macrina*, by Gregory of Nyssa, see C. White, *Lives of Roman Christian Women*, pp 20-48.
23. For Basil's contribution to monasticism and their life at Annesi, see S. Elm, *'Virgins of God' The Making of Asceticism in Late Antiquity* (Oxford: Clarendon Press, 1994), pp 78-136.

Pontus, just across the river Iris from Basil's monastery – which was the first to be founded in Asia Minor. The whole family was deeply shocked by the death of another son and brother, Naucratius, in a hunting accident. His mother was particularly affected by the sudden death of her son and Macrina was a great support both to her mother and to the rest of the family. They continued to live the monastic life at Annesi and the youngest brother, Peter, took over the management of the men's monastery.

Her mother, Emmelia, died in 373 when Macrina was in her early forties and she then gave away all her worldly goods and lived by the labour of her own hands. She died not long after in 379 in great poverty and was buried in the church of the Forty Martyrs of Sebaste. Her brother Gregory of Nyssa wrote her *Life* and he also wrote a treatise which took the form of a dialogue between himself and the dying Macrina called *De anima et resurrectione* ('On the soul and the resurrection'). He also reported miracles reputedly worked through the intercession of his sister. His *Life* was a very influential text.

Like Macrina in Pontus and Marcellina in Rome, some of these women never married, but others in the late-classical era who dedicated their lives to God were widows who took this step after the death of their husbands. Unlike widowhood in the scriptures, which meant poverty frequently akin to destitution and/or dependence on male relatives,[24] widowhood for wealthy upper class women in the Roman Empire bestowed a certain independence to order their lives as they wished which was denied to unmarried women by the customs of the times.[25] As widows they also had access to their deceased husbands' property and wealth and could usually dispose of this in accordance with their own wishes. Palladius describes the elder Melania[26] thus:

So much wealth did she spend in holy zeal, consumed in a

---

24. See the scriptural stories such as those outlined in the Book of Ruth.
25. See R. MacMullen, 'Women in Public in the Roman Empire', *Historia: Zeitschrift für Alte Geschichte*, Vol 29, No 2 (2nd Qtr, 1980), pp 208-218.
26. Melania was known as 'the elder' to distinguish her from her granddaughter of the same name. For her *Life* by Palladius, see C. White, *Lives of Roman Christian Women*, pp 50-56.

fire as it were, that not I but those rather who live in Persia should give the account. No one failed to benefit by her good works, neither in the east nor in the west, neither in the north nor in the south.

For thirty-seven years she practised hospitality; from her own treasury she made donations to churches, monasteries, guests, and prisons. Her own family and son and stewards provided the funds for this.[27]

It was the appropriate ordering of this wealth that constituted something of a problem for these women of the aristocracy who wished to consecrate their lives to God because the right disposal of wealth was seen as closely allied to the practice of true humility and this virtue was closely connected to other ascetic practices such as chastity and prayer. The two women who share the name Melania were two of the wealthiest and the best known for their ascetic endeavours of all these aristocratic women.

Melania, already mentioned several times previously, was the daughter of the Consul Marcellinus.[28] Her family had great possessions in Spain where she was born, probably around 342. She married at the age of fourteen and had three sons. When she was only twenty-two, two of these sons died, as well as her husband, in the same year. Jerome attributes to her the exclamation: 'Lord, I will serve you more easily, since you have relieved me of such burdens.'[29] She arranged for her remaining son to be taken care of and set off for Alexandria. She travelled for six months visiting the famous desert ascetics both in Egypt and Palestine. Together with Rufinus she founded a double monastery for both men and women on the Mount of Olives. After considerable travelling between Italy and Palestine, she eventually died in her monastery outside Jerusalem. Palladius had a great admiration for her and writes of her in Chapters 5, 10, 46 and 54 of his *Historia Lausiaca*. He introduces her as 'Melania, the thrice-

27. Palladius, *Historia Lausiaca*, pp 134-135.

28. A daughter according to Palladius and Jerome; a granddaughter according to Rufinus and Paulinus. See Palladius, *Historia Lausiaca*, p 205, note 401.

29. Jerome, *Epistola* 39, 5, quoted in E. Castelli, 'Virginity and its Meaning for Women's Sexuality in Early Christianity', *Journal of Feminist Studies in Religion*, Vol 2, No 1 (Spring, 1986), pp 61-88 at p 70.

blessed'. The following story which he recounts of her gives some idea of her wealth and her character and also the attitude of the desert fathers to riches:

> [T]he blessed Melania told me this: 'When I first came from Rome to Alexandria and heard about [Pambo's] virtue from the blessed Isidore, who showed me the way to him in the desert, I took him a silver coffer containing three hundred pounds of silver and invited him to share in my wealth. He was sitting weaving palm leaves, and he merely blessed me and said: "May God reward you!" And he told his steward Origen: "Take this and dispense it to all the brethren down in Libya and on the islands, for those monasteries are in greater need." He gave him orders not to dispense any of it in Egypt because that country was better off ... I was standing by and expecting to be honoured or praised by him for my donation, but I heard nothing from him, and so I spoke up to him: "So you may know, O lord, how much it is, there are three hundred pounds." He did not so much as raise his head, but said: "My child, he who measures the mountains knows better the amount of the silver. If you were giving it to me, you spoke well; but if you are giving it to God, who did not overlook the two obols[30] then be quiet".'[31]

In this story we see both the tremendous generosity of these aristocratic women, but also their desire for acknowledgement of this generosity. These traits surface again and again in all the *Lives* of these women.

Melania, 'the younger', was the daughter of Publicola, son of Melania the Elder, and his wife Albina.[32] She was born probably in 383 and when only fourteen years old was engaged to Valerius Pinianus, son of the prefect Valerius Severus. She thus moved in the highest Roman society and her father very much wanted a male heir through her. Melania, however, took the unusual (at that time) step of attempting to persuade her husband to live in continence, which at first he refused to do. Melania

---

30. A reference to the widow's mite in Luke 21:1-4.
31. Palladius, *Historia Lausiaca*, pp 44-45.
32. For her two *Lives*, one by Gerontius, one by Palladius, see C. White, *Lives of Roman Christian Women*, pp 180-234.

subsequently bore two children, both of whom died in infancy, and when she almost died as well after the premature birth of her second baby, Pinianus gave in to her desire and agreed that they should live as brother and sister. Her father strongly disapproved and only changed his mind shortly before his own death five years later, when he left all his estates to Melania, and repented of his treatment of her. This meant that she was an extremely wealthy woman, owning vast property and estates throughout Europe. Together with Albina, they left Rome and lived on a country estate where they put into practice all the corporal acts of mercy. They then decided to sell all their properties in Italy, which caused immense trouble with their relatives, who were devastated at the breakup of the enormous family fortunes, and other members of their social class. Having left Italy before the invading Goths, after various adventures, they reached their estates in North Africa, and eventually settled at Tagaste, and were warmly welcomed by Augustine in Hippo when they went to visit him there. Having built two monasteries in Africa, they eventually travelled on to Jerusalem, taking Albina with them. By this time, so generous had they been that their funds were running low. However, they travelled on again to visit the monks in the Egyptian deserts, and were so impressed that they returned to Jerusalem to try to put into practice what they had seen in Egypt. Here they were introduced to Jerome by Melania's cousin, Paula. Melania worked closely with Jerome and he thought very highly of her, calling her 'the devout lady Melanium' and praising her for being 'eminent among Christians for her true nobility'. When they had been in Palestine for about fourteen years, both Pinianus and Albina died within a year of each other. Melania buried them both on the Mount of Olives and eventually her own small cell near their graves grew into a large community of women, with another for men close by. She died on the day after Christmas in 439 in Bethlehem.[33]

33. The celebration of Christ's birth has a complicated history. A calendar of feasts dating from 243 gives March 28 as the date of the nativity. A Roman text of 354, the *Chronographia*, is the first reference to December 25: 'VIII *kal. Ian. natus Christus in Betleem Iudeae*'. In the East, the feast was observed in Constantinople in 379.

Probably the best known of all these aristocratic women is Paula, who was born into the Roman nobility, a descendant of both the Gracchi and the Scipio families.[34] She was born about 347, married well according to her status and bore four daughters, Blesilla, Paulina, Eustochium and Rufina and a son, Toxotius. She was widowed at the age of thirty two and after the death of her husband, which caused her great anguish, experienced a religious conversion. At the urging of another noble widow, Marcella ('the glory of the ladies of Rome' according to Jerome[35] and the first to adopt an ascetic way of life),[36] who had been a great comfort to her after the death of her husband, Paula and Eustochium joined Marcella's community of like-minded women, and when Jerome came to Rome in 382 he became involved with their direction. Jerome recounts how Marcella was inspired by Athanasius' *Vita Antonii* to adopt a monastic way of life and how she influenced Paula and Eustochium:

> At that time no high ranking Roman woman knew anything of the monastic way of life and no one dared go in for something that, because of its novelty, would be regarded with suspicion and contempt. Some priests from Alexandria (Bishop Athanasius and his successor Peter who fled to escape persecution by the Arian heretics – they had come to Rome as a safe haven where they could find people with similar beliefs) had told Marcella of the life of the blessed Antony who was still living at the time, of the Pachomian monasteries in the Thebaid and of the monastic rule for virgins and widows. She was not ashamed to adopt this way of life which she knew had been pleasing to Christ ... The much-respected Paula enjoyed Marcella's friendship and it was in Marcella's room that Eustochium, that paragon of virgins, was brought up – so it is easy to judge what the teacher must have been like if this is how her pupils turned out![37]

34. For her *Life* by Jerome, see C. White, *Lives of Roman Christian Women*, pp 72-108.
35. Jerome, Letter 127, *To Principia*.
36. For the *Life of Marcella*, by Jerome, see C. White, *Lives of Roman Christian Women*, pp 58-70.
37. Jerome, *Life of Marcella*, C. White, *Lives of Roman Christian Women*, pp 63-64.

Though still only in her mid-teens, Eustochium made a vow of perpetual virginity, with Jerome's encouragement.[38] When Blesilla, another of Paula's daughters, died (it was said, from extreme fasting and other ascetic practices, encouraged by Jerome), Jerome and Paula came under a cloud of disapproval in society and in 385 Jerome left Rome for the East. So much was Paula under the influence of Jerome that she and Eustochium soon followed him and after quite extensive travels through Palestine and to visit the ascetics in the deserts of Egypt, eventually set up monastic houses near Bethlehem, one for men and three for women, the latter directed by Paula with assistance from Eustochium. They also set up a hospice for visitors to the Holy Places.

Jerome was a controversial saint. He made enemies just as easily – in fact, possibly more so – than he made friends. After a classical education, in which he read both Latin and Greek authors fluently and mastered the art of rhetoric, which he later put to great, and sometimes satirical, use, he had a religious conversion, following a vivid dream and then for four years lived a life of great asceticism in the desert of Syria. Here, along with penitential fasting, he experienced severe temptations, which he later described graphically in a letter to his protégée, Eustochium. He also during these years, studied Hebrew, which enabled him later on to accomplish his great work as biblical scholar, translator, and commentator. After some time in Constantinople, where he studied the scriptures under Gregory Nazianzen, Jerome travelled on to Rome. Eventually, Pope Damasus asked him to work as his secretary, which he did while also writing some biblical commentaries. Although he left no Rule of his own composition, his writings, especially his *Vita* of Paul the Hermit helped to spread monastic ideals and practice and his deep love of the scriptures and his translation work made further links between scripture and monastic life.

Just as the bonds of family relationships were not disdained and their vast stores of wealth were not entirely distributed to the poor, but also administered in order to benefit churches and to found monasteries and so initiate monastic life, so education

38. See Jerome's Letter 22 to Eustochium, *On Choosing a life of Virginity*, C. White, *Lives of Roman Christian Women*, pp 110-148.

was not scorned but highly valued by these women. They were powerful and articulate, and by contemporary standards, were well educated and their understanding of the importance of intellectual prowess for the pursuit of theological and scriptural studies encouraged them to expand their learning by studying Hebrew and Greek. Paula and Marcella had mastered Greek while still in Rome in order to read the New Testament in the original, but now Paula and Eustochium were anxious to learn Hebrew in order to read the Old Testament. Jerome wrote of Paula: 'She succeeded so well that she could chant the psalms in Hebrew and could speak the language without a trace of the pronunciation peculiar to Latin.'

The support she gave Jerome in funding his literary activities and the founding and maintaining of her various monasteries drained Paula's vast finances and she died in Bethlehem in 404 in very impoverished circumstances. She was laid to rest under the altar of the church of the Nativity. Eustochium, having been with her mother throughout her life, was devastated by her death, but eventually overcame her grief and took on the direction of the various monastic houses. In 416 she was shattered by another traumatic experience when the monasteries were burned down and the inhabitants attacked by vandals. Eustochium was so deeply shocked by this that she never really recovered and died not long after.

As well as their attitude to wealth and to education, these women differed from the female desert ascetics in other significant ways, too. The records we have of the desert mothers preserve a few of their short sayings as worthy of remembrance and as having value for others pursuing the ascetic life. These female figures of third and fourth century desert monasticism seem to have discovered their own spiritual paths with little or no assistance from others, certainly not from the men who seem to have resented their presence. Marilyn Dunn notes this and comments:

> The question arises of who taught them in the first place. Were they former syneisakts[39] or members of urban ascetic groups who had then embarked on *anachoresis*?[40] Had they

---

39. The ascetic practice of a man and woman living together as brother and sister.
40. Withdrawal from secular life.

been amongst the visitors who ventured into the hermit colonies to learn from the greatest teachers – and if so where did they stay?[41]

On the other hand, the aristocratic women of the fifth century apparently relied far more on male guidance and teaching and were anxious to be under male clerical direction. We have lengthy letters addressed to them by the great theologians and scriptural teachers of the day: Augustine's letters to Proba,[42] and to Juliana[43] and also Jerome's letter to Demetrias[44] and also his infamous (because of its explicit sexual references) *Epistola* 22 to Eustochium.[45] Pelagius wrote to Demetrias also, and these letters of direction assumed such a length as to resemble treatises, becoming almost a literary genre in their own right, all giving these women detailed guidance in their ascetic endeavours,[46] the practicalities of their chosen way of life and their spiritual welfare.[47] The following is a short extract from Jerome's letter of

---

41. M. Dunn, *The Emergence of Monasticism* (Oxford: Blackwell, 2000), p 46.

42. *Epistula* 130 (NBA 22, 76). For a discussion, see G. D. Dunn, 'The Elements of Ascetical Widowhood: Augustine's *De bono viduitatis* and *Epistula* 130' in Mayer, Allen and Cross (eds), *Prayer and Spirituality in the Early Church*, Vol 4: *The Spiritual Life* (Strathfield, NSW: St Paul's Publications, 2006), pp 247-256. Passages from Augustine's *Letter to Proba* are used in the Roman Breviary Vol 3 today, forming a commentary on the scriptural readings from the book of Esther, Week 29 of the Year, pp 661-681.

43. *Epistula* 188; CSEL, 57, 119-130.

44. *Epistola* 130; CSEL 56/1, 175-201.

45. However, any letters that the women wrote to their male teachers and guides have not survived. See Castelli, 'Virginity and its Meaning for Women's Sexuality in Early Christianity', p 62: 'Jerome's letters to Paula, Marcella, Eustochium and other learned and literate women were collected and preserved while not a single letter of any of these women remains.'

46. See Castelli, 'Virginity and its Meaning for Women's Sexuality in Early Christianity', p 64 for full references.

47. See S. Elm, *Virgins of God*, p 14: 'In particular the then developing genre of the treatise *On Virginity*, as well as the hagiographical writings or *Lives*, both usually classified by the authors themselves as 'letters', are eminently normative in nature. They as well as numerous 'actual' letters were written with the sole and clearly stated intention of regulating and 'normalizing', and were understood as such by their addressees.'

advice to the teenage Eustochium giving an example of his direction:

> Choose as your friends those whom you can see have grown thin by fasting, whose faces are pale, who are of a suitable age and way of life and who every day sing in their hearts ... Be obedient to your parents; imitate your Bridegroom. Only go out in public very occasionally, seek out the martyrs in your bedroom. Do not eat large amounts and never let your stomach get full ... Spend much of your time reading and learn as much as possible. Let sleep steal upon you with the book in your hands and the sacred page catch your head as it droops. Practise fasting every day and do not eat so much that you get full ... Wash your bed and sprinkle your couch each night with tears. Stay awake and become like the sparrow in your solitude ... Do not harbour a secret thought that because you have ceased to be admired for clothes of gold, you might be admired for your shabby clothes. When you are in room full of brothers or sisters, do not take a seat at the far end, pleading that you are not worthy to sit anywhere else. Do not speak quietly on purpose as if your voice were weakened by fasting, and do not lean on someone else's shoulder as if you were feeling faint.[48]

Jerome descends into the minutiae of daily life and leaves this young woman no personal choices at all in the details of her life. His *Epistola* 107 to Laeta (Paula's daughter-in-law) on the education of little Paula is much more human in tone and content than his *Epistola* to Eustochium and is full of advice on bringing up Paula's granddaughter.[49] He leaves no stone unturned in his desire that these women should fit into his preconceived pattern of holiness from their earliest days.

Yet these women were so completely under the influence of their male clerical guides that they have left us practically nothing personal to themselves by which we can access their inner lives and their personalities. They have left us no pithy wisdom

48. C. White, *Lives of Roman Christian Women*, pp 122, 123,133
49. See Jerome's Letter 107 to Laeta, *On the Education of Little Paula*, C. White, *Lives of Roman Christian Women*, pp 150-163.

sayings as did the desert mothers, no down-to-earth aphorisms. Their spiritual experiences remain hidden behind those of their mentors. Whereas for the ascetics in the desert, so negative was their view of the female that the women monastics achieved holiness almost in spite of their male counterparts, women of the late classical world relied heavily on their male spiritual guides and mentors in their striving for sanctity. This was not because of any weakness either of will or of intellect; these were influential, aristocratic women, who in the absence of their husbands and after their deaths (it was the custom in late antiquity for wealthy Romans of the upper classes to marry much younger women,[50] therefore their husbands frequently predeceased them) had almost unlimited wealth at their disposal. Dunn describes the situation of these women:

> The death of a husband or father was a significant event in the lives of ascetically inclined female aristocrats, as they had little legal autonomy as wives or daughters. Sometimes married off at an early age – even before the legal age of consent – women had very limited rights and a large number of duties within the confines of family and married life. A woman could not act for herself in court. Laws regarding marriage were largely framed to protect property and upper-class marriages were undertaken for the advantage of the two family groups concerned, to gain property or perhaps to cement political alliances.[51]

Yet so all-pervading in Christianity was the idea that women were inferior to men in every aspect of their lives, that these women subjected themselves to the tyranny of Jerome and others without question. Jerome expressed a great regard for Paula and others under his direction precisely because they accepted his male chauvinism.[52] White comments in her short biography

---

50. See P. Brown, *The Body and Society*, pp 5-17.

51. Dunn, *The Emergence of Monasticism*, p 47.

52. In his *Life of Paula* (*Epistola* 108, which he wrote shortly after her death in order to comfort Eustochium) he says: 'If all my bodily limbs were to turn into tongues and if every limb could speak with a human voice, I would still be unable to give an account of the virtues of the holy Paula.' C. White, *Lives of Roman Christian Women* (London:Penguin Classics, 2010), p 74.

of Paula: 'She ... was regarded as particularly saintly for putting up with Jerome as he had a difficult personality: Palladius in the *Lausiac History* records the view of one holy man who commented that 'Paula who looks after Jerome will die first and be set free at last from his meanness. Because of him no holy person will live in those parts. His bad temper would drive out even his own brother'."[53]

The letters of spiritual guidance which Jerome and other church writers addressed to these women have much to say on the matter of property and its administration, family ties and the responsibility which came with high social status and the appropriate practice of celibacy. These were three key areas for ascetics in the late-classical period and they occasioned controversy and differing opinions among patristic ascetic and spiritual writers. Castelli quotes Cyprian who 'in the third century, does not require the group of virgins to whom he writes to give up their wealth, but to be generous with it.'[54]

Although some of these women, such as Melania, were famous for their ascetical practices, it seems that others of these formidable and aristocratic women adopted a considerably more 'moderate' form of ascetic living than their desert counterparts,[55] but even when they took upon themselves some of the austerities of the desert and gave away their fabled wealth, adopting a lowly and humble outward guise, something of the cultural attitudes of their social class remained very near the surface. This we see from an incident in the life of Melania herself. Although committed to an extremely ascetic way of life,[56] she was very much involved with the ecclesiastical politics of her day, and when monks who were suspected of Origenism were expelled from Nitria by Theophilus and fled to Palestine

---

53. C. White, *Lives of Roman Christian Women* (London: Penguin Classics, 2010), p 72.
54. Castelli, 'Women's Sexuality in Early Christianity', p 83.
55. See See B. Neil, 'On True Humility: An Anonymous Letter on Poverty and the Female Ascetic' in Mayer, Allen and Cross (eds), *Prayer and Spirituality in the Early Church*, Vol 4: *The Spiritual Life* (Strathfield, NSW: St Paul's Publications, 2006), p 236 for the technical use of the term 'moderate'. Its application to the Anici women is questioned by Dunn, 'The Elements of Ascetical Widowhood', p 250.
56. See the incident regarding washing in the previous chapter.

for refuge, it was Melania who took food to them at night in the disguise of a slave. She was arrested and thrown into prison by the local governor, because it had been forbidden to help them in any way. Melania's response was anything but servile:

> She rounded on him, instantly reassuming part of her old identity with all the imperious disdain of a *grande dame* accustomed to deference on account of her rank and declaring: For my part, I am So-and-so's daughter and So-and-so's wife, but I am Christ's slave. And do not despise the cheapness of my clothing, for I am able to exalt myself if I like and you cannot terrify me in this way or take any of my goods.[57]

Humble servility and deference to others did not come naturally to these aristocratic women and one suspects that their spiritual direction might not have been without its difficulties. Jerome even encouraged them to maintain a certain pride in their aristocratic birth, although he disapproved of their retaining the wealth and social obligations which membership of their privileged class brought with it. As an example of this aristocratic pride, in his *Life* of Paula, Jerome gives the text of the inscription which he himself had had carved on her tomb in Bethlehem; he obviously took very great pride in the aristocratic lineage of his protégées:

A woman descended from Scipio, whose parents belonged to the Pauli,
A descendant of the Gracchi, the famous offspring of Agamemnon
Lies in this tomb, to whom her parents gave the name Paula.
Mother of Eustochium, leading lady of the Roman Senate,
She went to live in rural Bethlehem to follow Christ in poverty.

But in spite of her noble birth, her commitment to asceticism was so extreme that it brought its censure from the society of the day. As described above, Paula's daughter Blesilla, young and recently widowed, threw herself into a life of penance and fasting, with more fervour than discretion. Within a few months she was dead, killed, so society said, by her imprudent austerities. Because of this, Paula and Jerome both fell under a cloud and

---

57. M. Dunn, *The Emergence of Monasticism* (Oxford: Blackwell, 2000), p 50.

first Jerome and then Paula, accompanied by Eustochium, left
Rome to travel to the Holy Land. Here they set up monastic life,
houses for women and one for men. In Paula's monastery,
which was reported to number at least fifty women, although
they dressed alike and shared the work and practices of community life, they were divided into three classes, according to the
social rank which had been theirs in secular life. Jerome commented:

> If a virgin were of noble birth she was not allowed to have an
> attendant belonging to her own household lest her maid fill
> her mind full of the doings of the old days and the licence of
> childhood and might, by constant converse, open old
> wounds and renew former errors.[58]

Although this division according to social rank does not
seem to be a way of living that sits easily with the gospel precepts, all the women, whatever their former social status gathered together in church for the hours of prayer. Paula made herself responsible for the ascetic formation of the sisters, taking
into consideration the character and weaknesses of each. To the
talkative, the argumentative and the boisterous she gave counsel and penance according to the need of each:

> If one of the women happened to arrive late for the psalms or
> was slow at her work, Paula would deal with her in different
> ways. If the woman was irritable, Paula would speak sooth-
> ingly; if she was apathetic she would rebuke her ... When
> people were arguing she would speak gently to them and
> make them come to an agreement. If the young girls became
> frisky with thoughts of sex, Paula would crush those tenden-
> cies by prescribing frequent and redoubled fasts, preferring
> the girls to have stomach pains rather than mental troubles.
> If she saw one of them rather elegantly dressed, she would
> rebuke the girl who was at fault with a frown and an expres-
> sion of displeasure, pointing out to her that elegance of ap-
> pearance and dress were indications of spiritual ugliness. A
> foul or dirty word should never be uttered by a virgin for

58. Jerome, *Letter to Eustochium*, quoted in Jo Ann McNamara, *Sisters in
Arms* (Massachusetts: Harvard University Press, 1996), p 78.

these were signs of a lewd mind ... When she found someone talkative or frivolous or insolent and the girl refused to correct her behaviour even after several warnings, Paula would make her pray among the younger ones, separated from the others, outside the dining room doors, and eat her meal apart so that if she could not be corrected by rebuke, shame might force her to amend her ways.[59]

Thus monastic life, even in an establishment as admirable as Paula's, was not always sweetness and light.

Jerome commented particularly on her loving and tender care for the sick and the weak. He wrote: 'Do I need to describe her compassion and committed care of the sick and the extraordinary devotion and concern with which she looked after them?'[60] This menial service was something quite extraordinary for a woman of noble birth, but both manual and intellectual work figured largely in the daily lives of these women and all the sisters had their own work to do, each according to her own abilities, whether it was making clothes for the community or copying manuscripts.[61] This was daily religious life as lived both by these aristocratic women, for whom manual labour would been unheard of in their previous secular lives, and those women of much lower social rank who would have toiled and laboured all their days. Paula died in 404; Jerome was devastated by her death; he concluded his *Life* of Paula with the words: 'Farewell, Paula, please pray for me in my final years, I who idolise you';[62] and he preached her eulogy at her funeral. The direction of the monastic houses passed to her daughter Eustochium, who continued in her mother's footsteps until her own death, around 419, brought on most probably by the trauma of the attack by the Vandals.

These were all valiant women who showed the sincerity of their desire for a life of prayer and austerity by giving away

---

59. Jerome, *Life of Paula the Elder*, in C. White, *Lives of Roman Christian Women* (London:Penguin Classics, 2010), p 96.

60. Jerome, *Life of Paula*, p 97.

61. Jo Ann McNamara, *Sisters in Arms* (Massachusetts: Harvard University Press, 1996), p 79.

62. See C. White, *Lives of Roman Christian Women* (London: Penguin Classics, 2010), p 107.

most, if not all, of their vast fortunes in the founding of monasteries, accepting exile and by taking on manual labour of various kinds, which would have been otherwise unthinkable for women of their social standing. However, the question remains: how much was this voluntary, how much forced on them in the face of the invasions and other social upheavals of the times, and how much imposed upon them by their male mentors? The practical contribution these women made to monasticism was to use their riches to further monastic living by building and founding monasteries, though even this distribution of their wealth was done under male direction. They were intelligent, spirited and articulate women, 'married to husbands for whom political and cultural activity involved endless travel to the centres of power' and who, during these absences 'were left by their husbands to manage the miniature empire of an aristocrat's estates'.[63] Ramsay MacMullen describes the influence these women could have in the political and social spheres of their days:

> At the centre of the Roman world, as any reader of Tacitus knows, women had a great deal to say about the decisions that determined the lives and fortunes of the most important people ... Claudius' reign offers the best illustration, pictured as wholly under the control of his latest wife ... and no one can doubt, though no evidence allows us to demonstrate, that, in such groups of the wives of the great in the capital, the strongest personalities stood out, and altered others' opinions, and those opinions were in turn carried home, there to influence at least some husbands, sons and fathers.[64]

However, this political and social influence and the articulateness that went with it, were not replicated in the religious and ecclesiastical spheres. Here, these women were expected to be unquestionably obedient to their male mentors and teachers. These women were courageous enough to undertake long and difficult journeys on pilgrimage to the deserts of the east and the

63. P. Brown, *The Body and Society*, p 15.
64. R. MacMullen, 'Women in Public in the Roman Empire', *Historia: Zeitschrift für Alte Geschichte*, Vol 29, No.2 (2nd Qtr, 1980), pp 208-218, at p 216.

holy places,[65] but they have left no wise sayings or other fruits of their lives of asceticism. The one letter purporting to come from the pen of Paula and Eustochium was, in all likelihood, actually written by Jerome and is included in the Collection of his Letters.[66] They do not speak to us directly down the centuries; we only know of them through the writings of the church fathers. They lived entirely in the shade of their male mentors and spiritual guides and their lives were organised down to the last practical details and their ascetic practices were dictated to them entirely by men. For this they were praised highly by these men but by acquiescing in this situation they perpetuated it for generations to come; in fact, it is still with us today.

65. See Letter 46, To Marcella, *On Visiting Jerusalem*, from Paula and Eustochium, C. White, *Lives of Roman Christian Women*, pp 166-177. For women and pilgrimage, see Elm, *'Virgins of God' The Making of Asceticism in Late Antiquity*, pp 272-275.
66. See C. White, *Lives of Roman Christian Women*, p 166.

CHAPTER FIVE

Queens and Slaves in the Early Medieval World – Women's Monasticism in England, Ireland and Gaul

We now move to the far west of the then known world, to Gaul, to Britain and even further west, to Ireland. Insular society in the early Christian centuries was a rich and complex mixture of a variety of cultures and peoples, which sometimes mingled, sometimes fused, sometimes contradicted and sometimes clashed violently. Bede famously described the situation in Britain thus:

> This island at present, following the number of the books in which the Divine Law was written, contains five nations, the English, Britons, Scots, Picts and Latins, each in its own peculiar dialect cultivating the sublime study of Divine truth.[1]

Thus the various nations were, according to Bede, joined together by the Latin language and by the Christian faith, but the situation was rather more complex than the impression which Bede gives. The tribes of Britain, some of which had intermarried with and otherwise been influenced by the Roman invaders, had, by the fifth century, been affected by Germanic influence in the form of the Anglo-Saxons. A parallel situation had occurred in Gaul, where Germanic tribes, the Franks, had taken over the remnants of Gallo-Roman society.[2] This chapter examines how society in Gaul and in the British Islands treated its

1. Bede, *HEGA*, 1,i.
2. Connections between the insular world and Merovingian and Carolingian society are discussed in some detail in D. Ó Cróinín, 'Merovingian Politics and Insular Calligraphy; The Historical Background to the Book of Durrow and Related Manuscripts', in M. Ryan, (ed) *Ireland and Insular Art A.D. 500-1200* (Dublin: RIA, 1987), pp 40-43. See also M. Carver (ed), *The Cross Goes North: Processes of Conversion in Northern Europe, AD 300-1300* (York: York Medieval Press, 2003).

womenfolk particularly with regard to their desire for monastic life.

When the new Christian faith came to lands inhabited by Celtic peoples there already existed a society in which women in some ways enjoyed greater freedom than contemporary women in other cultures, and yet at the same time were still very subordinate to their menfolk and very limited in their social rights. The place of women in the early medieval West is often portrayed in popular writing on 'Celtic spirituality' as being equal to that of men, but although Tacitus had written about powerful Celtic women leaders in Britain such as Boudica (*Annals* 14:35) and Cartimandua (*Annals* 12:40), and early Irish legends featured such influential women as Medb, Ness, Emer and Fedelma, women of such power and influence in Celtic society remained either very few and far between, or in the realms of myth and legend. The reality was much harsher, far more restricted and repressed, and much more complex as shown in texts from early Britain and Ireland. Reality for most women in the early middle ages was much more of a daily grind at the service of their husbands and masters than the feisty lifestyle portrayed in legends and folklore.[3] Also, this was a time of great political upheaval, conquest and rebellion, in many ways parallel to that we have witnessed in the last chapter. We do not know if the powerful women such as Boudica would have been tolerated as leaders by their tribesmen in more peaceful circumstances. Perhaps only the threat posed by the Roman invaders and the consequent need for immediate leadership made possible Boudica's adoption of tribal authority.

One valuable textual witness to the position of women in insular society is from the writings of St Patrick. Patrick was a fifth century Christian of the Roman Empire, who crossed the sea to an alien land, where he had previously lived and worked in captivity as a slave, to bring Christianity to its people. There, probably late in his life, he wrote an account of his life and ministry. In his account, his *Confessio* – which can be translated as his declaration – both in the sense of a refutation of his critics, a statement

---

3. For details of daily life in insular society, see Liam de Paor, *Saint Patrick's World* (Dublin: Four Courts Press, 1993, 1996).

of his faith, and an acknowledgement of the work of God in his life – gives a very vivid and graphic picture of the situation in which Christians on both sides of the Irish Sea found themselves in the fifth century. Regarding those women who wished to become Christians, he says:

> This, of course, is not to the liking of their fathers and they have to suffer persecution and false accusation from their parents. Yet despite this their number keeps increasing and we do not know the number of those born there from our begetting apart from widows and those who are celibate. But of all these women, those held in slavery have to work hardest; they are continually harassed and even have to suffer being terrorised. But the Lord gives grace to many of his maid servants and the more they are forbidden to imitate the Lord, the more boldly they do this.[4]

So even becoming a Christian was not easy for a woman in fifth century Britain and Ireland. If unmarried, she was still under the control of her father and he had the right to order her life. If married, her husband had total control over her. If she was a woman of lower social status and living in slavery, then her lot was even harder: she could be made to suffer physically and mentally at the hands of her master. A passage from an early Irish law tract says:

> Her father has charge over her when she is a girl, her husband when she is a wife, her sons when she is a 'woman of the kin' [i.e. with no other guardian], the church when she is a woman of the church [i.e. a nun]. She is not capable of sale or purchase or contract or transaction without the authorisation of one of her superiors.[5]

Other early collections of laws give us an insight into the legal status and position of women. An early collection of Irish canon law, the *Collectio Canonum Hibernensis*, gives relevant evidence on the place of women in that society. Although Irish in provenance, it was known and used throughout the insular

---

4. T. O'Loughlin, *St Patrick: the Man and his Works* (London, SPCK: 1999), p 78.
5. F. Kelly, *A Guide to Early Irish Law* (Dublin: 1988), p 76.

world, and even further afield; the earliest manuscript we have is from Anglo-Saxon Northumbria. In this collection we find that the evidence of a woman was not accepted, a daughter could not receive the principal part of an inheritance, a woman was classed with slaves, pilgrims, simpletons and monks living outside their monasteries (and therefore suspect because not subject to obedience to their rightful abbot), as one who could not act as a guarantor; women were not allowed to teach men, they were to be silent in church, they were not to receive any male or priestly office and a man could divorce his wife for any number of reasons (some of them very minor) but women did not have this same freedom with regard to their husbands.[6] A wife had to remain faithful and obedient even if her husband was a gambler, a drunkard or beat or abused or neglected her. She could not initiate separation or sue him for adultery. The code of law operative in Burgundy actually prescribed that a wife who tried to divorce her husband should be smothered in mire.[7] The Frankish historian, Hincmar of Rheims (806-882), wrote that men who accused their wives of adultery: 'lead them to the slaughter house to be butchered, and they bid the cooks to kill them with swords as it is the practice with sheep and pigs, or they personally murder them with the edge of their own swords, cutting them into pieces'.[8] Three hundred years earlier, Gregory of Tours (538-593/4), the main contemporary source for Merovingian history, had described the even more ferocious treatment of female prisoners of war:

> They put more than two hundred of our young women to death in the most barbarous way: they tied their arms round the necks of their horses, stampeded these animals in all directions by prodding them with goads, and so tore the girls to pieces; or else they stretched them out over the ruts of their roads, attached their arms and legs to the ground with

6. T. O'Loughlin, 'Collectio Canonum Hibernensis, Book 46' in A. Bourke *et al*, eds, *The Field Day Anthology of Irish Writing*, IV: *Irish Women's Writings and Traditions* (New York University Press, New York: 2002).

7. A. Lucas, *Women in the Middle Ages* (London: The Harvester Press, 1983), p 69.

8. S. Wemple, *Women in Frankish Society: Marriage and the Cloister, 500-900* (Philadelphia: University of Pennsylvania Press, 1981), p 104.

stakes, and then drove heavily laden carts over them again and again, until their bones were all broken and their bodies could be thrown out for the dogs and birds to feed on.[9]

We see a specific example of this brutal male treatment of women who were regarded as the spoils of war, in the life of Radegund, Princess of Thuringia. In Radegund's case this treatment did at least stop short of death.

She was born c.520, the daughter of Berthaire, the king of Thuringia, who was a pagan. While she was still small, her father was murdered by her uncle, who took charge of Radegund and her brother. When the Franks invaded Thuringia in 531, Radegund and her brother were carried off by the king, Clothaire I. Radegund had no wish to marry him, partly because of his cruelty and partly because she wished to become a nun, but she had no choice in the matter and he took her as his wife. One of her biographers, Venantius Fortunatus, wrote of her time as Clothaire's wife:

> At night, when she lay with her prince she would ask leave to rise and leave the chamber to relieve nature. Then she would prostrate herself in prayer under a hair cloak by the privy so long as the cold pierced her through and only her spirit was warm. Her whole flesh prematurely dead, indifferent to her body's torment, she kept her mind intent on Paradise and counted her suffering trivial, if only she might avoid becoming cheap in Christ's eyes. Re-entering the chamber thereafter, she could scarcely get warm either by the hearth or in her bed. Because of this, people said that the King had yoked himself to a monocha[10] rather than a queen. Her goodness provoked him to harsher irritation but she either soothed him to the best of her ability or bore her husband's brawling modestly.

Ten years into this marriage, which produced no heirs and must have been mutually unsatisfactory, Clothaire had Radegund's brother murdered, and this, coupled with Clothaire's

9. Gregory of Tours, *The History of the Franks*, trs Lewis Thorpe (London: Penguin Books, 1974), pp 167-168.
10. A nun.

brutal treatment, provoked her into fleeing from the Frankish court. She was eventually consecrated as a deaconess, and settled at Poitiers, where she built a monastery dedicated to the Virgin Mary. After the arrival of a relic of the True Cross, sent by the Emperor of Byzantium, the monastery was rededicated to the Holy Cross. The *Regula* Radegund adopted for her foundation was written by a male cleric: it was composed by Caesarius of Arles for his sister, Caesaria, and specified strict enclosure. It also required that the nuns be able to read and write and they devoted several hours each day to reading and copying the scriptures. This was very unusual at that time. Radegund died in 587, and two *Vitae* were written; one by the chaplain, the poet Venantius Fortunatus, and the other by one of her nuns, Baudonivia. The latter *Vita* is unique in that it is the life of a woman saint, written by a woman, and a woman who had actually known the subject of her work and lived with her. However, although it is of very great importance because it gives us an insight into women's own motivation, it is full of hyperbolised enthusiasm for Radegund and her austerities. Venantius Fortunatus' account of Radegund's virtues is a stereotyped version of Radegund as the hagiographer thought she should be – ascetic, remote and pious. In Baudonivia's version we have another description of her but this time with her motherly virtues emphasised showing her concern for her sisters, trying to make peace between the various warring factions of her husband's family and anxious that her religious foundation should be a place of prayer for the kings of Merovingian Gaul.[11] Her life shows vividly how much women, especially those of the ruling classes, were at the mercy of the men, who had total control of their lives and frequently exercised that control with brutality.

At the other end of the social scale, we have a graphic, and at times, spine-chilling insight into conditions of life for slave women in England and Ireland at the end of the seventh century which has been preserved in the Law of Adomnán – *Lex innocentium* in Latin. This law is unique among the laws of early medieval Ireland, because not only do we know the person responsi-

---

11. Margaret Wade Labarge, *A Small Sound of the Trumpet* (London: Hamish Hamilton, 1990), pp 7, 8.

ble for its promulgation, but we also know the exact year and the place of its promulgation. It was a great milestone in the history of Irish women as it was the earliest law to be concerned primarily with the welfare of women in Ireland. This law, intended to protect the weaker members of society, women, children and clerics, was promulgated at a great synod in Birr, Co Offaly, in 697, by Adomnán, the abbot of Iona. It was intended to be effective throughout Ireland, and also in England, especially in the north, where Irish influence was strong because of the links through Lindisfarne with Iona. It describes as follows how Adomnán emancipated women from fighting and performing servile work:

> 'Slavey' was the name for women until Adomnán came to emancipate them and this was the work of the slave: a pit was dug for the woman at the head of the sluice gate so that it hid her nakedness. One end of the crossbar was supported by her until the grinding of the load was done. After coming out of that hole in the earth, she dipped a candle four manfists in thickness into a mound of butter or tallow and that candle remained in her palm until dividing and distributing and bedmaking in the houses of kings and superiors had ended. That woman took no share in purse or basket nor did she live in the one house with the master of the house but in a cold hut outside the enclosure, lest any malevolence from land or sea befall her lord. The work which the finest of women used to do was to proceed to battle and battle field, division and encampment, killing and slaughter. On one side she carried her provision bag, on the other side her infant, her wooden pole upon her back, thirty feet in length. On one end of it (there was) an iron hook, which she would thrust into the opposite battalion at the hair of the other woman, her husband behind her, a fence-stake in his hand, flogging her on to battle. For at that time it was a woman's head or two breasts which were taken as trophies.[12]

---

12. Máirín Ní Dhonnchadha, 'The *Lex Innocentium*: Adomnán's Law for Women, Clerics and Youths 697 AD', in M. O'Dowd and S. Wichert (eds) *Chattel, Servant or Citizen: Women's Status in Church, State and Society* (Belfast: Historical Studies xix, 1995), p 64 (punctuation slightly altered).

Márkus is of the opinion that this description 'owes more to the imagination of the writer than to a knowledge of how things were for women in the seventh century',[13] and sees 'the appalling picture ...' as 'greatly exaggerated.'[14] However, he does concede that women were probably involved in battle and fighting, otherwise Adomnán's law would have been pointless. So maybe the description of woman's lot in *Cáin Adomnáin* is not too far off the mark.

Adomnán believed he had received divine guidance to make 'a law in Ireland and Britain for the sake of the mother of each one, because a mother has borne each one, and for the sake of Mary, the mother of Jesus Christ.' The attitude behind this legislation was expressed thus: 'Great is the sin when anyone kills the one who is mother and sister to Christ's mother.' It sought to protect women from offences rangeing from murder and rape to blackening the good name of a married woman. Polygamy was officially forbidden by the church, but it took place, along with rape, abduction, and physical abuse of all kinds. Adomnán and his mother had some kind of visionary experience on a battle field:

> Though they beheld the massacre they did not see anything which they thought more pitiful than a woman's head on one bank and her body on the opposite bank with a child asleep at the breast, a stream of milk on one cheek and a stream of blood on the other.[15]

So this was an age characterised by war, murder, treachery, apostasy and infant mortality in which women and their rights counted for very little indeed (and this is certainly true of slave women and women of the lower social classes) and in which it was her very biological function of motherhood which rendered a woman most vulnerable.

There does not appear to be any equivalent in the Irish or Welsh society of this period of the powerful women recorded by

13. Gilbert Márkus, *Adomnán's 'Law of the Innocents': Cáin Adomnáin* (Glasgow, Blackfriars Books: 1997), p 4.
14. Ibid, p 4.
15. Ní Dhonnchadha, 'The Lex Innocentium: Adomnán's Law for Women, Clerics and Youths 697 AD', pp 65-66.

Gregory of Tours and Bede in Frankish and Saxon society. For Gregory and Bede, royal women had, and were expected to have, great influence over the lives of their men folk. According to the chroniclers of the times, women generally were often responsible for the conversion of their men folk, and this was true for all countries where the gospel was influential. Women saw the possibilities in the gospel message for freedom from the grind of society. According to Bede, Bertha and Ethelburga were specifically charged by the Pope with the conversion of their husbands, and (indicating that this influence, though powerful, was not always for good) Bede lays the blame for Redwald's apostasy at the door of his wife, while Wilfrid's ultimate downfall was attributed by Eddius Stephanus to the bad influence of Egfrith's second wife, Iurmenberg.

But this situation may not be as straightforward as it seems, because in addressing the position of any early society we are at a disadvantage, and this is especially true of the insular world. Johnston writes of early Ireland, and this is true of the insular world generally:

> The surviving images of Irish women were filtered through a specifically male viewpoint. The voices of the women of early Ireland are lost, yet this lack of detail from women themselves is in contrast to the enormous amount of discourse concerning them, not only in Ireland but also in a Western European context. Medieval writers record a fundamental bipolarity – a bipolarity that excludes, with a few exceptions, actual female discourse from the written medium.[16]

So there is a fundamental prejudice against women in the literary sources at our disposal; and in stories from the lives of the saints, we see this prejudice against women in action. For example: Maedoc of Ferns cursed a woman for washing clothes in the stream which ran by his monastery; he feared pollution from her garments. Ciarán taught psalms to a local king's daughter, but never looked at any part of her body but her feet; he feared she would be a temptation to his virtue. Moling beat a woman

16. E. Johnston, 'Transforming Women in Irish Hagiography', *Peritia* 9, (1995), pp 197-220, at p 158.

with branches from a tree for making a pass at him; again, he
feared for his virtue. And Mac dá Cherda dived into a chilly
river and remained there all night just because he caught sight
of a woman walking along the river bank. And even if these
examples tell us more about attitudes prevailing at the time the
lives were written rather than the actual life of the saints themselves (they were often written two hundred years or more after
the events they purport to portray, when accurate details had
been lost in the mists of time), they show great fear on the part of
men where women were concerned. But on a lighter note, not all
women took this kind of treatment lying down. The story is also
told of a nun who requested hospitality of St Senan of Scattery
Island, in the mouth of the River Shannon. Senan made it very
clear that she was not welcome, because she was a woman, but
she had a suitable reply ready:

> How can you say that? Christ is no worse than you. Christ
> came to redeem women no less than men. He suffered for the
> sake of women no less than for men. Women have given ser-
> vice and ministry to Christ and his apostles. Women enter
> the heavenly kingdom no less than men.[17]

Whether this is a genuine saying of a holy woman remembered down the years, or whether it is attributed to her memory
by a later scribe, it would seem to indicate that although perhaps a few women had the spirit and courage (and the theology)
to rebel against the way their society and their men folk treated
them, on the whole life for women in early insular society was
grim.

Under Irish law, a woman's rights depended on the amount
of wealth (especially in terms of land) which she brought into
the marriage, but early Irish society was polygynous, so a
woman could be married but not necessarily be the primary
wife. In Irish society the most important function of a woman in
marriage was to provide sons, so if she proved to be barren, the
obvious solution was to take another. This was disapproved of

17. L. Bitel, 'Women's Monastic Enclosures in Early Ireland: a Study of
Female Spirituality and Male Monastic mentalities', *Journal of Medieval
History* 12, (1986), pp 15-36, at pp 31-32.

by the church, but was popularly justified on the biblical precedent of the patriarchs.

> MacCairthind, reputed ancestor of the Ui Meic Cairthind in Airgialla, was said to have had twelve sons, of whom four were by slave girls; Fland da Chongal, king of Ui Failge, is credited with the same number, with the same proportion by a slave girl. Such fertility was expected at that level, and admired; but with a heavy infant mortality, it was rarely attainable without a plurality of wives ... The church disapproved, predictably, of such pluralities ...[18]

So in pre-Viking Ireland, society was still strongly influenced by its pre-Christian customs and habits, no matter how much these might have incurred the censure of the church and the wrath of churchmen, and Gaul and Britain were not so very different, even if Bede does a certain amount of sanitising in his reports. Life for a woman in the early medieval European world was tightly circumscribed. She was strictly under the control of her father when she was a girl, and passed from his control to that of her husband when she married. If widowed, she was answerable to her sons; if she was a nun, then she was under the control of the church. She did not have the power to sell or purchase, or to make any sort of contract or transaction without the permission of those who oversaw her life. In antiquity, religious life did give women marginally more freedom, because women were the chattels of their men folk in name and in fact.

We have already looked at some evidence provided by the *Collectio Canonum Hibernensis*; O'Loughlin comments further on the place the society from which it emanates assigns to women in early insular society:

> The position of the *Hibernensis* on women reflects a basic attitude that women are only incidental to the concerns of society: and so far as the law is concerned, except for marriage, they only appear as a complicating factor in legal disputes.[19]

From this collection of early canon law we see that women

---

18. Gearóid MacNiocaill, *Ireland Before the Vikings*, (Dublin: Gill and Macmillan, 1972), p 58.
19. T. O'Loughlin, *Collectio Canonum Hibernensis*, Book 46, p 12.

had no significant place in male-dominated Irish society, either secular or religious; they were completely under the control of their nearest male relative.

Little in-depth research has been done so far on the place of women in the insular church, on women's monasticism, or critical appraisals of the lives of early women saints – with the exception of Brigid, who is in a class of her own, and has been the subject of numerous studies. This lack is partly because of the lack of evidence: it is unlikely that anything was written by women, little was written specifically about women, and what little there was, was written by men and from a masculine point of view. That there were women monastics in early insular territory is indisputable – from Patrick onwards they are there (he tells of the 'beautiful noble woman' who came to tell him of her resolve to consecrate herself to Christ), but they are shadowy figures in the background; their direct voices are lost to us.[20] We can only hear them through the darkened glass of male commentators. This is true of the writings of Bede, particularly with his description of the life and virtue of Etheldreda of Ely, which modern commentators think he is guilty of manipulating to suit his own hagiographical ends. But even through Bede's possibly rosy spectacles, we can see how unfree women of the Saxon aristocracy were in issues related to the choosing of their own path in life and how they were controlled by their menfolk, either fathers or husbands. Royal Anglo-Saxon abbesses, such as Etheldreda and Hilda, were powerful and determined women in the sphere of life reckoned as theirs,[21] capable during their married lives of ruling their husbands' territories and subjects when those husbands were absent on the battlefield, which they frequently were.

> [B]ecause prevailing political structures were rooted in the domestic sphere of the dynastic family and lordly household, women – in particular as wives and mothers – could

---

20. See Eoin de Bhaldraithe, 'The Three Orders of Irish Saints: New Light from Early Church Studies', *Milltown Studies* 61, (2008), pp 58-83.
21. See K. LoPrete, 'Gendering Viragos: medieval perceptions of powerful women' in C. Meek and C. Lawless (eds), *Studies on Medieval and Early Modern Women 4; Victims or Viragos?* (Dublin: Four Courts Press, 2005), pp 17-38.

find themselves at the centre of the public stage while play-
ing out their traditional, prescribed and 'feminine' household roles. Just how many women and with what frequency
they acted authoritatively in political affairs would depend
on personal, familial and wider political circumstances.[22]

All the more reason why it was so hard for these strong and
capable women to leave their households where they wielded
so much authority and power to enter monastic life. Once they
had managed to exchange their former way of life for that of the
cloister, their living voices were airbrushed out of the texts by
male clerical historians and annalists, in accordance with the received wisdom as to what was seen to be appropriate for holy
women. So these women have become shadowy, faceless and
almost characterless figures on the pages of history.

Bede writes with very great enthusiasm of Etheldreda, even
composing poetry in her honour. She fitted his picture of what
an ideal royal woman should be. She was born, according to
local tradition, at Exning, near Newmarket in East Anglia. One
of the daughters of Anna, the Saxon king of East Anglia, she was
related to Hilda of Whitby through her mother. Her family was
Christian; the area had been evangelised by Felix, a bishop from
Gaul, and also by Fursa, an Irish monk. She was thus the heir to
a spiritual tradition which blended together both the Romano-
Gallic and the Celtic elements. As one of the daughters of a royal
house, she was expected to marry in order to form political alliances with other noble families, so, as her elder sister, Sexburgh
had been married to the king of Kent, Etheldreda also was married, in her case twice and both times for dynastic reasons, first
to Tondbert, chief of the Southern Girvii, a man much older than
her, and after he died to one very much younger, Ecgfrith of
Northumbria. However, Bede claims, on the authority of
Wilfrid, her spiritual counsellor, that she remained a virgin
throughout both marriages because of her wish to consecrate
herself to Christ.[23] Wilfrid encouraged her in this desire, for

---

22. Ibid, pp 18-19.
23. Bede, whose interest was in royal women who were either nuns or
widows, does not record the impact of this unusual desire on the marriage; for him marriage was not important; however, for most people it
is supremely important – the biggest decision they ever make.

which Ecgfrith never really forgave him. Ecgfrith eventually gave in – reluctantly – to her wishes and agreed to her leaving the royal court to enter a monastery. She travelled north to the abbey of Coldingham where she learned of monastic life and practice from the abbess, Ebba, a kinswoman of her second husband, and then returned south to found the abbey of Ely on land granted to her by her first husband. Here she lived as abbess until her death several years later during an epidemic of plague. Bede puts onto her dying lips words of penitence for what he describes as her youthful pride in wearing beautiful necklaces. However, there is no certainty that we have here the actual words of Etheldreda herself; we may have instead what Bede considers to be an appropriate deathbed confession for a dying queen. However, at least one recent commentator is of the opinion that Bede is guilty of idealising the whole Etheldreda story:

> [I]n celebrating the perpetual virginity of a married woman who left her husband to found a monastery, Bede gives a mythic, idealising form of expression to the preponderance of widows and formerly married women among the founders of female monasticism.[24]

Bede describes Etheldreda's austerities in terms which recall the fathers and mothers of the desert:

> It is reported of her, that from the time of her entering into the monastery, she never wore any linen but only woollen garments, and she would rarely wash in a hot bath, unless just before any of the great festivals, as Easter, Whitsuntide, and the Epiphany, and then she did it last of all after having, with the assistance of those about her, first washed the other servants of God there present: besides she seldom did eat above once a day, excepting on the great solemnities, or some other urgent occasion, unless some considerable distemper obliged her. From the time of Matins she continued in the church at prayer till it was day.[25]

Bede is here giving full rein to his hagiographical tendencies

24. S. Hollis, *Anglo-Saxon Women and the Church: Sharing a Common Fate* (Woodbridge: The Boydell Press, 1992), p 72.
25. Bede, *HEGA* IV, xix.

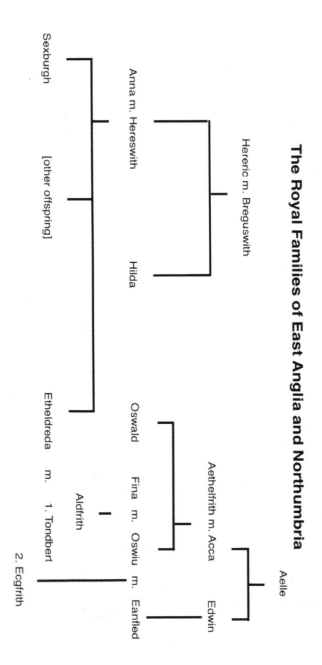

The Royal Families of East Anglia and Northumbria

and this passage immediately recalls such incidents in the *Historia Lausiaca* as the following:

> Up to the end of his life [Isidore] wore no fine linen except for a headband. He neither bathed nor ate meat.[26]

This ascetic determination to repress physical needs such as eating, sleeping and washing, already noted in the lives of the desert mothers, and the late classical women such as Melania, denies the intrinsic holiness of human existence and the fact that the body is the temple of the Holy Spirit. Since the incarnation, all matter is spirit-bearing and therefore has the potential for the sacred, which is denied when humanity (one's own, or another's) is treated harshly and made to suffer unduly.

Bede's retelling of the whole Etheldreda saga makes it clear that it was not seen to be easy for women of any rank in society in the seventh century, especially those of royal or noble birth, who had particular responsibilities to their own tribe or clan and thus to society at large, to follow a call they believed they had to enter the monastic life.

Bede preferred his royal women to be unmarried, virtuous and, if possible, monastic. As we have seen with regard to Etheldreda, he was not above manipulating his sources to this end. Another Anglo-Saxon royal woman who adopted monastic life was Hilda. Quite possibly she had been married and then widowed, but Bede is silent on these issues as they would not have fitted his preferred pattern of holiness. Widowhood would, however, explained her self-imposed exile, and, significantly, she is nowhere referred to as '*virgo*'.

Hilda was born in 614 AD into the royal family of Northumbria, the daughter of Hereric, a nephew of Edwin, King of Northumbria and was baptised with Edwin and the rest of the royal court on 12 April 627 by Paulinus, the Archbishop of York. Having lived, according to Bede, our source of information, virtuously in secular life, twenty years later Hilda decided to become a nun, and went to stay with her sister and family in East Anglia on her way to enter the monastery of Chelles in Gaul, as other of her relatives had done. She had planned to stay

---

26. Palladius, *Historia Lausiaca*, p 31.

in East Anglia for a year, but before this time was up, she received a message from Aidan, Bishop of Lindisfarne recalling her to the north. To begin with, she lived on the bank of the River Wear with a few companions on a small plot of land (a 'hide'[27]) given to her by Aidan of Lindisfarne, but she was chosen as Abbess of the double monastery of Hartlepool, to succeed Heiu. Some ten or so years later, in 657, Hilda moved to Streanaeshalch, where she founded a double monastery of monks and nuns. In this monastery, she gave great importance to education, and the copying, reading and studying both of scripture and of Latin literature were encouraged. Hilda's monastery was a cradle for bishops (at least five) and other clergy. Hilda had great influence at all levels of society, and her monastery was chosen as the venue for what came to be known as the 'Synod of Whitby', which took place in AD 664.[28] There are two sources for our information: Bede and Eddius Stephanus, though it would seem likely that Bede based his account on that of Eddius, editing and adding to it to serve his own purposes. According to Bede the chief purpose of the 'Synod' was to settle the correct date for the celebration of Easter, and so bring Northumbrian Christians into line with the practice of the rest of western Europe.

The date of Easter had become a cause of contention at the royal court of Northumbria, as the king kept Easter according to the Irish dating system which he had learned on Iona and the queen followed the continental practice in which she had been brought up in Kent. Sometimes their celebrations of the major feast of the Christian year were a week apart. Bede gives this as the main reason for the meeting at the place he refers to as Streanaeshalch, though other local practices where the insular church differed from Rome were discussed as well, such as the form of the monastic tonsure.

In spite of the title by which it has become known, this meet-

---

27. A 'hide' was the amount of land reckoned necessary to support a peasant family; its exact area differed in different parts of the country.
28. For the 'Synod of Whitby', see H. Mayr-Harting, *The Coming of Christianity to Anglo-Saxon England* (London: Batsford, 1972, 1977), pp 103-113.

ing was a Royal council and not an ecclesiastical synod. It has frequently been seen as a major conflict between 'Celtic' and 'Roman' forms of Christianity, and sympathy for the 'Celtic' cause has been espoused by those with an anti-Roman bias, but this is to read back into the seventh century disputes which stem from Reformation and post-Reformation theological positions. However, it is possible to exaggerate the significance of the 'Synod'. If, as Bede argues, it was the confusion caused by the disparity between the king's and the queen's observance of Easter that gave rise to the council, it is puzzling that this had not been addressed earlier, as they had been married some twenty years previously, so presumably the problem was long-standing.

Together with some confusion regarding the political background, the location has also been the object of scholarly attention in recent years. In near-contemporary sources the place is referred to as Streanaeshalch. The Scandinavian form of 'Whitby' does not appear before the Doomsday Book. This has caused scholars to suggest the village of Strensall in Yorkshire as linguistically a more plausible site. Strensall would also have been more accessible to the participants, being only 5 miles from York, the royal capital of Deira, than the remote site of Whitby. For the last seven years of her life, Hilda was chronically ill, though the nature of the actual illness itself is unknown. She died in 680.

In spite of the widespread masculine prejudice, many of the monastic houses founded in England from 630 onwards were, like Hilda's monastery in Streanaeshalch, 'double monasteries' – that is they housed both monks and nuns, though the living quarters were separate and the inhabitants only came together in the church for the Divine Office. Folkestone, founded in 630, was the earliest, but there were also double monasteries at Hartlepool, Coldingham, Minster-in-Sheppey, Minster-in-Thanet, Barking, Repton, Wimbourne, Ely, Much Wenlock and Bardney. Most of these religious houses were founded by royalty, and were headed by a woman of the local royal family. Many of these royal abbesses were widows whose husbands had been killed in battle and it seems that this was seen as a suitable way for a widowed royal woman (Sexburga, daughter of King Anna

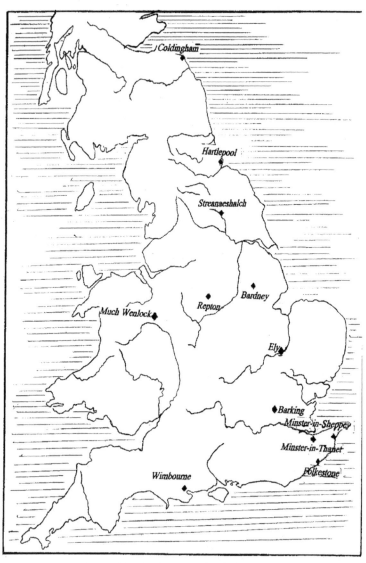

Early Monastic Britain

of East Anglia and sister to Etheldreda) or one who had been divorced (Etheldreda herself) to end her days,[29] especially if she was past the age of child-bearing and so had lost much of her value as a political or dynastic tool.[30] The position of abbess then passed to her daughter, sister or niece. This was the situation in Gaul, where women of both the Frankish and English royal houses entered monastic life, as Bede records, giving the reason why:

> Earcongota [daughter of King Earconbert of Kent] was a nun of outstanding virtue who served God in a convent in Frankish territory founded by the noble abbess Fara at a place called Brie [Faramoutiers], for as yet there were few monasteries built in English territory and many who entered conventual life went from Britain to the Frankish realm of Gaul for that purpose. Girls of noble family were also sent there for their education or to be betrothed to their heavenly Bridegroom, especially to the houses of Brie, Chelles, and Andelys.[31]

These religious houses where the abbess had been a royal queen, princess or widow were 'one of the most important political, religious and cultural institutions of seventh century England'.[32] Royal women had considerably more power and influence than their humbler sisters lower down the social scale, and although it might have been more difficult for them to attain their goal of entering religious life in the first place, as witness the lives of Radegund, Etheldreda and Hilda, among many others, once established, they were in a position to exercise the traditional aristocratic female role of counsellor, adviser and

---

29. Marilyn Dunn notes that: 'In English double houses in general, evidence for unmarried women flocking to join the religious life in great numbers is scarce', *The Emergence of Monasticism* (Oxford: Blackwell, 2000), p 205.

30. '[W]idowed queens and princesses became the religious specialists of the royal houses.' B. Yorke, 'The Adaptation of the Anglo-Saxon Royal Courts to Christianity', in M. Carver (ed), *The Cross Goes North: Processes of Conversion in Northern Europe AD 300-1300* (University of York: York Medieval Press, 2004), pp 243-257.

31. Bede, *HEGA*, III, 8.

32. M. Dunn, *The Emergence of Monasticism* (Oxford: Blackwell, 2000), p 202.

mediator. These functions are seen in many of the royal Saxon women who appear in the pages of Bede.[33]

However, this particularly northern European form of monastic living did not win the approval of Theodore, the Greek Archbishop of Canterbury when he arrived in England in 669. Although he stated his intention to 'respect the custom of the province', he also expressed his disapproval of double monasteries:

> It is not permitted for men religious to have women [among them], nor for women, men: nonetheless we shall not overthrow that which is the custom of this province.[34]

So the English and Frankish custom of the double house fell into disuse, and this not simply from the fact of Theodore's disapproval. Bede presents a darker side in his criticisms of the monastery at Coldingham in Northumbria, and claims that there were actual grounds for bringing this particular form of monastic life to an end. If Bede is to be believed, even though under the direction of the saintly Ebba, its shortcomings were many and serious.

> All of them, men and women alike, are either sound asleep, or else awake in order to do evil. Even the cells, which were built for prayer and study, are now converted into places for eating, drinking, gossip, or other amusements. When they have leisure, even the nuns vowed to God abandon the propriety of their calling and spend their time wearing fine clothes, which they employ to the peril of their souls, either to adorn themselves like brides, or to attract attention from strange men.

However, we know that Bede did not approve of double monasteries and he here produces the classic excuse for bringing this particular form of monastic life to an end.

If a slave woman had difficulty in becoming a nun, or even in

---

33. Dunn, *The Emergence of Monasticism*, pp 202-203.
34. Penitential of Theodore VI, 8, J. T. McNeill and H. M. Gamer, *Medieval Handbooks of Penance: A Translation of the Principle Libri Poenitentiales* (New York, 1938, 1990), p 204, quoted in Dunn, *The Emergence of Monasticism* (Oxford: Blackwell, 2000), p 206.

becoming a Christian, because her life was of such little value, the women from the upper strata of society, princesses and queens, had the same difficulty, but for the opposite reason – as potential wives and mothers of kings and princes, as tools in the network of social and political alliances, they were an extremely valuable resource – in fact, society depended on them. Offered in marriage to princes and kings of tribes with which an alliance was sought, they could save the lives, the territory, the future of their own tribe or race. They could ensure peace for tribes at war. They were far too valuable for their social and political potential, their ability to bear the sons who would be heirs, warriors and labourers, to be allowed to disappear into a monastery and waste their lives unproductively. This was how early medieval society saw its women folk, especially those from noble or aristocratic families. Slave women counted for nothing; noble women were a precious dynastic resource – so for both, becoming a nun was only accomplished with the greatest difficulty.

Some, however, as we have seen, did brave parental, and even marital, opposition and left the traditional structures of their society to enter monastic life. There, for a very few, there was access to power and influence nowhere else available to women. They had the responsibility for the organisation and carrying out of religious ritual; the running and overseeing of farms and estates. They shared, even if only in a limited way, in the social and political roles of male clerics, and most of all they were able, up to a point, to direct their own lives by their spiritual and religious commitment. Christianity, and particularly monastic life, did succeed in providing an alternative lifestyle for women, but it was still very limited, even for the few who were brave enough to risk social and familial disapproval to embark on this way of life. However, this new freedom to arrange their own lives could never be absolute: women relied on men for their access to the liturgical and sacramental life of the church, and also on the practical front for help with the heavier forms of labour. The theology and spirituality on which the monastic life was based was written by men. Whereas this was beginning to change, canon law, which came to govern their lives completely, was very definitely written by men. The monastic rules which ordered their lives down to the smallest detail were conceived and written by men.

In this whole question of the male view of women and their place in society and specifically in religious life, there is a possible connection between the liminal quality of sacred places, both Christian and pre-Christian, and the quality of femaleness as presented in hagiography.[35] The Irish in particular saw such sacred places as neolithic tumuli (Newgrange, for example) as gateways to the Otherworld, and in some *Vitae* the monastic enclosure was understood as sharing in this sacred quality. The sacred space of the monastic enclosure could, in some cases, only be inhabited by men, and this holy monastic space where the ascetic saint (male) dwelt was set apart from the unholy world outside (frequently symbolised by the female). Just as the pagan world outside the monastic enclosure was both a temptation to and a gauge of the monk's ascetic virtue, so too was the quality of femaleness, both in the concrete and in the symbolic, which is a theme frequently alluded to in the Sayings of the Desert Fathers. Lisa Bitel summed up the situation in the early insular world and the inference to be drawn from it:

> [D]enial of sex often became confused with the rejection of women. Women were sex, sex was a threat to celibacy, therefore women were a threat to the celibate elite. *Ubi enim fuerit ovis, ibi erit mulier, et ubi fuerit mulier ibi peccatum: ubi vero peccatum, ibi erit dyabolus, et ubi dyabolus, ibi infernus est.*[36] (For where there is a sheep, there will a woman be; and where there is a woman, there will be sin; truly, where there is sin, there will the devil be; and where the devil is, there is hell.)

This was the philosophy behind the *Vitae* of the male saints and their rejection of the feminine: where there was a woman there was sure to be sin; where there was sin the devil would be present and so, inevitably, there was the threat of hell and eternal damnation. One followed the other as sure as night followed day. Therefore women had to be controlled and preferably

35.E. Johnston, 'Transforming Women in Irish Hagiography', *Peritia* 9 (1995), pp 197-220.
36. L. Bitel, 'Women's Monastic Enclosures in Early Ireland: a Study of Female Spirituality and Male Monastic mentalities', *Journal of Medieval History* 12, (1986), pp 15-36, at p 31.

locked away where their presence would not be a threat to male virtue.

This is particularly noticeable in the *Vitae* of male Irish saints such as Maedoc, Ciarán and Moling quoted above. In stories from these lives, we see this prejudice against women in action. The *Vita* of Moninna is another example. Liam de Paor is of the opinion that the Life of Moninna would appear 'if we prune away a comparatively small accrescence of folk miracle-tales and a few diplomatic insertions (such as the obligatory appearance of St Patrick in the story) – to give us a plausible outline of the career of a female founder of the period.'[37] He points out that there are suggestions in the writings of Patrick of parallels between Jerome's and Augustine's and Ambrose's direction of noble ladies who sought their spiritual counsel, and that of the very different world in which Patrick found himself. Moninna appears as a devout woman being directed by a male counsellor in the traditional path we have already seen in late classical society. First of all she lived a life of prayer and seclusion in her own home; then she gathered other like-minded women around her. She lived for a while as a solitary to test the strength of her resolve, and finally she became the abbess of a large and flourishing community of nuns. Thus although her still semi-barbaric world was very different from that of Alexandria, Rome, and Constantinople, in her own circumstances and her own society, Moninna stands very firmly within the monastic tradition.

As remarked above, we have particular insights into the Irish monastic movement known as the Céli Dé, as there are several Rules which have their origin within this group still extant.[38] These monks had the accepted view of the early church and the

---

37. L. de Paor, *Saint Patrick's World* (Dublin: Four Courts Press, 1993, 1996), pp 46-47. For the 'Life of St Darerca or Monninna the Abbess', see idem, pp 281-294.

38. For the Céli Dé movement, see P. M. Rumsey, *Sacred Time in Early Christian Ireland* (London, T & T Clark, 2007); also W. Follett, *Céli Dé in Ireland: Monastic Writing and Identity in the Early Middle Ages* (Woodbridge: Boydell and Brewer, 2006). For an earlier view of the Céli Dé movement, see P. O'Dwyer, *Céli Dé: Spiritual Reform in Ireland 750-900* (Dublin: Editions Tailliura, 1977, repr. 1981); P. Ó Fiannachta, 'The Spirituality of the Céli Dé' in M. Maher ed, *Irish Spirituality*, (Dublin: Veritas, 1981), 22-32.

Middle Ages:[39] that menstruation and sexual relations[40] were a source of 'uncleanness':

> During the monthly sickness of daughters of the church they are excused from vigils, morning and evening, so long as it lasts, and gruel is to be made for them at Tierce, at whatever time this happens, because it is right that this sickness should have attention. They do not attend communion in such case, for they are unclean at these times.[41]

---

39. But that a more enlightened view was also held, cf Gregory's reply to Augustine's questions in Bede, *HEGA*, 88-95, at 93: 'Nevertheless a woman must not be prohibited from entering a church during her usual periods, for this natural overflowing cannot be reckoned a crime: and so it is not fair that she should be deprived from entering the church for that which she suffers unwillingly ... A woman ought not to be forbidden to receive the mystery of the Holy Communion at these times. If, out of deep reverence she does not venture to receive it, that is praiseworthy; but if she has received it she is not to be judged.' Wood comments on Gregory's reply: '[I]ts quiet sanity marks a milestone in the history of women, a milestone which announced that henceforth Christianity was abandoning all those demeaning taboos with which earlier cultures had invested menstruation, thereby limiting the freedom of half their people. With Gregory, the old Levitican prohibitions were gone forever, dropped by a man who had begun to see that, much as he and his intellectual heirs might continue to fear the sexual attractiveness of women, the menstrual process itself was less a defiling threat than a normal and natural phenomenon, at least as such phenomena existed under the constraints imposed by the fall.' C. T. Wood, 'The Doctor's Dilemma: Sin, Salvation, and the Menstrual Cycle in Medieval Thought', *Speculum*, Vol 56, No 4 (Oct, 1981), pp 710-727, at p 726.
40. Leviticus 15 with its provision of rituals for the 'cleansing' of 'impurity' caused by normal sexual functions gave the justification for this attitude and has been the source from which most of the sexual taboos in the Judaeo-Christian tradition take their origin. Ross Kraemer makes the interesting point that: 'Frustratingly, early Christian sources make no mention one way or another of the observance of menstrual purity regulations. We would expect Christians to reject these along with circumcision and food laws, since such regulations functioned as signifiers of purity and therefore of social boundaries, which Christians were in the process of redefining and broadening.' For the full exploration see: Kraemer, *Her Share of the Blessings: Women's Religions Among Pagans, Jews and Christians in the Greco-Roman World* (New York, Oxford University Press: 1992), pp 143-144.
41. *Rule of the Céli Dé*, n 50.

However, although this text reveals these commonly held ideas about women, it is of positive value, as it shows that women monastics followed the same rule as their male counterparts. Kathleen Hughes notes the Céli Dé view that 'women, in particular, were an added source of danger ... and were not to be trusted ... in the later *Vita* of Máel Rúain woman is spoken of as man's "guardian devil".'[42] It is indicative of the ambivalent attitude towards women that a monastic group with such negative feelings towards women could yet preserve sayings and memories of the abbess Samthann.

In Samthann, (d. 793) the abbess of Clonbroney in Co Meath, we have a very interesting woman. We have very few *Vitae* of Irish women saints, only those of Brigid, Monninna, Ita and Samthann. The latter is closely connected with the monastic group known as the Céli Dé,[43] and even though a woman she seems to have been highly regarded by these monks. She had a particularly close relationship with either Máel Rúain or Ferdácrích (both were founding figures of the movement but the text is not clear as to which one Samthann desired to have as her 'soul-friend') and whichever monk it was regarded it as a great compliment to be so sought out by this abbess. Various teachings of hers have been recorded and she seems to have been sought out as a wise counsellor. To her are attributed the oft-quoted sayings that one should pray in every position: 'lying, sitting or standing', and also in every place: 'God is close to all who call upon him' so 'we are under no obligation to cross the sea' to find him; 'the kingdom of heaven can be reached from every land'. According to her *Vita*, she had a high regard for poverty, refus-

---

42. Hughes, op. cit., p 177.
43. This is a somewhat enigmatic branch of early Irish monasticism. P. O'Dwyer's study, *Céli Dé: Spiritual Reform in Ireland 750-900* (Dublin: Editions Tailliura, 1977, repr. 1981), for long the standard work on the subject, interprets them as a monastic 'reform' movement. More recent works see them as an 'elitist' group; see P. M. Rumsey, *Sacred Time in Early Christian Ireland* (London: T&T Clark, 2007) and also W. Follett, *Céli Dé in Ireland: Monastic Writing and Identity in the Early Middle Ages* (Woodbridge: Boydell and Brewer, 2006). Perhaps the most we can say with certainty is that there were monks in Ireland in the eighth and ninth centuries who called themselves 'companions of God' and that there were nuns connected with them.

ing to own land and never having more than six cows. This was of the greatest significance in early Ireland, where land and cattle were the chief expressions of prosperity and wealth.

However, whatever the views and opinions held about women, by the seventh century, monasticism was being both patronised by queens, princesses and women of the highest ranks of the nobility, and monastic communities were being headed by such women. Monastic life had come a long way since its humble beginnings in the deserts of Egypt and Palestine. But although male writers such as Bede and Anselm praise the virtues of these aristocratic ladies and many of them were quite undoubtedly holy – witness the great respect accorded to Hilda, and her hosting of the Council and also the great honour paid to Etheldreda after her death – she is recorded as being the most well known saint in pre-Conquest England, and even the invading Normans gave devotion to her, though using their own form of her name – the spiritual wisdom of the desert mothers had now been translated into political influence – converting kings, administration of family and tribal land and wealth. Apart from a few sayings recorded by Bede, which may, or may not, be genuine *dicta* of those concerned, and the sayings attributed to Samthann, we have no spiritual wisdom recorded from these women monastics. Even Hilda has left no words to remember her by. The tradition of Christian women is silent.

Largely due to the benefactions which were bestowed upon them by royal and aristocratic patrons, monasteries, both of men and women, were on their way to becoming the centres of art, learning and culture which they had become by the eleventh century. R. W. Southern in his study of the early Middle Ages, having described monastic life as it had come to be lived by the eleventh century, makes the following comment:

> It was a majestic life, incomparable perhaps in this respect to any form of the Christian life developed before or since. It is a far cry from the fastnesses of Subiaco where the Benedictine life was born, to the rich hills of Burgundy with Cluny in their midst ...[44]

44. R. W. Southern, *The Making of the Middle Ages* (London: Hutchinson, 1967), p 157.

So as we move towards the end of the first millennium, monastic life as lived in Europe had come a long way since its humble beginnings in the far off deserts of Egypt and Syria. It was now well on the way to its medieval destination – a revered and highly regarded institution, favoured by kings and nobles with large grants of land and financial donations in the expectation of Masses and prayers being offered in perpetuity for the donors.[45] Instead of the austere monastic houses in the deserts of Syria and Egypt, European monasteries were frequently large, prosperous and wealthy. This change in emphasis and in the practical living of the religious life helps to explain the outlook and ideals of the women we will meet in the next chapter.

45. The development of the practice of offering 'Mass stipends' is a crucial issue; see T. O'Loughlin, 'Treating the "Private Mass" as Normal: Some unnoticed evidence from Adomnán's *De locis sanctis*', in *Archiv für Liturgiewissenschaft* 51 (2009), pp 334-344.

CHAPTER SIX

'The Privilege of Having No Privileges' – Empresses and Heiresses in Medieval Europe

With this chapter on Clare of Assisi and her early companions, we reach a watershed in the history of women's monasticism. In some areas, and for some women, life was beginning to open up a little. Although these areas were still rather restricted, life for women was beginning to show signs of change. Now a woman had some say in the choice of her marriage partner and – at least in theory – could refuse to marry a man if she did not wish to do so; there were some possibilities of education for women, and – of great significance for this study – canonization required a formal process with the testimonies of witnesses and was also beginning to move away from assuming that to be canonised the prospective saint had to be noble. We will look at each of these processes in greater detail.

The marriage canons of Gratian's Decretum stated: 'No woman should be joined with a man, except by her own free will.'[1] Though this had been written into earlier law codes of various European peoples, its interpretation and application had varied enormously, but it was here made explicit in a major collection of canon law for the first time and we see it in operation in the lives of women such as Clare.

It was becoming possible for women to attain at least a basic level of education, though these were mostly of the upper classes (Héloise was Abelard's pupil while he was teaching in the school that later – in 1204 – became the University of Paris). This meant that at least some women were able to express them-

---

1. *Decretum Gratiani* C.31 q.2 d.p.c. 4. For the problems of its application in this context, see J. A. Brundage, *Medieval Canon Law* (London, Longman: 1995), pp 165-168. On Gratian, see J. A. Brundage, *Medieval Canon Law*, pp 44-69. The exact date of the *Decretum*, which was the fundamental text book of the Middle Ages, is uncertain, but probably c. 1140.

selves not only verbally in their own local language or dialect, but also formally, in Latin, the language of scholarship, in a way that could be transmitted, preserved and respected in books and letters.

Clare of Assisi (1194-1253) and Agnes of Prague (1211-1282) are prime examples of this growth and expansion in the social and ecclesial position of women, so this chapter will outline an analysis of their road to sanctity. Agnes in particular, being of royal birth, was familiar with the complex exigencies involved in the exercise of power and diplomacy in the politics of the papal court and numerous letters of hers are still extant in the Vatican Archives, helping us to date and to understand what was going on in the battle the Poor Ladies were raging with the Papacy to obtain their desired goal.

From shortly before the time of Clare, for sanctity to be recognised by formal canonisation for both men and women, an official canonisation process had to be declared, with the holiness of the protagonists being formally attested to on oath by witnesses. So, although conventional *Vitae* were still being produced in accordance with the stereotyped hagiography, for the first time we are now in touch with individual human beings, both through their own writings and through the sworn testimonies of those who knew them and lived with them. Clare of Assisi is described in the Process of her Canonisation as the 'New Woman in the Valley of Spoleto'. This appellation is very true in many ways. Although very much a child of her times and social setting, she pioneered an innovative way of life for women, and broke out of the accepted pattern of holiness for women as it had been seen up till then. Though much romanticised in art and legend, her life was a constant struggle to be true to her ideals. For many centuries Clare was obscured by Francis and it is only comparatively recently that she has been recognised as a strong, vibrant and independent personality in her own right, and her contribution to the wider field of Franciscan studies and spirituality has been acknowledged.[2]

---

2. This has come about largely through the pioneering work of such internationally renowned scholars as Regis Armstrong, Margaret Carney, Joan Mueller and Frances Teresa Downing.

She was born in 1193 or 1194, the eldest daughter of Favarone Offreduccio, one of the noble lords of Assisi in Umbria. However, she came into the world in turbulent times, and when she was still a very small child, her family had to flee to Perugia for refuge after their palazzo had been set on fire by a rebel mob during an uprising of the '*minores*' (the rising merchant class within feudal society) in Assisi. They returned to their home town in 1205, when Clare was about twelve years old, but the friendships she had made with young girls from similarly aristocratic houses in Perugia remained with her all her life. Devout and pious from her early childhood, partly through the influence of her mother Hortolana, while she was still quite young she came under the influence of 'Francesco' Bernadone, who inspired her with ideals similar to his own – a desire to live the gospel in a life of great simplicity and total poverty. She heard Francis preach during Lent in the Church of San Giorgio in Assisi and she asked his assistance in achieving her desire to follow Christ in the religious life. But a woman of her social class was not free to make her own life decisions; marriage and child-bearing were expected of her. So to escape the disapproval of her family which would have rendered the choice of religious life impossible, under the inspiration of Francis and possibly with the knowledge of the Bishop of Assisi, she ran away from home on the night of Palm Sunday 1212, using a little-used side door to escape detection.[3] With a companion, she made her way to the little chapel of St Mary of the Angels of the Porziuncula, outside the walls of Assisi, which was one of the tiny churches Francis had repaired himself and her vows were accepted by Francis in the presence of his small band of like-minded young men. They escorted her to a local Benedictine house in Bastia, San Paolo delle Abbadesse, a couple of miles from Assisi. Her male relatives, having discovered her whereabouts, came to bring her home the next day. Clare clung to the altar, claiming

---

3. Traditionally, this has been known as the 'door of the dead' through which corpses were carried out for burial, and the symbolism in Clare's case, of 'dying' to family relationships and social position have been noted and commented upon; however, see the translator's note in A. Fortini, *Francis of Assisi* (trs H. Moak) (New York, Crossroads: 1981), p 329.

the right of sanctuary, but it was only when she pulled off her veil and they saw her shorn hair, proving her monastic tonsure and consecration and therefore her 'unmarriageability' that her uncles retreated in disgust and frustration at her stubbornness. Like Francis, she was claiming by her actions to be under ecclesiastical rather than civil jurisdiction. She worked for a short while in the monastery as a domestic. Francis then took her to a community of devout women, who may have been Béguines, at San Angelo in Panzo, but 'her soul was not at rest'. Eventually, Francis found sanctuary for Clare and her younger sister Agnes, who had also incurred parental wrath by coming to join her, in the little monastery of San Damiano, outside the walls of Assisi which Francis had rebuilt in the early days of his own conversion. Here Clare lived in great poverty and austerity for the next forty years. In the early days, Francis had given her a very short *formula vitae* to live by, probably consisting mostly of passages from scripture, which may have been similar to the 1209 *forma uitae* which Francis had composed and Pope Innocent III (1160-1216) had approved for the friars. Her life's work was the composing of her own *Forma Vitae*, which included that given her by Francis, but expanding this to cover more of the life of the sisters. Successive popes, though full of admiration for her holiness (at least in the early days), thought her austere way of life too difficult and tried to impose their own ideas and their own written rules upon her but, although forced to accept these rules in practice, she remained stubbornly faithful to Francis' teaching and ideals, even long after his death. There is some evidence that towards the end of her life Clare fell out of favour with the authorities. In Thomas of Celano's first *Life of Francis*, he waxes enthusiastic about Clare and her acknowledged sanctity:

> Noble by lineage, but more noble by grace, chaste in body most chaste in mind, young in mind, mature in spirit, steadfast in purpose and most eager in her desire for divine love, endowed with wisdom and excelling in humility, bright in name, more brilliant in life, most brilliant in character.[4]

4. I. Peterson, 'Clare of Assisi: Hidden behind which image of Francis?' in J. Hammond (ed), *Francis of Assisi: History, Hagiography and Hermeneutics in the Early Documents* (New York, New City Press: 2004), pp 39-63, at p 42.

However, in his second *Life of Francis*,[5] she is hardly mentioned.[6] Pope Gregory IX, on his flight from Rome in the wake of attack by the Emperor Frederick at Easter in 1228, had stopped in Assisi and gone to speak with Clare, and had offered her land and possessions in order to ensure security for her and her sisters in their way of life. These she had been unwilling to accept, in accordance with her total commitment to poverty. The Pope said that if she was worried about keeping her vow of poverty he would absolve her from it. Clare is reported to have said, with strong feeling: 'Absolve me from my sins, Holy Father, but not from following Jesus Christ.' Gregory departed in anger and his admiring attitude towards Clare was never quite the same.[7] It was only on her death bed that she received the confirmation of her Rule, by the Papal Bull *Solet annuere* on 9 August, 1253. The few remaining early companions of Francis were present at her death (Brother Leo sobbing into the bedclothes); they revered her as the embodiment of all that Francis held dear. Although she saw herself as Francis' 'Little Plant'[8] and for a long time re-

5. See Regis Armstrong and Ignatius Brady (eds), *Francis and Clare: The Complete Works* (New York, Paulist Press: 1982), p.107: 'The development of the Rule of the Friars Minor is one of the areas of Franciscan research that has prompted the greatest attention throughout the centuries.' This Rule evolved gradually over the years through three recognisable stages: 1) the *'propositum uitae'*: the primitive legislation composed mainly of scriptural texts which Francis assembled for the early friars, approved verbally by Pope Innocent III in 1209 or 1210; 2) the Earlier Rule (the *Regula non bullata*) of 1221 which, it was claimed, was lost; 3) the Later Rule (the *Regula bullata*) of 1223. These texts can be found and their relationships studied in more detail in Regis Armstrong and Ignatius Brady (eds), *Francis and Clare; the Complete Works* (New York, Paulist Press: 1982), especially pp 107-145, and references.
6. M. Bartoli develops this fact as the premise of his book, using it even to question Clare's existence. See *Chiara: Una donna tra silenzio e memoria* (Edizioni San Paolo, 2001, 2003), Eng. trs F. T. Downing, *Saint Clare: Beyond the Legend* (Cincinnati: St Anthony's Messenger Press, 2010).
7. See I. Peterson, 'Clare of Assisi: Hidden behind which image of Francis?' in J. Hammond (ed), *Francis of Assisi: History, Hagiography and Hermeneutics in the Early Documents* (New York, New City Press: 2004), pp 39-63, at p 42.
8. This expression is now thought to have been a kind of 'code' for those who had known Francis in the very early days and had remained faithful to his original ideals. Bernard of Quintavalle, his earliest companion, is also described as the 'little plant' (*plantula*) of Francis

mained in his shadow, she is very much a saint in her own right, though this has become recognised more clearly as a result of recent scholarship.

The first Rule for women in the history of the church to be written by a woman was the *Forma uitae* of the Poor Clares, by Clare herself – although we have here moved out of the tribal society of the early Middle Ages into the feudal society of the world of Clare, this shows what an innovator she actually was. However, it took her the whole of her life to have this *Forma uitae* recognised and only on her death bed did Papal approval reach her.[9]

In our sources for the study of Clare, we are much more fortunate than in previous chapters; now we have writings from the hand of Clare herself, her Letters, her Testament, and her Rule.[10] And for the first time, we have a canonisation document, giving the details of the process and the testimony of many witnesses, all of whom had known Clare personally, some for the whole of her life. A text such as this is one of the richest sources for information about the saint, especially when it was conducted, as was the case with Clare, within a couple of years of her death.[11] The evidence was given by people who had known her intimately and had lived with her on a day-to-day basis. Now at last, we can feel we are in touch with a real person, even though those witnessing at the Process were convinced of her holiness and gave testimony to this conviction, and also the fact that over

---

9. Just as with the Rule of the Friars, the Poor Clare Rule is a complex text. The following sources can be identified: 1) the Rule of the Friars; 2) the Rule attributed to Benedict; 3) the Rule of Cardinal Hugolino; 4) the Rule of Pope Innocent IV. With the exception of 2), these texts are available in *Clare of Assisi: Early Documents*, Regis J. Armstrong, ed, (NY: Paulist Press, 1988).

10. See *Clare of Assisi: Early Documents*, Regis J. Armstrong, ed., (NY: Paulist Press, 1988).

11. Throughout the first Christian millennium the recognition of an exemplary and virtuous life by the local community of believers pre-dated the later explicit canonisation by a centralised ecclesiastical authority. See A. W. Haddon, 'Canonisation' in W. Smith and S. Cheetham eds, *A Dictionary of Christian Antiquities* (London: John Murray, 1908), p 283. The date of the first formal canonisation is controversial, but a decree of Pope Alexander III in 1170 AD gave the prerogative of formal canonisation to the Pope as far as this applied to the Western church.

a long period of time that authentic personality became obscured with layers of popular piety and devotion.

Among Clare's earliest companions was her own blood sister, Catherine. Some two weeks after Clare had run away from
home to join Francis and his brothers, Catherine, who was about
fifteen at the time, went to join her at San Angelo di Panzo. She
'told her that she wanted to serve God completely. Embracing
her with joy, Clare said: "I thank God, my dearest sister, that he
has heard my concern for you".' (*Legend of St Clare*, 24) But the
family, still smarting under the disgrace of Clare's defection (as
they saw it) and the consequent loss of the family honour and
reputation which were so important in medieval Europe, was
not going to let this second daughter escape so easily; the uncles
set out to bring Catherine home: 'Twelve men burning with
anger and hiding outwardly their evil intent, ran to the place'
(*Legend* 24). This account says that though they initially managed to pick the girl up and carry her a short distance, her body
suddenly became so heavy (which was attributed to the prayers
of Clare, who was in great distress and was interceding for her
younger sister) that the men could carry her no further and
dropped her. One of the uncles, in his frustrated rage, lifted his
arm to hit her, but he suffered sudden agonising pain and his
arm remained in mid-air. Francis then cut Catherine's hair and
gave her the religious name of Agnes, and took the two sisters to
San Damiano, where he instructed them in gospel living. Agnes
lived here with Clare and the others who came to join them, including their own mother and other relatives. Eventually Clare
sent her as abbess to the monastery in Florence, which parting
from her sister seems to have cost her a very great deal of suffering. She wrote to Clare from Florence: '[Y]ou would know,
Mother, that my soul and body suffer great distress and immense
sadness, that I am burdened and tormented beyond measure
and am almost incapable of speaking, because I have been physically separated from you and my other sisters with whom I had
hoped to live and die in this world.' From this we can gather
that she was particularly close to Clare. However, she remained
in Florence probably for over twenty years until in 1253 she returned to Assisi during Clare's last illness. Agnes died later that
same year.

Another Agnes who eventually followed Clare was a princess of the royal house of Bohemia and, as a royal woman was destined even more inexorably than Clare to become a pawn in the dynastic politics of medieval Europe. She was born in the early thirteenth century, the daughter of Premysl Ottokar, King of Bohemia and his second wife, Constance of Hungary. She was born in Prague and educated at the Cistercian abbey at Trebnitz. She was twice betrothed, but her two prospective suitors (the infant Duke of Silesia, and Henry of Austria, son of the Emperor Frederick II) died in infancy, and she herself refused Frederick's offer of marriage, in order to found, and then enter, a Poor Clare monastery in Prague. She was a powerful and influential woman, with an intimate knowledge of thirteenth century diplomacy, both in ecclesial and secular political circles, as is shown by her extant correspondence with the popes of her day[12] and her insistence in gaining papal permission to adopt a similar lifestyle to that lived by Clare and the sisters at San Damiano. Regis Armstrong makes this point clearly:

> A number of documents emerge providing directives to Agnes in Prague. These are important because they frequently relate to Clare's letters to Agnes and because, once again, they show the widespread papal scrutiny of enclosed women. Because Agnes was a royal princess and because her father, Ottokar I, and her brother Vaclav III, were successively Kings of Bohemia, her political influence was potentially beneficial to the papal court. Real questions persisted regarding the financial and material provisions for enclosed communities. It took four years for Agnes and her sisters to re-

---

12. See *Sincerum animi*, 30 August, 1232; *Cum relicta saeculi*, 18 May, 1235; *Cum saeculi vanitate*, 4 April 1237; *Pia credulitate tenentes*, 15 April, 1238 (granting the privilege of not receiving any other property than their hospital); *Pia meditations pensantes*, 5 May, 1238 (granting dispensations from some prescriptions of the Rule because of the cold climate); *De Conditoris omnium*, 9 May, 1238 (encouraging Agnes and her sisters in their observance of 'evangelical perfection'); *Angelis gaudium*, 11 May, 1238 (discussing various points of observance of the Rule); *Ex Parte carissimi*, 18 December, 1238 (dispensing the Prague community from the observance of some of the fasts of the Rule); *In divini timore nominis*, 13 November, 1243 (discussing the observance of the monastery); *The Lady: Clare of Assisi, Early Documents*, pp 351 et seq.

ceive papal approbation to live without common property in the manner of Clare.[13]

Although as far as we know the two women never met in the flesh, they had a very deep and long standing friendship: Clare called Agnes 'half my own soul' and Clare's letters to Agnes provide some of the deepest insights we have into Clare's spirituality and theology and her understanding of monastic life. Agnes died in Prague in 1282. Her body was originally buried within the monastery in Prague, but was subsequently reburied, according to tradition, by the sisters in the grounds of the monastery to avoid desecration at the time of the Hussite Wars, but has never been found.[14] The people of Prague revered her particularly as her canonisation took place on 12 November 1989, shortly before the revolution against Communism took place in her homeland of Czechoslovakia.[15]

But this is to jump forward several centuries. In Europe in the High Middle Ages, women were seen to be dangerous, not only to themselves, but to those around them, and it was the responsibility of the husband to keep them under control. A French writer from the thirteenth century (that is, contemporaneous with Clare) wrote:

> In a number of cases men may be excused for the injuries they inflict on their wives, nor should the law intervene. Provided he neither kills nor maims her, it is legal for a man to beat his wife when she wrongs him ... It is the husband's duty to be his wife's chastiser.[16]

13. *The Lady: Clare of Assisi, Early Documents*, p 344.
14. However, in late 2009 a team of restorers claimed they had possibly found the grave of Agnes under the floor of the church of St Hastal in Prague.
15. See *Sarosata Herald Tribune*, November 13, 1989: 'More than 9,000 Czechoslovaks, including a Government delegation, packed St Peter's basilica to watch the canonisation of the princess who turned nun and laid a framework for social work in thirteenth century Bohemia'. Also *Los Angeles Times*, November 13, 1989: 'Pope John Paul II canonised Princess Agnes of Bohemia, a medieval Czechoslovak nun on Sunday in the first papal ceremony broadcast on state television in the Communist nation'.
16. Quoted in F. Beer, *Women and Mystical Experience in the Middle Ages* (Woodbridge: The Boydell Press, 1992), p 3.

Jacques de Vitry (1170-1240), Bishop of Acre and eventually a cardinal and member of the Roman Curia, who was later to be very much involved with groups of religious women in Europe expressed himself in very similar terms:

> [T]he husband is his wife's head, to rule her, correct her (if she strays) and restrain her (so she does not fall headlong). For hers is a slippery and weak sex, not to be trusted too easily. A wanton woman is slippery like a snake and mobile as an eel; so she can hardly be guarded or kept within bounds. Some things are so bare that there is nothing by which to get hold of them ... so it is with woman: roving and lecherous once she has been stirred by the devil's hoe.[17]

De Vitry was, actually, much more sympathetic towards women than this extract would suggest. In the next chapter we see how he championed the cause of the Béguines in the Low Countries.

Marriage was weighted very much in the man's favour.[18] But by Clare's day, the wishes of the woman with regard to entering into marriage were beginning to be taken into account due, largely if not entirely, to the already mentioned concordance of Canon Law complied by Gratian, who claimed that according to Jerome and other fathers of the church, no woman should be married to anyone except by her own free will. Previously, 'the actual desire and feelings of the woman to be married seem to have been of little significance. Parental or kinsman's will and approval were what decided her fate in marriage, and in the first instance at any rate, conversion to Christianity did nothing to improve the situation.'[19] However, times were beginning to change and for the first time, the woman was legally free to refuse if she so wished and we know Clare refused several offers of marriage from eligible suitors, to the chagrin of her family, who had put a great deal of pressure on her to make an advanta-

17. A. Blamires (ed), *Woman Defamed and Woman Defended: An Anthology of Medieval Texts* (Oxford: Clarendon Press, 1992), p 146.
18. For a discussion of the institution of marriage in the Middle Ages, see A. Lucas, *Women in the Middle Ages: Religion, Marriage and Letters* (London: The Harvester Press, 1983), pp 61-134.
19. Lucas, *Women in the Middle Ages*, p 66.

geous match. Pietro de Damiano, a neighbour of Clare's family while she was still living in her parental home, spoke of this grave concern of her family at her canonisation process more than forty years later:

> At the time, Lady Clare, a very young girl at that time, lived in a spiritual way, as was believed. He saw her father, mother, and relatives who wanted her to marry magnificently, according to her nobility, to someone great and powerful. But the young girl, at that time about seventeen or so, could not in any way be convinced because she wanted to remain in her virginity and live in poverty, as she demonstrated since she sold all her inheritance and gave it to the poor.[20]

When Pietro de Damiano was asked 'how he knew these things' he replied that 'he had seen her because he was her neighbour'. He had witnessed Clare's resolve about her future life at first hand, and saw that she had no intention of accepting any of the suitors who came to ask for her hand in marriage. One of these suitors, Lord Rainieri de Bernardo of Assisi, was also still alive at the time of her canonisation process and he too gave witness, speaking from his own experience. He said:

> Because she had a beautiful face, a husband was considered for her. Many of her relatives begged her to accept them as a husband. But she never wanted to consent. Since the witness himself had many times asked her to be willing to consent to this, she did not even want to hear him; moreover, she preached to him of despising the world.[21]

Although Clare had a completely different way of life in view, she was not free to pursue it because of the expectations of her family, hence her flight from home in the middle of the night. And even when she had achieved her goal of religious life, the pattern of holiness for women in the masculine world of the Middle Ages into which she had been born and in which she had been brought up was not woman-friendly. To become holy, to become a saint, a woman had to get rid of her femininity and

---

20. Regis J. Armstrong (ed), *Clare of Assisi: Early Documents* (New York: Paulist Press, 1988), pp 173-174.
21. *Early Documents*, pp 172-173.

become masculine. To be a woman was something to be ashamed of. Sandra Schneiders describes the situation thus:

> [W]omen early in life developed a fairly pronounced and much emphasised sense of sacral unworthiness. Not only could they not be ordained; they were not even to be in the sanctuary while divine service was taking place. They were not to touch the sacred vessels nor read the word of God in public.[22]

Although Schneiders is writing for the position of women in the present day, this was just as true of Clare's time. Women then, as now 'could not have any access to the divinity except through the mediation of men.'[23] Women were, to all intents and purposes, treated as being on the same level as children. They were weak, irresponsible, fickle, emotional and untrustworthy. If they wanted to be taken account of, they had to overcome these supposedly female traits and adopt masculine attributes. A German writer, Gottfried von Strassburg, wrote at about this time:

> When a woman grows in virtue despite her inherited instincts and gladly keeps her honour, reputation and person intact, she is only a woman in name, but in spirit she is a man! ... When a woman lays aside her woman's nature and assumes the heart of a man, it is as if the fir tree dripped with honey, a nettle bore roses above ground![24]

The pattern and ideal for holiness was still masculine, as it had been in earlier centuries. For a woman to be considered holy, she had to adopt masculine virtue.

The early years of Clare's religious life were marked by exaggerated fasting and penance, although she grew through this phase into a more whole and holy acceptance of herself as a woman, as even the saints had to grow in their spiritual understanding. Could this pattern of masculine holiness which was

---

22. S. Schneiders, 'The Effects of Women's Experience on their Spirituality', *Spirituality Today*, Summer 1983, vol 35, No 2, pp 100-116, at p 101.
23. Ibid.
24. Gottfried von Strassburg, *Tristan*, trs A. T. Hatto (Harmondsworth, 1960), p 277; quoted in F. Beer, *Women and Mystical Experience*, p 5.

expected of women be another clue to Clare's excessive fasting – was she endeavouring to lose her femininity? Clare was a very devout girl, from a family where all the women were very devout; she fasted and did penance because she wanted to accompany Christ in his sufferings and she went without food to help the poor and those less well-off than herself. 'To be more of a saint one had to be less a woman' – or preferably not a woman at all – this was the powerful philosophy of the world she grew up in; was she trying to reproduce the pattern of holiness accepted by those around her and passed on to her? If so, then the way she eventually transcended that model of holiness and grew into something much more feminine and totally original is very significant. She not only grew into psychological self-acceptance, but she grew into her own new conception and understanding of what holiness could mean for a woman, and what it meant for her. This she expressed in her first letter to Agnes of Prague, using poetic phrases from the Divine Office for the feast of St Agnes of Rome, virgin and martyr:

> Thus you took a spouse of a more noble lineage, Who will keep your virginity ever unspotted and unsullied, the Lord Jesus Christ:
>> When you have loved Him, you shall be chaste; when you have touched Him, you shall become pure; when you have accepted Him, you shall be a virgin.
>> Whose power is stronger,
>> Whose generosity is more abundant,
>> Whose appearance more beautiful,
>> Whose love is more tender,
>> Whose courtesy more graciousness.
>> In whose embrace you are already caught up;
>> Who has adorned your breast with precious stones
>> And has placed priceless pearls in your ears
>> and has surrounded you with sparkling gems
>> as though blossoms of springtime
>> and placed on your head a golden crown as a sign to all of your holiness.
> Therefore, most beloved sister, or should I say, Lady, worthy of great respect: because you are the spouse and mother and

the sister of my Lord Jesus Christ, and have been adorned resplendently with the sign of inviolable virginity and most holy poverty: Be strengthened in the holy service which you have undertaken out of an ardent desire for the Poor Crucified ...[25]

Clare in her later years is a woman at peace; at peace with herself and very clear in her ideals. She is no longer tormented by self doubt; she is no longer trying to attain something impossible. She acknowledges to Agnes that 'our flesh is not bronze, nor is our strength that of stone. No, we are frail and inclined to every bodily weakness!' She counsels Agnes to be prudent and sensible in her own observance of fasting:

> I beg you, therefore, dearly beloved, to refrain wisely and prudently from an indiscreet and impossible austerity in the fasting that you have undertaken. And I beg you in the Lord to praise the Lord by your very life, to offer the Lord your reasonable service, and your sacrifice always seasoned with salt.[26]

This is a far cry from the young Clare who had to be commanded under obedience by both Francis and the Bishop of Assisi to eat at least once a day because she was endangering her own health by her overzealous fasting.

Her spirituality as we find it in her letters, her Rule, and the stories told about her, is intensely feminine. Her imagery stresses the feminine – in her earlier letters we have the Bride, betrothal, symbols of betrothal in jewels, rings and flowers, the beauty of the Bridegroom, nuptial imagery abounds, and in her later letters, as well as these bridal images, we have images of motherhood, nurturing and nursing – all totally feminine. In her third letter to Agnes, written possibly in 1237-38, Clare says:

> May you cling to His most sweet Mother who gave birth to a Son whom the heavens could not contain. And yet she carried Him in the little enclosure of her holy womb and held

25. *Clare, First Letter to Agnes*, Regis J. Armstrong (ed), *Clare of Assisi: Early Documents* (New York: Paulist Press, 1988), pp 35-36.
26. *Clare, Third letter to Agnes*, Regis J. Armstrong (ed), *Clare of Assisi: Early Documents* (New York: Paulist Press, 1988), p 46.

Him on her virginal lap ... As the glorious Virgin of virgins carried [Him] materially, so you, too, by following in her footprints, especially [those] of poverty and humility, can, without any doubt, always carry Him spiritually in your chaste and virginal body.[27]

Here we have a woman at home with her sexuality and able to use it metaphorically in a creative way and with originality as a paradigm for her own spiritual journey. Frances Teresa comments: 'The integration of her own sexuality expressed itself in everything she did.'[28] In this, she totally transcends the pattern offered to her by a masculine dominated church down through the centuries until her own day. The Clare we find in her letters has no intention whatsoever of 'being overwhelmed with shame at the thought that she is a woman'. Clare delights in her womanhood and all its attributes; in this she completely overturns the paradigm of holiness for women accepted from the earliest days of Christianity down until her own time.

As the abbess in the community at San Damiano (though she accepted this position with the greatest reluctance and only then because Francis ordered her to under obedience to him), she was responsible for teaching and training the sisters in the ways of holiness. In the *Legend of Saint Clare* her instructions in the ascetical life to her sisters are quoted and she is reported as follows:

First of all she taught them to drive every noise away from the dwelling place of the mind so that they might be able to cling to the depths of God alone. She taught them not to be affected by a love of their relatives and to forget the homes of their families so that they might please Christ.[29]

But although she is here said to have instructed her sisters to flee human relationships and to forget their families, she is notable as the saint of friendship. Some of the girls who had been her

---

27. *Clare, Third letter to Agnes*, Regis J. Armstrong (ed), *Clare of Assisi: Early Documents* (New York: Paulist Press, 1988), p 45.
28. F. T. Downing, *This Living Mirror: Reflections on Clare of Assisi* (London, Darton, Longman and Todd, 1995), p 107.
29. Anon, *The Legend of St Clare*, Regis J. Armstrong (ed), *Clare of Assisi: Early Documents* (New York: Paulist Press, 1988), p 222.

childhood playmates during her family's exile in Perugia were among the first to join her community in San Damiano. Her mother and another sister as well as Agnes also joined the community, as did at least two nieces. Her friendship with Francis is one of the best known in medieval European history, and her correspondence with Agnes of Prague reveals her as a loving, affectionate and deeply caring woman. Among her many expressions of deep affection for Agnes we find the following:

> In this contemplation, may you remember your poor little mother, knowing that I have inscribed the happy memory of you indelibly on the tablets of my heart, holding you dearer than all others. What more can I say? Let the tongue of the flesh be silent when I seek to express my love for you; and let the tongue of the Spirit speak, because the love I have for you, O blessed daughter, can never be fully expressed by the tongue of the flesh, and even what I have written is an inadequate expression. I beg you to receive my words with kindness and devotion, seeing in them at least the motherly affection which in the fire of charity I feel daily toward you and your daughters, to whom I warmly commend myself and my daughters in Christ.[30]

Here is a woman of deep maturity, who is not afraid of her emotions nor afraid to express them with great warmth and tenderness. She loves Agnes because of the goal they share in their understanding of religious life, and this creates a strong bond between them.

The many stories recounted about her which illustrate this motherly care and concern for her community tell of her tucking up her sleeping sisters in bed, taking on herself the unpleasant tasks which are the inevitable part of the care of the sick and healing the various illnesses suffered by nuns in the community by compassionately making the sign of the cross over them. Reading between the lines in one incident, it appears that one of the sisters, so tormented by the pain of a fistula, tried to commit suicide; Clare did not condemn her but spoke to her with compassion, and healed the condition.

---

30. *Clare, Fourth letter to Agnes*, Regis J. Armstrong (ed), *Clare of Assisi: Early Documents* (New York: Paulist Press, 1988), p 50.

These stories, while illustrating various character traits which Clare is traditionally held to have possessed, also demonstrate another Franciscan characteristic: some religious orders treasure written texts – rules, homilies, sermons, treatises, works of scholarly erudition – which enshrine their history and / or their defining characteristics, but Franciscans have *stories*. Some of these stories are of dubious authenticity and are more in the genre of folk-history (such as that of her meal with Francis at the Porziuncula), but they are cherished for the expression they give to the Franciscan charism. Franciscans treasure the stories and tell and retell them; in these stories are found the concrete examples left by Francis, by Clare and their companions. These stories reveal Franciscan theology and spirituality lived out in the practicalities of daily existence. They reveal Franciscan theology incarnated in the lives of the holy ones who founded this particular religious family.

This was a time when many small houses of religiously minded women were springing up all over Europe and many experiments in what today would be called 'alternative lifestyles' were being made. It was a time when people were beginning to read the gospels for themselves, and to make negative comparisons between what they read there and what they saw going on around them. Not unnaturally, these groups of women were causing the official church no little anxiety.[31] Cardinal Hugolino, Papal Legate in Tuscany and Lombardy, was deputed by the Pope, Honorius III (born 1148, Pope from 1216-1227), to oversee these groups of religious women and, if possible, bring them into some kind of association or unity. The Fourth Lateran Council in 1215 had refused to approve any new religious Rules:

> In order to avoid an excessive diversity of Orders in the church of God causing serious confusion, we prohibit with force from now on the founding of an Order. But if someone wishes to seek conversion in the life of an Order, let him take one of the accepted Orders. Likewise if someone wishes to

31. J. Mueller, *The Privilege of Poverty: Clare of Assisi, Agnes of Prague and the Struggle for a Franciscan Rule for Women* (Pennsylvania: Pennsylvania University Press, 2006), pp 12-21.

renew an already established house of an Order, let him adopt the Rule and attitude of one of the approved Orders.[32]

So Hugolino, wanting to provide some kind of stability and security, gave Clare and the Poor Ladies of San Damiano a *Rule of Life*, based on that attributed to Benedict, and it was in accordance with this Rule that she lived for nearly all her religious life.[33] Hugolino expressed his insistence that his Rule be obeyed in no uncertain terms, terms so strong, in fact, that they suggest he might have had concerns about the 'virtue of obedience' he was enjoining:

> Every true Religion and approved institute of life endures by certain rules and requirements, and by certain disciplinary laws. Unless each sister has diligently striven to observe a correct rule and discipline for living, she will deviate from righteousness to the degree that she does not observe the guidelines of righteousness. She runs the risk of falling at the point where, in virtue of her free choice, she neglected to set for herself a sure and stable foundation for making progress ... Therefore, in virtue of obedience we strictly enjoin each and every one of you, and we command that you humbly and devotedly accept this form of life, fully explained below, which we are sending you, and that you and those who follow you strive to observe it inviolably for all time.[34]

Hugolino's 'disciplinary laws' were minutely detailed. His prescriptions for the keeping of enclosure, for silence, for the singing of the Divine Office, and for fasting were all spelled out precisely. Let us take his regulations on the nuns' clothing as an example:

> The following should be observed regarding clothing: each one may have two tunics and a mantle besides a hair shirt or a woven one if they have it, or one of sackcloth. They may also have scapulars of smooth, religious cloth or of woven

---

32. Regis J. Armstrong (ed), *Clare of Assisi: Early Documents*, fn 1, p 83.
33. For the full text of this Rule, see 'The Rule of Cardinal Hugolino (1219)', Regis J. Armstrong (ed), *Clare of Assisi: Early Documents* (New York: Paulist Press, 1988), pp 87-96.
34. Rule of Cardinal Hugolino, *Early Documents*, p 88.

cloth, if they wish, which are of fitting width and length as the nature and size of each one demands. They should be clothed in these when they are working or doing something which they cannot fittingly do wearing a mantle. If they wish to have the scapulars together with the mantles, or even wish to sleep in them, they are not prohibited from doing so. They can be without them sometimes, if it seems fitting to the Abbess, when perhaps because of excessive heat or the like they are too heavy for the sisters to wear. If this precept about wearing the scapular seems too burdensome or troublesome for some to the extent that they cannot be inclined or induced to accept it, the Abbess may dispense with it. But those who accept the scapular are acting much more uprightly and are much more pleasing to us, and we believe that they are much more pleasing to God as well.[35]

The editors have here added a footnote to say: 'The exhortation to wear the scapular implies some lack of agreement between the Cardinal and the sisters as to its use.'[36] The Cardinal was busying himself so minutely about the nuns' clothing because it was an issue of authority; authority required a cleric and therefore a male. Clare's own prescriptions regarding clothing were of the simplest and appealed to practicality and common sense rather than authority:

[O]nce her hair has been cut off round her head and her secular clothes laid aside, she may be permitted three tunics and a mantle ... The sisters may also have little mantles for convenience and propriety in serving and working. In fact, the Abbess should with discernment provide them with clothing according to the diversity of persons, places, seasons and cold climates, as it shall seem expedient to her by necessity.[37]

Clare has far less to say about the practicalities of clothing than Hugolino, but reveals her farsightedness in her prescription regarding 'persons, places, seasons and cold climates.'

35. Rule of Cardinal Hugolino, *Early Documents*, p 92.
36. Ibid.
37. Clare, *Rule,* Regis J. Armstrong (ed), *Clare of Assisi: Early Documents* (New York: Paulist Press, 1988), pp 63, 64.

The originality of both Clare and Francis spring from the importance they gave to poverty in their interpretation of gospel living. This importance, in its turn, was largely a reaction to the increasing wealth and consequent status of the merchant class in medieval society. Marygrace Peters describes the social upheavals of the twelfth century, which had such a profound effect on Francis and Clare, thus:

> As feudalism declined, a new class of people arose in urban communities. These merchants and trades people of the towns appeared during the transition from a gift economy, in which goods and services were exchanged, to the market economy, in which things were expected to have an assigned value ... The sharp contrast between wealth and poverty became more striking in the towns, as the ranks of the urban poor swelled. Many revelled in the new opportunities for acquiring fortune and for indulging consumption. Still others were repelled, seeing in these opportunities the lure of Satan. These latter often felt impelled to renounce all property, power and privilege. Such craving for renunciation cut across all class distinctions, so as to include even the merchants who derived the most material benefits from these new conditions ... Nobles, artisans, those with a substantial education, secular clergy who protested against the worldly pomp of ecclesiastical prelates – persons from all walks of life were attracted to the cult of voluntary poverty.[38]

Of such were the first followers of Francis and of Clare. Clare had been inspired by Francis and his vision of poverty, whom he addressed as the 'Lady Poverty',[39] finding in his words the echo of what was taking place deep within her own heart. In her

---

38. M. Peters, 'The Beguines: Feminine Piety Derailed,' *Spirituality Today* (Spring 1991, Vol 43 No. 1, pp 36-52, at pp 36, 37.

39. See Anon, *Sacrum commercium sancti Francisci cum domina Paupertate* ('The Sacred Exchange between Saint Francis and the Lady Poverty') in Regis Armstrong, J. A. Wayne Hellman, W. J. Short (eds), *Francis of Assisi: Early Documents* Vol 1: *The Saint* (New York, New City Press: 1999), pp 521-554. The Introduction describes this text as: 'An allegory offering insights into Francis's vision of poverty ... [weaving] a luxuriant tapestry of images held together by the strong threads of a biblical theology ... The allegory is an exhortation written to encourage Francis's followers to live in an authen-

Testament, she described the early days of her religious life, according to the teaching of Francis:

> After the most high heavenly Father saw fit in His mercy and grace to enlighten my heart, that I should do penance according to the example and teaching of our most blessed father Francis, a short while after his conversion, I, together with a few sisters whom the Lord had given me after my conversion, willingly promised him obedience, as the Lord gave us the light of His grace through his wonderful life and teaching. When the blessed Francis saw, however, that, although we were physically weak and frail, we did not shirk deprivation, poverty, hard work, trial, or the shame and contempt of the world – rather, we considered them as great delights, as he had frequently examined us according to the example of the saints and his brothers – he greatly rejoiced in the Lord ... Afterwards he wrote a form of life for us, especially that we always persevere in holy poverty. While he was living he was not content to encourage us with many words and examples to the love of poverty and its observance, but he gave us many writings that, after his death, we would in no way turn away from it, as the Son of God never wished to abandon this holy poverty while He lived in the world. And our most blessed father Francis, having imitated His footprints, never departed either in example or in teaching from this holy poverty that he had chosen for himself and his brothers.[40]

Her understanding of the renunciation involved in living out this vision of poverty which she had learned from Francis, operated on varying levels, each level taking the understanding deeper into the mystery of 'sine proprio': 'nonappropriation'. In its widest external sense, as it affected the whole community, it involved the foregoing of land and property rights, which were so important in the Middle Ages. Clare was a daughter of the

---

tic way the saint's biblical vision of poverty. The central figure of the work is Lady Poverty, the personification of biblical Wisdom and, at times, of the church'. 'The Sacred Exchange between Saint Francis and the Lady Poverty', p 523.

40. Clare, *Testament*, Regis J. Armstrong (ed), *Clare of Assisi: Early Documents* (New York: Paulist Press, 1988), p 56.

aristocracy who understood wealth as meaning the ownership of land and the vast estates in the country necessary to support a great household in the city. Fortini describes the great estates of the Offreducio clan in the environs of Assisi thus:

> Their vast possessions extended below the leper hospital, reached to Castelnuovo, went up the hill beyond Cannara, this not counting the lands of Chiagina conceded *in precarium* to the canons. An opulent *curtis* [manor], capable of supplying every kind of produce, was established below the wall of Moiano, between Sant' Anastasio and the Valecchie road. They had serfs, men and women, and men-at-arms.[41]

This was the world familiar to Clare, into which she had been born and in which she had been brought up from childhood; it was the world she had renounced so decisively. For her, wealth meant land and estates, which signified security; poverty meant the non-appropriation of these estates:

> Just as I, together with my sisters, have ever been solicitous to safeguard the holy poverty which we have promised the Lord God and blessed Francis, so, too, the Abbesses who shall succeed me in office and all the sisters are bound to observe it inviolably until the end: that is to say, by not receiving or having possession or ownership either of themselves or through an intermediary, or even anything that might reasonably be called property.[42]

In this, as a daughter of the aristocracy, her understanding of what it meant to be truly poor differed from that of Francis, the merchant's son, for whom wealth meant money, and for whom poverty translated as not having money, which he saw as tainted. In his Earlier Rule of 1221, he had written very emphatically:

> [N]one of the brothers, wherever he may be or wherever he goes, should in any way carry, receive, or have received [by another] either money or coins, whether for clothing or books or payment for any work – indeed for no reason – un-

41. See A. Fortini, *Francis of Assisi* (trs H. Moak) (New York, Crossroads: 1981), p 329.

42. Clare, *Rule*, Regis J. Armstrong (ed), *Clare of Assisi: Early Documents* (New York: Paulist Press, 1988), p 69.

less it is for the evident need of the sick brothers; for we must not suppose that money or coins have any greater value than stones. And the devil would like to blind those who desire it or consider it better than stones ... [The brothers] should beware of money. Likewise all the brothers should beware of running around the world for filthy gain.[43]

In the Later Rule of 1223, these words are abbreviated, but his legislation is just as strong: 'I firmly command all the brothers that they in no way receive coins or money, either personally or through an intermediary.'[44] In contrast to Clare who never mentioned money, for the newly emerging merchant class, to which the Bernadone family belonged, wealth meant money and money brought power and the ability to control others. To shun money meant to be needy and in physical want; it also meant to be powerless and vulnerable, without influence or status.

But however it was expressed, the concept of poverty which inspired both Francis and Clare differed from that of the existing monastic Orders. The Benedictines practised poverty on a personal level and the Rule attributed to Benedict allowed those who followed it to have:

> ... all things that are necessary: that is, cowl, tunic, stockings, shoes, belt, knife, pen, needle, handkerchief, and tablets; so that all pretext of need may be taken away.[45]

However, it upheld very strongly the virtue of personal poverty and was adamant that no one should violate it. No monk should:

> have anything as his own, anything whatever, whether book or tablets or pen or whatever it may be; for monks should not have even their bodies and wills at their own disposal ... let it be unlawful to have anything which the abbot has not given or allowed ... But if anyone shall be found to indulge in this

43. Regis Armstrong and Ignatius Brady, *Francis and Clare: the Complete Works* (New York: Paulist Press, 1982), pp 116, 117.
44. Ibid, p 140.
45. Benedict, *Regula*, trs Justin McCann (London: Sheed and Ward, 1976), p 61.

most wicked vice, let him be admonished once and a second time; if he do not amend, let him undergo punishment.[46]

However, even though the personal poverty of the individual monk was strict and was legislated precisely, with appropriate punishment for infringements, by the time of Francis and Clare, the Benedictines as an Order, and the individual monasteries within the Order, frequently owned lands and estates which were often vast. In fact, the author of the *Rule* attributed to Benedict deliberately wanted his monasteries to be self-supporting: each to be like a small village with everything necessary for the lives of the monks to be at hand so they did not need to go outside the monastery property for anything that they needed:

> The monastery should, if possible, be so arranged that all necessary things such as water, mill, garden, and various crafts may be within the enclosure, so that monks may not be compelled to wander outside it, for that is not at all expedient for their souls.[47]

This was especially necessary for such reforms of the Benedictine family as the Cistercians, who were farmers and who needed large granges and tracts of grazing land for the animals on which they depended. But in contrast, Clare, not wishing her sisters to possess these great estates, wrote:

> Nevertheless, let both [the sister] who is in office, as well as the other sisters, exercise such care and farsightedness that they do not acquire or receive more land about the place than extreme necessity requires for a vegetable garden. But if, for the integrity and privacy of the monastery, it becomes necessary to have more land beyond the limits of the garden, no more should be acquired than extreme necessity demands. This land should not be cultivated or planted but remain always untouched and undeveloped.[48]

46. Benedict, *Regula*, trs Justin McCann (London: Sheed and Ward, 1976), p 40.

47. Benedict, *Regula*, trs Justin McCann (London: Sheed and Ward, 1976), p 74,

48. Clare, *Testament*, Regis J. Armstrong (ed), *Clare of Assisi: Early Documents* (New York: Paulist Press, 1988), p 58.

So Clare had no desire for her nuns to possess any more land than 'extreme necessity requires'. And again in Chapter Six, the heart of her Rule, as already referred to above, she wrote:

> Just as I, together with my sisters, have ever been solicitous to safeguard the holy poverty which we have promised the Lord God and blessed Francis, so, too, the Abbesses who shall succeed me in office and all the sisters are bound to observe it inviolably to the end: that is to say, by not receiving or having possession or ownership either of themselves or through an intermediary, or even anything that might reasonably be called property, except as much land as necessity requires for the integrity and proper seclusion of the monastery, and this land may not be cultivated except as a garden for the needs of the sisters.[49]

That Clare practised what she legislated can be shown by the existence of a mandate, attributed by Luke Wadding in the *Annales Minorum* to the year 1238,[50] in which Clare and her community at San Damiano sold a field. Although Regis Armstrong in the short Introduction claims that this document 'is of little spiritual importance',[51] I find it of the greatest significance in the independent witness it gives to Clare's fidelity to her own principles. She wished that the financial affairs of the community should be handled by a procurator;[52] and this is expressly stated in the mandate: 'a procurator or treasurer who will sell or hand over in her name and in that of the monastery a certain enclosure in Compiglione'. She wished that the whole community should be consulted in any important affairs,[53] and that has manifestly been done in the matter of the selling of this field: 'by the will of the ladies or sisters listed below' and all their names

---

49. Clare, *Rule*, Regis J. Armstrong (ed), *Clare of Assisi: Early Documents* (New York: Paulist Press, 1988), pp 69-70.
50. The original document was discovered in the archives of Assisi by that indefatigable Franciscan scholar, Arnaldo Fortini.
51. Mandate, Regis J. Armstrong (ed), *Clare of Assisi: Early Documents* (New York: Paulist Press, 1988), p 107.
52. Clare, *Rule*, Regis J. Armstrong (ed), *Clare of Assisi: Early Documents* (New York: Paulist Press, 1988), p 67.
53. Clare, *Rule*, Regis J. Armstrong (ed), *Clare of Assisi: Early Documents* (New York: Paulist Press, 1988), p 67.

are listed at the conclusion of the document where, 'Lady Clare and her sisters have placed the seal of this monastery's chapter'. From this we can tell that in 1238 there were fifty sisters living at San Damiano.

So, although there are some elements in Clare's Rule which she took from that attributed to Benedict, her words to her sisters when praying for the deliverance of the town of Assisi from the army of Vitalis d'Aversa show that she in no way saw her community as being self-sufficient according to the Benedictine model. According to the Benedictine understanding the local urban community depended on the monastery for its sustenance and for its survival; the Benedictine monastery provided employment, security, possibilities for trade and barter, refuge in time of warfare or conflict, medical aid, education for the young, spiritual comfort both in life and death and even a certain amount of prestige. But Clare completely reversed the situation and saw herself and her sisters as dependant on the local community; both for their daily sustenance and for their survival. She was very conscious that she and her sisters depended on the citizens of Assisi for their subsistence and so owed them a debt of gratitude in return expressed in prayer:

> Dearest children, every day we receive many good things from that city. It would be terrible if, at a proper time, we did not help it as we now can.[54]

Her desire to have no privileges or possessions at all was in sharp contrast to the religious experience of most monastic women in her day, who relied on the income from land and property for their livelihood. Joan Mueller sums up the issue succinctly:

> Most women involved in the religious movement of her day did not share Clare's desire to be radically poor. Monastic women willingly accepted land grants and tax exemptions given them by wealthy relatives and solicitous popes.[55]

---

54. Anon, *The Legend of St Clare*, Regis J. Armstrong (ed), *Clare of Assisi: Early Documents* (New York: Paulist Press, 1988), pp 212-213.
55. J. Mueller, *The Privilege of Poverty: Clare of Assisi, Agnes of Prague and the Struggle for a Franciscan Rule for Women* (Pennsylvania: Pennsylvania University Press, 2006), p 2.

But Clare fought throughout her life, and as time went on, Agnes of Prague fought with her, for the 'privilege of having no privileges'; the 'privilege of poverty'. She wished her sisters to earn their living by the work of their own hands, as did the poor. It was precisely this continued insistence on poverty, seen as total dependence on God, which made her proposed way of life so suspect in the eyes of the church authorities. To them, it was imprudent to the point of foolhardiness.

When it came to the practice of poverty by individual members of the Order, Clare was not as explicit as Benedict as to what items were actually allowed each nun. Apart from stipulating that each sister be allowed 'three tunics and a mantle' and that the Abbess should make provision for 'persons, places, times and cold climates' as she might deem necessary and appropriate, Clare does not descend into legislating specific details, but she made the heartfelt plea:

> I admonish, beg, and exhort my sisters to always wear cheap garments out of love of the most holy and beloved Child Who was wrapped in such poor little swaddling clothes and laid in a manger and of His most holy Mother.[56]

So she understood poverty as something to be exercised at the level of the community as a whole (lands and estates); at the level of the individual (clothes and personal belongings), but these two were to be the expression of something far deeper: a sharing in the self-emptying of Christ at the incarnation. She returns to this theme over and over again in her writings:

> O God-centred poverty,
> whom the Lord Jesus Christ
> Who ruled and now rules heaven and earth,
> Who spoke and things were made,
> condescended to embrace before all else! ...

> If so great and good a Lord, then, on coming into the Virgin's womb, chose to appear despised, needy and poor in this world so that people who were in utter poverty, want and absolute need of heavenly nourishment might become

---

56. Clare, Rule, Regis J. Armstrong (ed), *Clare of Assisi: Early Documents* (New York: Paulist Press, 1988), p 64.

rich in Him by possessing the kingdom of heaven, be very joyful and glad! Be filled with a remarkable happiness and a spiritual joy! Because, since contempt of the world has pleased You more than its honours, poverty more than earthly riches, and you have sought to store up greater treasures in heaven rather than on earth, where rust does not consume nor moth destroy nor thieves break in and steal, Your reward is very rich in heaven![57]

Thus does Clare express poetically her desire to live truly poor in imitation of the poor Christ, who 'being rich, became poor that he might enrich us by his poverty'.[58]

In this she faithfully imitated Francis, for whom, although external poverty was so important, the interior spirit of poverty was even more so:

[They are not truly poor in spirit] who are scandalised and quickly roused to anger by a single word which seems injurious to their person, or by some other things which might be taken from them.[59]

For both Francis and Clare, poverty in outward things such as money, possessions, buildings and land expressed the inner poverty of spirit. However, it was this very insistence on outward poverty and a way of life with no security or guarantees that brought Clare into conflict with church authorities. There were many other such groups of women in the church at that time and some of them were suspected of heresy. There is some evidence that towards the end of her life, Clare fell into quite serious disrepute and disgrace with church authorities, probably because of the insistence both she and Agnes of Prague demonstrated in their determined desire to obtain papal recognition for their request to live in total poverty. (There is even a suggestion in the writings of Angelo Clareno that Clare might have been issued with a decree of excommunication, but he is not the

---

57. Clare, *Rule*, Regis J. Armstrong (ed), *Clare of Assisi: Early Documents* (New York: Paulist Press, 1988), pp. 36-37.
58. 2 Cor 8:9.
59. Francis of Assisi: *Admonitions*, Regis J. Armstrong and Ignatius Brady (eds) *Francis and Clare; the Complete Works* (New York, Paulist Press: 1982), p 32.

most reliable of witnesses, having an axe of his own to grind.)
There is a letter from Cardinal Hugolino (the Cardinal who had
been given special responsibility as Protector of the Order[60]) to
Clare, written possibly in 1220, in which he addresses Clare in
reverential terms: she is his 'very dear sister in Christ and mother
of his salvation'. He continues:

> From that very hour when the necessity of returning here
> separated me from your holy conversation and tore me away
> from that joy of heavenly treasure, such bitterness of heart,
> such an abundance of tears and such an immensity of sorrow
> have overcome me that, unless I find at the feet of Jesus the
> consolation of his usual kindness, I fear that I will always en-
> counter such trials which will cause my spirit to melt away ...
> Therefore, I entrust my soul and commend my spirit to you,
> just as Jesus on the cross commended his spirit to the father,
> so that on the day of judgement you may answer for me ...[61]

These are strong emotions for a cardinal of the church to ex-

60. At the request of Francis himself, Cardinal Hugolino had taken on
the responsibility of Cardinal Protector of the Order. Francis wrote in his
Later Rule: 'In addition, I command the ministers through obedience to
petition the Lord Pope for one of the cardinals of the holy Roman
Church, who would be the governor, protector, and corrector of this
fraternity, so that, always submissive and prostrate at the feet of the
same holy church, and steadfast in the Catholic faith, we may observe
the poverty and the humility and the holy gospel of our Lord Jesus
Christ which we have firmly promised', Francis of Assisi, 'The Later
Rule', Regis J. Armstrong and Ignatius Brady (eds), *Francis and Clare: the
Complete Works* (New York, Paulist Press: 1982), p 145. Clare made the
same request for the sisters: '[T]he sisters are firmly obliged to have always that Cardinal of the Holy Church of Rome as our governor, protector, and corrector, who has been delegated by the Lord Pope for the
Friars Minor, so that, always submissive and subject at the feet of that
holy church, and steadfast in the Catholic faith, we may observe forever
the poverty and humility of our Lord Jesus Christ and of his most holy
Mother and the holy gospel which we have firmly promised.' Clare of
Assisi, 'The Rule', Regis J. Armstrong and Ignatius Brady (eds), *Francis
and Clare: the Complete Works* (New York, Paulist Press: 1982), p 225. The
position of Cardinal Protector of the Franciscan Order was discontinued
after Vatican II in 1965.
61. Letter of Cardinal Hugolino to Clare, Regis J. Armstrong (ed), *Clare of
Assisi: Early Documents* (New York: Paulist Press, 1988), pp 97, 98.

press to a nun; yet eight years later, when he wrote to Clare again, this time as Pope Gregory IX, the tone of his letter is quite different. Now, although still addressing her conventionally as 'my beloved daughter', rather than expressing his own affection for Clare and his need for her companionship and support, he seems to be putting pressure on her to accept issues she finds hard and distasteful:

> We certainly hope and have confidence that, if you pay careful and diligent attention, those things which now seem bitter will become wholesome and sweet for you, what is hard will become soft and what is rough will become smooth, so that you will exult, if you merit to suffer these things for Christ who endured for us the passion of an infamous death.[62]

Probably these 'bitter ... hard ... and rough' things to which she had to 'pay careful and diligent attention' were his repeated insistences that Clare should follow the Rule he himself had given her, based on that attributed to Benedict.

Agnes of Prague felt so strongly about this issue that she explicitly requested that mention of the Rule of Benedict be excluded from the Rule granted to her and her sisters; the reply she received from Rome (the pope by this time was Gregory's successor, Innocent IV [1243-1253]) was not sympathetic and read as follows:

> [Y]ou humbly request that the two phrases by virtue of holy obedience and the Rule of Blessed Benedict be stricken from the afore mentioned document and you ask Us to restore the special indults granted to your monastery by Pope Gregory, Our predecessor of happy memory. After taking counsel, We cannot see our way, for a variety of reasons, to grant this request.[63]

Innocent went on to explain these reasons in detail: the abbesses and sisters in San Damiano and all the other members

---

62. Letter of Pope Gregory IX to Clare, Regis J. Armstrong (ed), *Clare of Assisi: Early Documents* (New York: Paulist Press, 1988), p 99.

63. *The Lady: Clare of Assisi, Early Documents*, Regis J. Armstrong, ed, (New York, London: New City Press, 2006), p 372.

of the Order had professed Gregory's Rule; they had observed this rule 'in a praiseworthy manner' from their profession until that time; and because the Rule itself prescribes that it be 'uniformly observed in all places by all who make profession of it' any alterations 'could result in serious and intolerable scandal'.[64]

However, Clare never gave up and, as she lay dying, the papal document *Solet annuere*, dated 9 August 1253, confirming 'the form of life that Blessed Francis gave' arrived and was placed in her hands. The original text was discovered in 1893, and is today preserved in the Protomonastery in Assisi. In the margin were written the words: 'Blessed Clare touched and kissed this many times out of devotion.' She was the first woman in the history of the church to be granted papal approval for a rule she had written herself.[65]

Mueller rightly comments on Clare's life and witness:

> Always a daughter respectful of church hierarchy, Clare never sacrificed the discernment born of prayer and the discipline of monastic living for a blind unthinking obedience.[66]

'Discernment' was a favourite word of Clare's, used frequently in her writings; she wished her sisters to have this discernment and to use it circumspectly and frequently in the daily events of communal living within the monastery.[67] She lived it out in her life and taught others to do the same.

By her dedication to her chosen way of life, her loyalty to the church in the figure of the Pope, and her unswerving faithfulness to the ideals she had learned from Francis, her male teacher and mentor, Clare stayed within the bounds set by convention for religious women of her time and was truly a 'daughter of the church' although that same church did not always understand

---

64. *The Lady: Clare of Assisi, Early Documents*, Regis J. Armstrong (ed), (New York, London: New City Press, 2006), p 371-373.
65. Regis J. Armstrong (ed), *Clare of Assisi: Early Documents* (New York: Paulist Press, 1988), pp 60-61.
66. Mueller, *The Privilege of Poverty*, p 124.
67. The abbess should provide clothing 'with discernment' (Rule, chapter 2); the Novice Mistress is to be chosen from among 'the more discerning' sisters (Rule, chapter 2); the abbess' council is to be chosen from among 'the more discerning sisters' (Rule, chapter 4); the portress is to be 'discerning' (Rule chapter 11).

her ideals and sometimes, in the persons of ecclesiastical figures of high authority, put great pressure on her to abandon them. But by her insistence on her right to live according to her own ideals –and in her interpretation of those ideals she exercised considerable originality and was far from being the carbon copy of Francis as she is sometimes portrayed – even though these ideals conflicted with the church's legislation for religious women at that time, and by her originality in expressing them both in her own life and in writing for future generations, she moved right outside the parameters set for cloistered women in the Middle Ages. As pointed out above, the Franciscan vision of poverty was, to a large extent, reaction against the strong social currents of the time, but it inspired one of the greatest and most original women in the history of the church. And if this is so, then we have to ask why has she – until very recently – been so less well known than Francis?

CHAPTER SEVEN

'Veni Sponsa Christi' – Medieval Monastic Mystics

Regular prayer at defined times of the day and night has been part of the Christian tradition since the beginning, as witness the *Didache*, an important text from the early church,[1] where the first generation of Christians were expected to say the 'Our Father' three times a day, presumably at morning, noon and evening. In the *Didache*, the belief – already found in the Old Testament[2] and in the practice of the Judaism within which Christianity appeared – is made explicit that the use of sacred time by the community of believers praying together was considered more important and more powerful than when the believer prayed alone. In this three times daily recitation of the 'Our Father' we see the Liturgy of the Hours in its earliest and most rudimentary form.[3] Gradually, however, the Liturgy of the Hours was seen less and less as the prayer of all believers, and more and more as the prayer of 'the professionals': priests, monks and nuns. By

---

1. See T. O'Loughlin, *The Didache: A Window on the Earliest Christians* (London: SPCK, 2010).
2. See 1 Kings 18:36: 'At the time when the offering is presented, Elijah the prophet stepped forward. "Yahweh, God of Abraham, Isaac and Israel," he said, "let them know today that you are God in Israel, and that I am your servant, that I have done all these things at your command"'; Judith 9:1: '*At the same time in Jerusalem the evening sacrifice was being offered in the Temple of God,* Judith said ....'; Dan 9:21; Tobit 3:17. In the first three of these references, even greater potency is accorded to prayer offered with others at the same time that sacrifice is being offered in the Temple (added emphasis).
3. For a full treatment of the Liturgy of the Hours, see Taft, R., *The Liturgy of the Hours in East and West: The Origins of the Divine Office and its Meaning for Today* (Collegeville, Minnesota: Liturgical Press, 1986, 1993), also Woolfenden, G. W., *Daily Liturgical Prayer: Origins and Theology* (Aldershot: Ashgate, 2004). For the development of the Liturgy of the Hours in the insular world, see P. Rumsey, *Sacred Time in Early Christian Ireland* (London:T & T Clark, 2007).

about the end of the first millennium, it had become the monastic prayer *par excellence*. So monks and nuns prayed the various Offices, which were composed mainly of psalms and other passages from scripture, by day and by night in the church or chapel of the monastery, coming together as a community at set times according to the horarium of the house. However, public liturgical prayer, at arranged times and places and according to prescribed forms, was not the only way to pray: there were other ways of finding God and being found by him. This chapter examines a more deeply personal, non-liturgical and mysterious way of finding God, which could take place anywhere, not just in the monastic Choir during set hours of prayer with the rest of the community. This chapter looks at 'mystical prayer'.[4] We will first examine the meaning of this phrase and then see how it affected the lives of monastic women (and men) in the later Middle Ages.

'Mysticism' has a long history in Christian spirituality. Origen (185-254) laid the foundations for later Christian understanding of the term by setting out a procedure of ascetic purification based on the scriptures and union with the Word made flesh which was taken up with enthusiasm by the desert monastics in their search for God. Clement of Alexandria was the first to use the term 'mystic things' (*ta mystika*) to refer to the hidden realities of Christian life and faith, primarily the scriptures, but also Christian sacraments and rituals and even the vision of God. The anonymous author pseudo-Dionysius, writing about 500 AD, coined the term 'mystical theology' and also 'mystical union' and was probably the most influential writer from among the early mystics. So early monastic 'mysticism' was essentially both scriptural and liturgical. Other influential monastic writers on mysticism were Evagrius Ponticus (d. 399),

---

4. There is a vast literature on all aspects of mystical prayer. See, for instance, the classic E. Underhill, *Mysticism: a study in the nature and development of man's spiritual consciousness* (London: Methuen, 1911); D. Knowles, *What is Mysticism?* (London: Burns and Oates, 1967); D. Turner, *The Darkness of God: Negativity in Christian Mysticism* (Cambridge: Cambridge University Press, 1995, 1996, 1998, 1999); V. Lossky, *The Mystical Theology of the Eastern Church*, Eng. trs Fellowship of St Alban and St Sergius (London: James Clark & Co, 1957, repr. 1968, 1973); O. Clément, *The Roots of Christian Mysticism* (London: New City, 1993).

Cassian (d. 435), Gregory of Nyssa (d. 395), Ambrose of Milan (d. 397), Augustine of Hippo (d. 430), and Gregory the Great (d. 604). Dionysius' 'negative theology,' where God is found in the darkness of unknowing, was introduced to the West through the translations of John Scottus Eriugena in the ninth century. By the twelfth century, there was an enormous growth in first-person accounts of visionary experience on the part of both men and women, in contrast to the more sober, scriptural and liturgical approach of the patristic era, and the Cistercians, exemplified in Bernard of Clairvaux (1190-1153), developed a mysticism using unambiguously erotic language based on their interpretation of the Song of Songs.[5] Bernard used this love poetry of the Old Testament as an allegory of the relationship between God and the individual human being, expressing this in terms of marital intimacy. This genre of spiritual writing opened the way for a type of less specialised theological expression, in contrast to the highly systematised and analytical presentation of the scholastics. This was where the women were to find their particular niche. Schneiders is describing the situation today, but her words are equally relevant for this period in the history of the church:

> [T]he fact – undoubtedly deplorable in itself – that women have always been totally dependent on men for official religious participation has led women to specialise in the only religious activity they could engage in without male permission or help – namely, personal prayer ... Women, ... often through their restriction to devotional prayers and their exclusion from the public sphere of ministerial activity, have frequently found their way through to genuine affective prayer, often of a high order.[6]

Partly through this female influence, the later Middle Ages saw the blossoming of a 'new mysticism', heavily influenced by the Franciscans and Dominicans and their stress on devotion to the humanity of Christ, including, especially, his suffering and death:

---

5. See E. A. Matter, *The Voice of My Beloved: The Song of Songs in Western Medieval Christianity* (University of Pennsylvania Press, 1990).

6. S. Schneiders, 'The Effects of Women's Experience on their Spirituality', *Spirituality Today*, Summer 1983, vol 35, No 2, pp 100-116.

The visualisation and imitation of Christ were central to thirteenth- and fourteenth-century spirituality. Saints and holy people increasingly focused their spirituality through the bodily re-enactment or re-presentation of Christ's Passion. Images, and thus the sense of sight, were central in religious practice. Representations of the Passion, in the form of paintings or sculptures, led to its imitation on the part of the viewer. Visual stimuli, real or imagined, provoked physical reactions.[7]

This applied to all manner of medieval persons, male as well as female. Dominic Guzmán, the eventual founder of the Order of Preachers, was frequently seen praying with his arms extended in the form of a cross.[8] The vision of Francis of Assisi when the crucifix in San Damiano spoke to him and told him to 'Rebuild my church which is falling into ruins' is so well known as to be part of the Christian hagiographical patrimony, as is also his identification with the crucified Christ to the extent of bearing the stigmata, the wounds of his crucifixion in hands, feet and side.[9] (But it is part of the contradictory nature of Francis' psychological makeup [and he is not alone in this] that he was deeply devoted to the humility and condescension of the humanity of Jesus manifest in the self-emptying (*kenosis*) of the incarnation and yet had a very low view of human nature, his own in particular, and thus a negative view of the body, to the point where he apologised to 'Brother body' at the end of his life for having treated his body so harshly and cautioned his friars that they should not copy him in this.)

---

7. C. Warr, 'Representation, imitation, rejection: Chiara of Montefalco (d. 1308) and the passion of Christ' in C. Meek and C. Lawless (eds), *Studies on Medieval and Early Modern Women 4: Victims or Viragos?* (Dublin: Four Courts Press, 2005), pp 89-101, at p 89.

8. Ibid, p 90.

9. However, E. F. Hartung and others have suggested that Francis' stigmata may have had medical and/or psychological causes. Francis suffered from malaria (which was probably the cause of his death) and possibly also from a form of leprosy (perhaps contracted while nursing the lepers in the early days of his conversion), both of which diseases could have produced symptoms similar to the stigmata. See E. F. Hartung, 'St Francis and Mediaeval Medicine', *Annals of Medical History* 1935, 7: pp 85-91; C. J. Simpson, 'The Stigmata: Pathology or Miracle?' *British Medical Journal*, Vol 289, Dec 1984, pp 1746-1748.

The 'visual stimuli ... provoking physical reactions' of which Warr wrote, were deemed to be 'particularly relevant to mystics and women viewers, who were held to be more susceptible to visual imagery and who were also more easily affected by the emotions.'[10] Thus this chapter is mainly concerned with women mystics from the twelfth to the sixteenth centuries.[11] During these years there was a 'proliferation of new religious roles for women'[12] and the influence these women had reached far into the future. Hildegard of Bingen went so far as to say that: 'the decadent society and church of her time were the result of masculine weakness of a kind that must be overcome through the agency of women of integrity. This, she said, "was the *tempus muliebre*, the era of women".'[13]

The devotional approach with its emphasis on imaginative and subjective renderings of the person of Christ had already appeared in the writings of Bernard of Clairvaux:

> [T]he Word became flesh and now dwells among us. He dwells in our hearts through faith, he dwells in our memory and thoughts, he penetrates even to our imagination. For what could a man conceive of God unless he first made an image of him in his heart? ... But how? you may ask. I answer: lying in a manger, resting on a virgin's bosom, preaching on the mount, spending the night in prayer; or hanging on the cross, the pallor of death on his face, like one forsaken among the dead, overruling the powers of hell; or rising again on the third day, showing the apostles the print of the nails, the sign of victory, and finally ascending from their sight into heaven.[14]

This meditative approach to the life and person of Christ was

---

10. Warr, 'Representation, imitation, rejection: Chiara of Montefalco (d. 1308) and the passion of Christ', p 92.
11. Simpson quotes Imbert-Gourbeyre who found that 'of the 321 people with stigmata that he discovered since the time of St Francis, 41 were men and 280 were women'. A. Imbert-Gourbeyre, *La stigmatisation* (Clermont, Bellet: 1894). Quoted in Simpson, op. cit., p 1746.
12. M. Peters, 'The Beguines: Feminine Piety Derailed,' *Spirituality Today* (Spring 1991, Vol 43 No 1, pp 36-52 at p 38.
13. Quoted in Peters, 'The Beguines: Feminine Piety Derailed,' p 38.
14. Bernard, *Sermo de Aquaeductu, Opera omnia, Edit. Cisterc.* 5 [1968], 282-283.

built on the monastic tradition of earlier times, but had a new
focus in its insistence that mystical experience was open to all
Christians. For this reason, and because it was frequently expressed in the vernacular tongues of Europe, rather than the
learned language of Latin, which was the prerogative of clerics
and the schools, it was open to women, who soon became enthusiastic participators. Women discovered a realm of spiritual
expression which was widely accessible to them and which appealed to their christological vision. A mysticism strongly influenced by personal devotion to Christ and expressed in highly
charged sexual imagery characterised such female mystical
writers as Mechthilde of Magdeburg (1210-1285), Gertrude
(1256-c.1302) and Mechthild of Helfte (1240/41-1298), Clare of
Assisi (1194-1253), Angela of Foligno (c.1248-1309), Catherine of
Siena (1347-1380), Beatrice of Nazareth (1200-1268) and
Hadewijch (thirteenth century). These are only a few of the host
of female visionaries who flourished from the thirteenth century
onwards. Of all of these, Julian of Norwich (1342-c.1416), who
became an anchoress in one of England's most prosperous
medieval towns, became one of the most popular. Julian lived as
an anchoress attached to the church of St Julian in Norwich in
the second half of the fourteenth century. Her '*Showings*' – a series
of sixteen visions revealing the love of God, and Christ in his
Passion, received when she was seriously ill in 1343, probably
while she was still living at home as she mentions the presence
of her mother at her bedside – which are notable for the 'home-
liness' of her style and her great emphasis on the forgiving love
of God, have made her one of the best-loved and most widely
read mystics. Apart from the little she tells of her own circumstances, details of her life are lacking. She tells us that she received her revelations in May 1373 when she was thirty years
old, so she was born in 1342 but it is not certain exactly when she
died. Three extant wills name her as a beneficiary and the latest
of these is dated 1416. By then she would have been well into
her seventies – a good age for those times. It has been assumed
that she was a devout woman who became an anchoress as a result of the visions she had experienced,[15] but we do not know if

15. C. Wolters, *Julian of Norwich: Revelations of Divine Love* (London: Penguin
Books, 1966), p 15.

she was a professed nun, Benedictine or other. At a time when
great emphasis was placed on the fear of God, Julian stressed
God's immense love for all his creation and especially for the
human race. Although she lived at a time of great hardship and
suffering (she lived during the outbreak of the Great Plague – ie.
the Black Death in 1348-49), her writings are full of optimism
and her phrase 'All shall be well, and all manner of thing shall
be well' is one of the best known in spiritual literature. There is
nothing negative about Julian; even in the midst of her graphic
'seeing' of the suffering of Christ in his passion, she experienced
'heartfelt joy':

> And at once I saw the red blood trickling down from under
> the garland, hot, fresh, and plentiful, just as it did at the time
> of his passion when the crown of thorns was pressed on the
> blessed head of God-and-Man, who suffered for me. And I
> had a strong, deep, conviction that it was he himself and
> none other that showed me this vision.
>
> At the same moment the Trinity filled me full of heartfelt
> joy, and I knew that all eternity was like this for those who at-
> tain heaven. For the Trinity is God, and God the Trinity; the
> Trinity is our Maker and keeper, our eternal lover, joy and
> bliss – all through our Lord Jesus Christ.[16]

Her 'seeings' are overwhelmed with the experience of God's
love:

> And he showed me more, a little thing, the size of a hazel-
> nut, on the palm of my hand, round like a ball. I looked at it
> thoughtfully and wondered, 'What is this?' And the answer
> came, 'It is all that is made.' I marvelled that it continued to
> exist and did not suddenly disintegrate; it was so small. And
> again my mind supplied the answer, 'It exists, both now and
> forever, because God loves it.' In short, everything owes its
> existence to the love of God.[17]

Although her pages are filled with the realisation of God's
overwhelming goodness and his great love for her and expressions of her love for God, her writing is largely free from the

---

16. Wolters, *Julian of Norwich*, p 66.
17. Wolters, *Julian of Norwich*, p 68.

eroticism so characteristic of other women mystics of the era. Typically Julian in its simplicity, wholesomeness, and gentle wisdom, is the following:

> God showed me too the pleasure it gives him when a simple soul comes to him, openly, sincerely, and genuinely. It seems to me as I ponder this revelation that when the Holy Spirit touches the soul it longs for God rather like this: 'God, of your goodness give me yourself, for you are sufficient for me. I cannot properly ask anything less, to be worthy of you. If I were to ask less, I should always be in want. In you alone do I have all.' Such words are dear indeed to the soul, and very close to the will and goodness of God. For his goodness enfolds everyone of his creatures and all his blessed works, eternally and surpassingly. For he himself is eternity, and has made us for himself alone, has restored us by his blessed passion, and keeps us in his blessed love. And all because he is goodness.[18]

This 'goodness' of God is one of her favourite themes, and one, along with his 'enfolding love', to which she returns over and over again.

In contrast to the quintessential 'Englishness' of Julian were the Spaniards Teresa of Avila (1515-1582) and John of the Cross (1542-1591). The reform of the Carmelite Order in sixteenth-century Spain produced some of the greatest mystics of all time. Teresa's writings included the important mystical classics, her autobiographical *Life*, the *Way of Perfection* and *The Interior Castle*.[19] The latter is the chief source of her mature reflections on the interior life and the life of contemplative prayer, and reveals the depth of her own mystical experience. Teresa Sanchez Cepeda D'Avila y Ahumada was born in Avila in Old Castile on 28 March 1515. Her father was Don Alonso Sanchez de Cepeda. His first wife had died and he remarried; his second wife was

---

18. Wolters, *Julian of Norwich*, pp 68-69.
19. *Autobiography*, trs E. Allison Peers (New York, Doubleday, 1991), which was written mainly for her director and was written before 1567; *The Way of Perfection*, trs and ed E. Allison Peers (New York, Doubleday: 1991), written for the instruction of her sisters, before 1567; and *The Interior Castle*, ed E. Allison Peers (New York, Doubleday: 1972), written in 1577.

the devout Dona Beatriz D'Avila y Ahumada. Teresa was educ-ated by the Augustinian nuns, but had to leave because of ill health. She entered the Convent of the Incarnation when she was eighteen. The religious life in this house was not particularly taxing and she lived there quite comfortably until in her late for-ties she experienced a conversion to a more strict way of life. She founded the first reformed convent of the Order in Avila in 1562, and from then on until her death in 1582 she was tirelessly founding new houses. At the same time as she was criss-cross-ing Spain in her travels to open new convents, she was experi-encing mystical states of prayer which she wrote down under obedience to her confessors. These writings came to be regarded as classics both of guidance in mystical prayer and of Spanish literature. But even women with such strong, forceful and at-tractive personalities as this 'mother of Carmel' saw themselves as second class citizens in the church, somehow deficient and to be despised. Teresa uses the whole of the first chapter of her *Conceptions of the Love of God* to explain the difficulties of under-standing scripture, and shows herself to be a daughter of her age when she insists that this is true particularly for 'we women', who 'need not entirely refrain from enjoyment of the Lord's riches: what we must not do is to argue about them and ex-pound them, thinking that we can do so successfully without having first submitted our opinions to learned men.'[20]

However, despite their low opinion of themselves, these women visionaries of the later Middle Ages had an influence way beyond their own times in that several of them were re-sponsible for the inauguration of feasts inspired by their own experiences and writings and later accepted into the liturgical calendar of the church, such as that of Corpus Christi, due to the devotion of St Juliana of Mount Cornillon (in 1264 by means of the Bull *Transiturus* issued by Pope Urban IV) and that of the Sacred Heart, which became known publically through the reli-gious experiences of St Margaret Mary Alacoque. The daily praying of the Divine Office was part of their religious life that

20. Teresa of Jesus, *Conceptions of the Love of God* in *The Complete Works of St Teresa of Jesus* Vol II, trs and ed E. Allison Peers (London: Sheed and Ward, 1946), p 362.

was taken for granted; it was the tremendous emphasis placed on Eucharistic devotion and the humanity of Jesus, particularly his Passion, that was stressed by these women mystics and their hagiographers. These women identified themselves with the person of Jesus to a degree that today would be considered psychologically unhealthy; many of them claimed (or it was claimed for them) that they bore the stigmata as a result of concentration on the wounds suffered by Jesus in his Passion; some claimed (or it was claimed for them) that they ate no food but the Eucharist; this severe fasting served to unite them to Christ's sufferings and to lead to states of ecstasy and mystical visions. They saw themselves as mystically wedded to Christ. Castelli claims: 'The notion of the virgin as the bride of Christ is present from the earliest patristic writings' and 'a vow of virginity is an irrevocable marriage contract with Jesus.'[21] She writes:

> This motif of eroticism and erotic substitution is present in the earliest narratives concerning women's asceticism, the Apocryphal Acts of the Apostles, and it continues as an important theme, especially in the lives of holy women.[22]

To illustrate her point, she cites examples from the lives of Macrina, Olympias and Melania the Younger. This particular approach to God has become known as 'Bridal Mysticism' and had a long history, which can be traced back into the Old Testament, but is also found in the New.[23] The erotic imagery of the Song of Songs was interpreted by the rabbis as expressing the closeness of the relationship between God and Israel. As a metaphor for the relationship between God/Christ and the church it passed into Christian theology. Origen was the first Christian writer to apply the imagery to the relationship between Christ and the individual. However, Peter Brown makes the point:

21. E. Castelli, 'Virginity and its Meaning for Women's Sexuality in Early Christianity', *Journal of Feminist Studies in Religion*, Vol 2, No 1 (Spring, 1986), pp 61-88, at p 71.
22. Castelli, 'Virginity and its Meaning for Women's Sexuality in Early Christianity', p 72.
23. cf Mk 2:18: 'The wedding guests cannot fast while the bridegroom is with them ...'; 2 Cor 11:1: 'I promised you in marriage to one husband, to present you as a chaste virgin to Christ.'

This concern for the continuous, unbroken loyalty of the virgin gave a quite distinctive flavour to the [...] image of the virgin as the 'bride' espoused to Christ. It is noticeable that the language of the Song of Songs, which had been applied by Origen to the relation of Christ with the soul of every person, male or female, came, in the course of the fourth century, to settle heavily, almost exclusively, on the body of the virgin woman.[24]

Church fathers such as Evagrius, Athanasius and Ambrose wrote at length on the subject of consecrated virginity, using the same potent imagery. Jerome, 'still struggling with his own physical nature'[25] in his *Letter 22* set before the young Eustochium a vividly erotic image of the meaning of consecrated virginity:

> When sleep overcomes you, he will come behind the wall, will thrust his hand through the aperture and will caress your belly; and you will start up all trembling and will cry, 'I am wounded with love'.

This graphic sexual imagery became common coinage in the mystical literature of later centuries. Bernard of Clairvaux famously preached a series of Sermons on the Song of Songs to his monks; the following is a short extract, typical of his use of bridal imagery:

> The Bridegroom's love, that Bridegroom who is himself love, seeks only reciprocal love and loyalty. She who is loved may well love in return! How can the bride not love, the very bride of Love? Why should Love itself not be loved? The bride, duly renouncing all other affections, submits with all her being to love alone; she can respond to love by giving love in return. When she has poured forth her whole being in love, how does her effort compare with the unending flow from the very source of love? Love itself of course is more abundant than a lover, the Word than a created soul, the Bridegroom than the bride, the Creator than the creature.[26]

---

24. P. Brown, *The Body and Society, men, women, and sexual renunciation in early Christianity* (New York: Columbia University Press, 1988), p 274.
25. M. Dunn, *The Emergence of Monasticism* (Oxford: Blackwell, 2000), p 56.
26. Bernard of Clairvaux, Serm 83, 4-6: *Opera omnia*, Edit. Cisterc. 2 (1958).

It is largely through the writings of Bernard that this imagery drawn from the descriptions of physical love in that scriptural book became part of the Cistercian heritage, as other abbots – Guerric of Igny, John of Ford – following in his wake. From then on, it gradually became common currency in the highly charged mysticism of the Middle Ages. For instance, the Béguine, Mechtilde of Magdeburg, put the following words onto the lips of the Deity in her account of her mystical experiences, *Flowing Light of the Godhead*:

> You are like a new bride whose only love has left her sleeping from whom she cannot bear to be parted for even one hour ... I await you in the orchard of love and pick for you the flower of sweet reunion and make ready there your bed.

Some of these writings are so sexually explicit as to be pathological; the cultured Flemish mystic Hadewijch is no less explicit in her writing as the following extract shows:

> With that he came in the form and clothing of a Man, as he was on the day when he gave us his Body for the first time; looking like a Human Being and a Man, wonderful and beautiful, and with glorious face, he came to me as humbly as anyone who wholly belongs to another. Then he gave himself to me in the shape of the Sacrament, in its outward from, as the custom is; and then he gave me to drink from the chalice, in form and taste, as the custom is. After that he came himself to me, took me entirely in his arms, and pressed me to him; and all my members felt his full felicity, in accordance with the desire of my heart and my humanity. So I was outwardly satisfied and fully transported.[27]

Very little is known of Hadewijch with certainty. It seems that she was writing in the early-to-mid thirteenth century. She is thought to have belonged to the Béguines, a movement for religious lay women (there was a male equivalent known as the 'Beghards' but they were not as numerous as their female counterparts), which flourished in Belgium, Germany, parts of

---

27. Hadewijch, 'Visions' in Elizabeth A. Petroff, *Medieval Women's Visionary Literature* (New York: Oxford University Press, 1986), p 196.

France and the Netherlands in the thirteenth century.[28] Hadewijch was Flemish and is traditionally thought to have lived in Antwerp. She may have come from an aristocratic background as her writings reveal a knowledge of courtly love lyrics that betoken a high standard of education. She knew Latin and French as well as her native Flemish, and seems to have travelled fairly widely.

Beatrice of Nazareth was an approximate contemporary of Hadewijch. She was born into a wealthy Flemish family in 1200. Her mother died when she was about seven and she was sent to live with the Béguines in Zoutleeuw. She eventually entered the Cistercian monastery at Bloemendaal (Florival) in present-day Belgium and was sent from there as prioress to found the new monastery at Nazareth near Lier in Brabant. Although her health was poor and her physical penances severe, she still spent fifty-eight years as a Cistercian nun, dying in 1268. She wrote of her mystical experiences in *Seven Manieren van Minne* (*Seven Experiences of Love*), notable both because of its content and subject matter and because she was the first to write in the Flemish dialect. She is reported to have had frequent ecstasies especially related to her reception of Communion. She was one of a number of contemporary Cistercian mystics, some of whom had previously been closely connected with the Béguine movement: Ida of Nivelles (1199-1231); Alice of Schaarbeek (d. 1250); Juliana of Cornillon (d. 1258); Ida Lewis (d. c.1273) and Ida of Leuven (1211?-1290?).[29]

The biographer of Beatrice of Nazareth described her desire for Communion thus:

> Caught up into an ecstacy of mind, she saw the sweetest spouse of her soul, the Lord Jesus Christ, standing and waiting at the altar with arms outstretched ... He attracted her so strongly with the bond of that love which surpasses all human understanding that she could scarcely await the usual time for Communion. With open heart and enlarged

28. See A. Stoner, 'Sisters Between: Gender and the Medieval Beguines', http://userwww.sfsu.edu/~epf/1995/beguine.html
29. See R. De Gank, *Life of Beatrice of Nazareth* (Cistercian Fathers Series, Number 50), *Beatrice of Nazareth in her Context* (Cistercian Studies Series, Number 121), *Towards Unification with God* (Cistercian Studies Series, Number 122) (Kalamazoo, Michigan: Cistercian Publications, 1991).

veins, as if she were mad with excessive desire, she aspired ...
to receive the Lord's saving Body. Refreshed by this health-
giving Communion, Beatrice suddenly felt her whole soul
diffused through all her bodily members, so vehemently
drawn together in such a wonderful embrace of the Godhead
that even her frail body in each of its members seemed gathered up by this mighty embrace. In the union of this sweet
embrace the Lord applied his chosen one's heart to his own
heart, and absorbed her spirit wholly into himself.[30]

Yet again, explicit use is made of sexual imagery in an attempt to 'spiritualise' the experience of physical human relations. In this use of graphic language, the 'spousal marriage'
conveyed by the phrase *'veni sponsa Christi'*[31] is seen as the perfect, 'spiritual' counterpart of normal human marriage relations.
However, the fact is often overlooked in analyses of the mystical
experience, that in this process, it is necessary to begin with the
material reality and the evidence of the senses: this forms the
basis of the human encounter with God through the sacrament-
ality of the Christ. Therefore, this interpretation can be seen as
serving the psychological needs of the individual. Moreover, in
setting up this 'comparison' of 'spiritual marriage' with the
purely human experience of marriage, marriage is reconstructed
as 'material marriage' and seen as less perfect than the 'spiritual.'
It is not a true comparison because it claims to compare a
notional, intellectually constructed concept ('spiritual marriage')
with a real divinely-created reality (marriage); and the outflow
of this confused thinking is that a piece of human reasoning un-
dermines our appreciation of a central aspect of God's creation.[32]

---

30. *Vita*, 193, 15. Quoted in R. De Gank, *Beatrice of Nazareth in her Context*
(Kalamazoo, Michigan: Cistercian Publications, 1991), pp 239-240.
31. These are the first words of the Latin anthem *'Veni sponsa Christi, accipe
coronam quam tibi Dominus praeparavit in aeternam'* ('Come bride of Christ, receive the crown which the Lord has prepared for you for ever'). It has been
used liturgically at the traditional Profession ceremonies of nuns and also as
the Magnificat Anthem for the feasts of virgins.
32. Practically all the women mystics who recorded their experiences were
unmarried; if they had had more experience of the reality of sexual relations
their writings might have been less idealised. I owe this telling insight to
Katy Parkin, a married woman who kindly read an early draft of this book.

These efforts to 'spiritualise' marriage and sexuality by using metaphors (explicit and implicit) by means of which to raise the earthy physical reality of sexual relations to a 'higher' level, which have been a preoccupation of spiritual writers throughout the Christian centuries, reveal deeper underlying fears and anxieties. Castelli comments:

> The underside of these metaphors of spiritualised marriage and sexuality is a persistent suspicion of the flesh and its passions, a suspicion not solely Christian in origin, but found throughout the Stoic philosophical tradition which influenced much Christian thinking about virginity.[33]

Thus, any stirrings of sexual feelings were seen at worst as sinful, but even at best as an obstacle to 'perfection.' Castelli quotes Eusebius of Emesa who said:

> Among the virgins whom the ardent desire of God has touched, lust is dead, passion killed. Nailed to the cross with its vices and desires, the body is like a stranger to them; it does not feel what you feel, it is no longer of the same nature as your body. The resolution of virginity has transported it to heaven; the human nature of the virgin is not long on earth with you.[34]

According to this view, the church fathers and various Codes of Canon Law[35] regarded a consecrated virgin who had yielded to the passions as an adulteress. Castelli says the virgin was 'committed to an irrevocable and mystical marriage with Christ and violation of the tie was considered sacrilegious adultery.'[36] She quotes Gregory of Nyssa and says:

---

33. Castelli, 'Virginity and its Meaning for Women's Sexuality in Early Christianity', p 73.

34. Eusebius of Emesa, *Homilia* 7, 13 (Amand de Mendieta, 784), quoted in Castelli, 'Virginity and its Meaning for Women's Sexuality in Early Christianity', p 73.

35. See, for example, Canon 19 of the Council of Ancyra (314 CE): 'All those who have consecrated their virginity and who have violated their promise ought to be considered bigamists', Castelli, 'Virginity and its Meaning for Women's Sexuality in Early Christianity', p 73.

36. Castelli, 'Virginity and its Meaning for Women's Sexuality in Early Christianity', p 71. Also includes references to church fathers.

He uses eros-language throughout the text [of his *De Virginitate*], and it would appear that he understands virginity to be a spiritual version of sexual love. To yield to passion is to commit adultery against the celestial bridegroom; virginity demands the mistrust of all flesh.[37]

However, in spite of what this genre of spiritual literature saw as inherent dangers to the life of the spirit and also the temptations which it identified, it became extremely popular in these circles in the Middle Ages, and remained so for several centuries, influencing women's religious experience and its expression right down to our own day.

Approximately a hundred years after the Cistercians and Béguines mentioned above, Catherine Benincasa was born in Siena (according to tradition) in 1347. She was the twenty-fifth child of a wool-dyer and received the habit of a Dominican tertiary when she was sixteen. She did not wish to marry or to enter conventional religious life and lived in her own home where she practised severe penances, and her visions and other extraordinary spiritual experiences became frequent. However, as her reputation for holiness spread abroad a group of devotees gathered around her. In the midst of tireless work for the poor, sick and unfortunate of the city she had profound mystical experiences which she described in her writings. The most famous of these is the *Dialogue On Divine Revelation*, which she dictated to disciples in 1378. A short extract from this gives some idea of the spiritual experience which was hers:

With the light of my understanding, in your light I have tasted and seen the abyss which you are, eternal Trinity, and the beauty of your creation. Then looking at myself in you, I have seen that I am your image; this is a gift that I receive from you in your power, eternal Father, and in your wisdom, which is attributed to your only-begotten Son. The Holy Spirit who proceeds from you, Father, and from your Son has prepared me, giving me a will to love you.

Eternal Trinity, you are the Creator, I the creature. I have

---

37. Castelli, 'Virginity and its Meaning for Women's Sexuality in Early Christianity', p 71.

come to know, in the new creation you made of me in the blood of your Son, that you are in love with the beauty of your creature.[38]

At the same time as receiving these mystical experiences, she was deeply involved in the affairs of both the church and secular society, and was instrumental in persuading Pope Gregory XI to return to Rome from Avignon. She died in Rome in 1380. Although only 'monastic' in the very broadest sense of the term, as she belonged not to the Dominican nuns, but to the Third Order – the *'mantellata'* – and as such and not living in a religious community, had greater freedom to carry out works of mercy for the poor, sick and destitute of her city. She was very much aware that her contemplative prayer and life of penance would be of more avail for the church than any human actions, no matter how good in themselves.

Clare of Assisi was less involved in the public affairs of the church and the papacy, but she could write to Agnes of Prague using the same imagery and counsel her:

...may you cry out: Draw me after you, we will run in the fragrance of your perfumes, O heavenly Spouse! I will run and not tire, until you bring me into the wine-cellar, until your left hand is under my head and your right hand will embrace me happily, and you will kiss me with the happiest kiss of your mouth.[39]

This excerpt from Clare's letters also illustrates the use the mystics made of the Song of Songs. Notably, almost identical passages occur in the writings of St Thérèse of Lisieux, from nineteenth century France, showing how widespread and enduring the influence of this literary genre on the thought and writing of religious women actually was. Thérèse wrote to her sister Céline: 'It was love that taught us to find, here on earth, the Bridegroom that we searched for. "He came upon us alone

---

38. Catherine of Siena, *Dialogue: On Divine Revelation*, Ch 167, *Gratiarum action ad Trinitatem*: ed. Lat., Ingolstadii 1583, f. 290v-291.
39. Clare, *Fourth Letter to Agnes*, Regis J. Armstrong (ed), *Clare of Assisi: Early Documents* (New York: Paulist Press, 1988), pp 49-50.

and greeted us with a kiss: henceforward we need fear no contemptuous looks".'[40]

For many of these women, their experiences were felt to be so intense that they describe their visionary experiences as a 'mystical marriage' and some, such as the Dominican Catherine dei Ricci, even claimed to have received a ring from Christ to seal their relationship. Even Teresa of Avila, described as 'the saint of sound common sense, of sane good humour' could indulge in such sensuously charged passages as the following in her *Conceptions of the Love of God:*

> But when this most wealthy Spouse desires to enrich and comfort the Bride still more, He draws her so closely to Him that she is like one who swoons from excess of pleasure and joy and seems suspended in those Divine arms and drawn near to that sacred side and to those Divine breasts. Sustained by the Divine milk with which her Spouse continually nourishes her and growing in grace so that she may be enabled to receive His comforts she can do nothing but rejoice.[41]

The imagery used in this passage develops from that of nuptials into those of motherhood and nurturing. It is characteristic of this form of mystical writing that the metaphors are drawn quite explicitly from natural functions (and as such were frequently condemned by the church, as in the case of Marguerite de Porete), but this was probably the only language these women (and some men, too – most famously John of the Cross) had in which to describe their graphic and overpoweringly vivid sense of union with God. The reasons for this are complex; as well as the already-mentioned emphasis on the humanity of Christ as preached by the Franciscans and Dominicans, they include sociological and economic factors, such as increased opportunities for at least some women to have access to education and therefore to be able to put their visionary experiences into

---

40. Thérèse of Lisieux, *Autobiography of a Saint*, trs R. Knox (London: Harvill Press, 1958), p 135.
41. Teresa of Jesus, *Conceptions of the Love of God* in *The Complete Works of St Teresa of Jesus* Vol II, trs and ed E. Allison Peers (London: Sheed and Ward, 1946), p 384.

writing; the invention of printing which rendered the written word more accessible; and the work of the mendicant friars which brought mysticism out of the monasteries and into the market place. In order to do this, the friars popularised such devotional practices as the Stations of the Cross, the Rosary, the Angelus, the Crib – all of which enabled the devotee in his or her imagination to follow in the footsteps of Christ and share in the events of his life, Passion and death. As pilgrimage to the Holy Land became possible in the wake of the Crusades, this became a reality, and some women (including notably, Hortolana, the mother of Clare of Assisi) were intrepid enough to do this, in spite of the many and real dangers. All of these devotional practices increased the worshippers' sense of identification and intimacy with the historical person of Jesus. He was no longer seen as the brooding and distant Pantocrator high above the worshipper in the frescoed apses of the early basilicas, or as the subject of the theological and philosophical debates of learned church fathers, but now he was seen as the human Jesus walking this earth, in sympathy with ordinary people, especially women, and with whom they could identify.

But perhaps the most potent reason is the very simple one that most of these women had very little philosophical or theological training; on the whole they were not versed in the language or the concepts of the schools, and as well as using the familiar language of the vernacular in which to express themselves, they also instinctively used images drawn from those aspects of life with which, as women, they were familiar, which appealed to them, and for which, in the world of their time, they were particularly responsible – courtship, betrothal and marriage; childbearing, nursing and motherhood. In these homely terms and with these familiar images, they could express the intimacy of their relationship with Jesus.

However, in spite of this and in spite of its enormous popularity and ubiquity in Western spiritual writing, this genre of spiritual expression never became common currency in Eastern Christianity which, in personal devotion, relies instead on the sobriety of the Jesus Prayer. Vladimir Lossky offers another possibility for the distinction between the mystical literature and experiences of the West and of the Christian East.

The individual experiences of the greatest mystics of the Orthodox Church more often than not remain unknown to us. Apart from a few rare exceptions the spiritual literature of the Christian East possesses scarcely any autobiographical account dealing with the interior life, such as those of Angela of Foligno and Henry Suso, or the *Histoire d'une âme* of St Teresa of Lisieux. The way of mystical union is nearly always a secret between God and the soul concerned, which is never confided to others unless, it may be, to a confessor or to a few disciples. What is published abroad is the fruit of this union: wisdom, understanding of the divine mysteries, expressing itself in theological or moral teaching or in advice for the edification of one's brethren. As to the inward and personal aspect of the mystical experience, it remains hidden from the eyes of all. It must be remembered that it was only at a comparatively late period, towards the thirteenth century in fact, that mystical individualism made its appearance in Western literature ... It was necessary that a certain cleavage should occur between personal experience and the common faith, between the life of the individual and the life of the church, that spirituality and dogma, mysticism and theology, could become two distinct spheres; and that souls unable to find adequate nourishment in the theological *summae* should turn to search greedily in the accounts of individual mystical experience in order to reinvigorate themselves in an atmosphere of spirituality. Mystical individualism has remained alien to the spirituality of the Eastern Church.[42]

The phenomenon of these women mystics of the Middle Ages is a complex one, but it marks a significant stage in medieval studies. Labarge comments perceptively on the reasons for the importance of these women in the study of medieval society:

[T]hese medieval female mystics were historically important because their visions reflected some of the deepest spiritual currents in the life of their day and made them respected interpreters of ideals to which medieval society gave at least

---

42. V. Lossky, *The Mystical Theology of the Eastern Church*, Eng trs Fellowship of St Alban and St Sergius (London: James Clark & Co, 1957, repr. 1968, 1973), pp 20-21.

lip service. Because their lives were naturally uneventful, clues to their personalities normally come from their visions, as they themselves wrote them down or had them recorded by others.[43]

Women had discovered an area where they could stand on an equal footing with men; perhaps indeed, precisely because of their sex, which had brought them into so much disrepute through the ages, they had an advantage over men in the mystical field where they could claim a relationship with Jesus which did not hold the same significance for men. (Although some men, notably Richard Rolle and John of the Cross, also claimed a spousal relationship with him.) In this field women were beginning to find a voice and to articulate the experiences which they believed were genuinely theirs. Christopher Morris comments on aspects of women's life in the sixteenth century which may have contributed to the growth of mystical experience:

> There came to be more emphasis on God's mercy and less on God's judgement, and a new interest in the human life of Christ. It is possible that the growth of devotional fervour centred on His Mother corresponds with the growing importance of family life and domesticity. Moreover, the high place accorded to woman in Renaissance society was, in a sense, foreshadowed by her idealisation in the late medieval world of chivalry.[44]

As Morris suggests here and as we have already seen above, possibly the choice made by these women mystics of language and metaphor in which to express their spiritual experience was coloured by the place and responsibilities they held in the society of their own day. Now, instead of the literary silence of women during the first thousand years of Christianity, we are overwhelmed by a veritable avalanche of writing by women, although much of it was done at the suggestion or command of male confessors or spiritual guides, and, in the institution of the Inquisition, men still retained control, which was sometimes

---

43. M. Wade Labarge, *A Small Sound of the Trumpet* (London: Hamish Hamilton, 1990), p 130.
44. C. Morris, *The Tudors* (London: Fontana/Collins, 1977), p 50.

merciless. These various social and religious aspects can be seen in a study of the Béguine movement, to which, as mentioned above, many of these women belonged (there was also a male equivalent, the 'Beghards' though these were never as numerous as their female counterparts).[45]

These groups of dedicated laywomen were coming into existence, mostly in the Low Countries,[46] originally from around Liège, from the late twelfth century, c.1170-80, and flourished in the thirteenth and fourteenth centuries. The time in which the movement was born has been aptly described by Marygrace Peters as 'a bubbling cauldron of diverse and colliding energies, fired by an immense mixture of conflicting concerns.'[47] The béguines have been seen as the first popular, distinctive movement specifically for women in Christian history.[48] Unlike professed religious, they took no explicit vows, except that they agreed to live in chastity while living in the béguinage, which they were free to leave. These béguinages consisted of groups of small houses near to a church, where they met at regular times for prayer. Each béguine supported herself by her own work, usually needlework and embroidery, or teaching children or caring for the sick and elderly. Theirs was a very simple life, the heir in some ways to the older eremitical tradition, although they observed a certain amount of common life, so it was also in a sense, the forerunner of some of the later women's apostolic congregations in the active works they undertook. Stonor comments:

> With their freedom of movement, economic independence and spiritual creativity, the Beguines carved out an unusually expansive – and controversial – niche for female religious expression.[49]

45. For a fuller account of the Béguines, see M. Wade Labarge, *A Small Sound of the Trumpet* (London: Hamish Hamilton, 1990), pp 115-120. See also A. Stonor, 'Sisters Between: Gender and the Medieval Beguines', http://userwww.sfsu.edu/~epf/1995/beguine.html.

46. There were no Béguine houses in England.

47. M. Peters, 'The Beguines: Feminine Piety Derailed,' *Spirituality Today* (Spring 1991, Vol 43 No. 1 pp 36-52.

48. C. Walker Bynum, *Holy Feast and Holy Fast: The Religious Significance of Food to Medieval Women* (Berkeley: University of California Press' 1987), p 6.

49. A. Stonor, 'Sisters Between: Gender and the Medieval Beguines', http://userwww.sfsu.edu/~epf/1995/beguine.html

Their spirituality was expressed in a simple but very deep and sincere devotion to the mysteries of Christ's life, especially his childhood, and also to the Eucharist. One of the originators of this movement was Marie d'Oignies (1177-1213), described by Peters as 'the prototype Beguine'[50] whose *Vita* was written by an admiring Jacques de Vitry.[51] Like Cardinal Hugolino in the last chapter, he had been made responsible for these groups of women, and obtained approbation for their way of life from Pope Honorius III in 1216.

Some of the women connected with this movement remained associated with it throughout their lives, although they had taken no formal vows and so were free to leave. Others however, as we have seen, went on to join established Orders within the church. Beatrice, for example, joined the Cistercians. The phenomenon of mystical prayer occurred across the spectrum of the contemplative Orders and even outside the recognised Orders, among those dedicated to a life of seclusion in their anchorholds and the groups of béguines.

However, although they were on the whole highly regarded, some of the béguines had to pay a high price for their spiritual experiences when they fell foul of church authorities who accused them of heresy and even of witchcraft. Peters remarks:

> The risk of heresy and aberration inherent in practices surrounding enthusiastic attachment to the passion of Christ is quite real in every age. An overzealous craving for the miraculous associated with the eucharist, exaggerated ecstasies and the visionary trances that came to be associated with the spirituality of some of the Beguines were destined to become the source for later suspicion as to their conformity to orthodox belief.[52]

Thus, a béguine from Hainault, Marguerite de Porete, was burned at the stake in Paris in 1310, having been accused and found guilty of heresy. Even so, as Fiona Bowie indicates 'in a

---

50. M. Peters, 'The Beguines: Feminine Piety Derailed,' p 38.
51. He was the future Bishop of Liège and cardinal legate to Pope Gregory IX. As such he was closely involved with the Order of Poor Clares, as mentioned in the last chapter.
52. M. Peters, 'The Beguines: Feminine Piety Derailed,' p 38.

society which undervalues female perceptions and accords women little authority, mystical or ecstatic experience enable a woman to transcend the normal boundaries of her existence and to claim direct inspiration from God.'[53] However, the movement was officially condemned, under pain of excommunication, by Pope Clement V, at the Council of Vienne in 1311, in the decree *Cum de quibusdam mulieribus*. The main objections to their way of life were that they 'discussed the Holy Trinity and matters of faith and sacraments', and that they 'professed no obedience to any one' – both seen to be very dangerous occupations for women. The relevant passage from the decree is as follows:

> We have been told that certain women commonly called Beguines, afflicted by a kind of madness discuss the Holy Trinity and the divine essence, and express opinions on matters of faith and sacraments contrary to the catholic faith, deceiving many simple people. Since these women promise no obedience to anyone and do not renounce their property or profess an approved Rule, they are certainly not 'religious' although they wear a habit and are associated with such religious orders as they find congenial ... We have therefore decided and decreed with the approval of the Council that their way of life is to be permanently forbidden and altogether excluded from the church of God.[54]

In other words, these women were not under the control of the hierarchy, they meddled in theological affairs not deemed appropriate for women, and they kept their hands on their own property. Therefore they were dangerous and had to be eliminated.

These were women whose 'search for a plausible religiosity was authentic'[55] but the institutional church was too suspicious of their motives.

It has always been widely acknowledged that the physical phenomena associated with the mystical experiences of these

---

53. F. Bowie (ed, trs O. Davies), *Beguine Spirituality: Mystical Writings of Mechtild of Magdeburg, Beatrice of Nazareth and Hadewijch of Brabant* (New York, Crossroad Publishing Company, 1990), p 28
54. Quoted by Peters, 'The Beguines: Feminine Piety Derailed,' p 50.
55. Ibid.

women were open to abuse and the possibility that they were
the fruit of fertile imagining and/or psychological imbalance
has always been recognised. Many readers today find the eroticism of their writings unpalatable and unhealthy. However, at
their best these women had a strong and lively faith and piety;
they were genuinely seeking a form of life which would 'chan-
nel the restless yearning for God, symptomatic of the age'.[56]
There were those in the church who appreciated them, like
Caesarius of Heisterbach: 'In the midst of worldly people they
were spiritual, in the midst of pleasure seekers they were pure
and in the midst of noise and confusion they led a serene,
eremitical life.'[57] These women sought to serve others in practical ways and in their writings they stressed the importance of
humility and obedience and mostly they lived these virtues out
in their own lives, which has always been regarded as the genuine sign of authenticity.

---

56. Ibid.
57. B. Bolton, 'Mulieres sanctae', in *Studies in Church History*, Vol 10
(Oxford, Blackwell, 1973), pp 77-95, at p 87, quoted in Peters, 'The
Beguines: Feminine Piety Derailed,' p 50.

CHAPTER EIGHT

'Preparing the New Paradise' – Monastic Martyrs

In more recent centuries priests, monks and nuns have been killed in great numbers and with particular savagery during the French and Russian Revolutions, and under the Nazi and Communist regimes, right into our own times with the slaughter of the Cistercian monks of Tibherine in Algeria in 1996. This chapter will examine the concept of martyrdom in the early church and briefly trace its development through the centuries down to the twentieth century where I will look in detail at the lives of two Orthodox nuns who were martyred for their Christian faith and practice.

For much of the first three centuries of the Christian era the threat of martyrdom, either actual or potential, was present throughout the Roman Empire, and martyrdom was held in the highest esteem as sharing in a very literal way in the passion and death of Jesus. From the second half of the first century onwards, martyrdom was highly regarded as the supreme way to attain holiness, in imitation of the apostles and even of Jesus himself, the greatest of all the martyrs. Early Christian writings accorded the greatest respect to those who gave their lives for Jesus.[1] To be worthy of the title 'martyr',[2] meaning 'confessor' or 'witness', was the greatest honour for a Christian in the early church. Cyprian (d. 258) expressed his veneration for his fellow Christians in prison awaiting their execution in the following terms:

I greet you, brethren, and I only wish I could see you face to

---

1. See Apoc 7:9-17; 14:1-5; 15:1-4.
2. For a full examination of the development of the term in Christian history and theology, see E. Bickersteth Birks, 'Martyr' in W. Smith and S. Cheetham (eds) *A Dictionary of Christian Antiquities* (London: John Murray, 1908), pp 1118-1132.

face, if conditions permitted me to visit you. I could long for nothing that would make me happier than to be with you. Then you could clasp me with those hands which, pure and innocent, kept their loyalty to Christ and rejected the sacrilegious offerings to idols. What could be more joyful or more uplifting for me than to embrace you, for you received grace to confess the Lord? What could be better than to be looked at by your eyes which rejected the world and were worthy to behold God? ... Happy the prison which your presence illuminates! Happy the prison which despatches the men of God to heaven! The darkness of this prison is brighter than the sun, it is more brilliant than this world's light. Here your bodies have now become temples of God, sanctified by your profession of faith.[3]

This passage expresses graphically the respect and admiration felt for the martyrs in the first Christian centuries. Even the squalid prison in which they awaited their final sufferings and death was made glorious by their confession of faith. Just as their fellow Christians upheld them in their time of trial by their prayers, so did the martyrs give encouragement to their brothers and sisters in the Lord by their example of steadfast faith and endurance in their sufferings. Peter Damian (c.1007-1072) used the example of the martyr George (date uncertain; possibly late third century; enormously popular in Eastern Christianity even before the crusaders brought him to England as their patron saint) to encourage those listening to his sermons:

Clearly Saint George was transported from one kind of military service into another, since he laid aside the earthly office of tribune to join the ranks of the army of Christ. Like a truly keen soldier he first threw away the burden of his earthly possessions by giving all he had to the poor, and thus free and unencumbered and wearing the breastplate of faith, he advanced into the thick of the fray, a valiant soldier of Christ ... My dear brothers, let us not merely admire this soldier of the heavenly army: let us also imitate him. Let us raise up our spirits to think on that heavenly reward, and fix our

---

3. Cyprian, *Letter* 6, 1-2. CSEL 3, 480-482.

hearts on it in contemplation, and so never flinch whether the world smiles on us with its blandishments or menaces us with adversities.[4]

Although George, like other so-called warrior saints so popular in the East, such as Mennas, Demetrius and Mercurius, was most likely a real person who did actually die for his faith in the Christ, the details of his life are pious romanticism. But even if the details of their lives were embroidered, this did not prevent preachers and teachers in the church holding up the martyrs, both men and women, as both examples and intercessors for those still fighting the good fight in this world while looking to heaven for their reward, particularly during the years of persecution. That martyrdom was not just held in high esteem, but was actively yearned for, can be seen in writings such as those of Ignatius, the second Bishop of Antioch after St Peter. Having been sentenced to death in the arena by being thrown to the wild beasts, he was taken to Rome by a detachment of soldiers for this sentence to be carried out. On the way there he wrote letters to the various churches he passed through, in these letters expressing his desire to die as a martyr for the Christian faith.

> For my part, I am writing to all the churches and assuring them that I am truly in earnest about dying for God ... pray leave me to be a meal for the beasts, for it is they who can provide my way to God. I am his wheat, ground fine by the lions' teeth to be made purest bread for Christ. So intercede with him for me, that by their instrumentality I may be made a sacrifice to God ... so far as I am concerned, to die in Jesus Christ is better than to be monarch of earth's widest bounds ... Here and now as I write in the fulness of life, I am yearning for death with all the passion of a lover ... I want no more of what men call life.[5]

For men and women like Ignatius, martyrdom was the gateway to eternal life with God. Thus they had no fear of the sufferings involved, or, if they did, they reckoned the suffering a small price to pay for the heavenly glory to come.

---

4. Peter Damian, *Serm 3, De sancto Georgio*: PL 144, 567-571.
5. Ignatius of Antioch, *Letter to the Romans*, Cap 4, 1-2; 6, 1-8,: Funk 1, 217-223.

Another early martyr, Polycarp, Bishop of Smyrna, was put to death around AD 156 by being first burnt on a funeral pyre and then being stabbed to death by the executioner in the city stadium. In the *Acts* of his martyrdom, he was portrayed as follows:

> And so he was bound, putting his arms behind his back, like a noble ram taken from a large flock for a sacrifice, a burnt offering acceptable to and made ready for God. then he gazed up to heaven and said: 'O Lord God Almighty, Father of your beloved and blessed child Jesus Christ, through whom we have received knowledge of you, God of the angels and the powers and of all creation, God of the whole race of the righteous who live in your sight; I bless you, for you have thought me worthy of this day and hour to share the cup of your Christ, as one of your martyrs, to rise again to eternal life in body and soul in the immortality of the Holy Spirit. May I be taken up today into your presence among your martyrs, as a rich and acceptable sacrifice ...'[6]

This is the first account we have of Christian martyrdom, and it was written within a year of Polycarp's death. The above passage shows the great reverence the early church had for its martyrs and how they were seen to have a particularly close affinity with Jesus in his suffering and death, and how this was understood as leading straight to eternal life in heaven.

The *Acta* of these martyrs and the *passiones* (detailed and often eye-witness accounts of their trials, tortures and deaths) were recorded and circulated among neighbouring churches for the edification and encouragement of their Christian brothers and sisters. The *Acts* of the martyrdom of St Justin, who is the earliest Christian apologist and who was born at the beginning of the second century, are particularly graphic. Justin was born into a pagan family in modern Nablus in Samaria. His philosophical investigations led him to Christianity, which he defended in his writings. He opened a school of philosophy in Rome where he taught and where he was martyred with several

---

6. *Letter of the Church of Smyrna on Polcarp's Martyrdom*, Chap 13, 2-15, 3: Funk 1, 297-299.

companions about the year 165, under the Emperor Marcus Aurelius. The following is a description of his trial.

After the saints had been taken prisoner, they were led to the Roman prefect, whose name was Rusticus. When they had been brought before the court, Rusticus the prefect said to Justin: 'Believe in the gods above all things and obey the princes.' Justin replied: 'We cannot be blamed or condemned for obeying the commands of our Saviour Jesus Christ.' 'What doctrine do you hold?' asked Rusticus. Justin answered: 'I have tried to become acquainted with all doctrines, but I have adopted the true doctrines, those of the Christians, even if they are not acceptable to those who hold false beliefs.' The prefect then said: 'So those are the teachings which you accept, you wretch?' To which Justin replied: 'Yes, I follow them according to the right rule of faith.' ... Rusticus said: 'So you are a Christian then?' And Justin replied: 'Yes, I am a Christian.' ... The prefect said: 'So you imagine that you are going to heaven and will receive some appropriate reward?' To this Justin replied: 'It is not a case of imagining. I know: I am certain.' Rusticus said: 'Let us come to the essential point, to what you must do. You must all sacrifice to the gods together.' And Justin said: 'No one in his right mind is going to turn away from the worship of the true God to worship false gods.' The prefect insisted: 'Unless you do as you are told, you will be tortured without mercy.' Justin said: 'We have prayed that we may suffer for the sake of our Lord Jesus Christ and in this way be saved ... And all the other martyrs said the same: 'Do what you like to us. we are Christians and we do not sacrifice to idols.' The prefect then passed sentence: 'These men have refused to sacrifice to the gods and to obey the Emperor's commands. Let them be taken away and flogged, and then put to death in accordance with the law'. The holy martyrs went out to the usual place of execution glorifying God. There they were beheaded and so won their martyr's crown professing their faith in the Saviour.[7]

---

7. *Acts of the Martyrdom of Justin & Companions* [extract]: Chap 1-5: PG 6, 1566-1571.

This passage is significant for several reasons, hence its quotation at such length. Whether or not it is (as it claims to be) a verbatim account of the trial of Justin, it shows what the beliefs of the early church were about the importance and uniqueness of the Christian faith and about the value and meaning of martyrdom. Justin claimed that, as an educated and discerning man, he had examined all the belief systems current in his day, and found what he believed to be the truth in Christianity. This faith told him that there was an existence after death and that he would then go to heaven if he was faithful to the teaching of Christ and did not worship false gods.

Women no less than men suffered martyrdom in the early centuries;[8] both were seen as icons of the crucified Christ. Eusebius of Caesarea, in describing the martyrdom of Blandina, one of the martyrs of Lyons in the late second century, wrote: 'In this battle, they saw with their bodily eyes, in the form of their sister, the One who had been crucified for them.'[9] The accounts of the martyrdom of women such as the married women Perpetua, Felicity and Cecilia, and the unmarried Agatha, Lucy, and Agnes were treasured in the church, both East and West. Tavormina, in examining the chants in the liturgy for the consecration of virgins, shows that the idealised legends of Agnes and Agatha, composed to be read on their feast days, present 'different but complementary aspects of virginity'[10] designed to be held up for emulation by their hearers.[11] She says:

---

8. 'However, there was one area where women had long since joined the battle and had proved that their fierceness and determination equalled, or even surpassed, that of men: martyrdom', S. Elm, *'Virgins of God' The Making of Asceticism in Late Antiquity* (Oxford: Clarendon Press, 1994), p 268.

9. Eusebius of Caesarea, *Hist. Eccl.* 5. 1. 1-63, at 41, quoted in E. A. Johnson, *She Who Is: The Mystery of God in Feminist Theological Discourse* (New York, Crossroad: 1992), pp 73-74.

10. M. T. Tavormina, 'Of Maidenhood and Maternity: Liturgical Hagiography and the Medieval Idea of Virginity', *American Benedictine Review*, Vol 31, 1980, pp 384-399, at p 398.

11. Tavormina specifies that her study concentrates on the consecration ceremonies as they are found in England from the tenth century onwards. See Tavormina, op. cit., p 384 for a description of the consecration texts used.

St Agnes' legend emphasises a virgin's immutable state of innocence and depends heavily on the nuptial metaphor to describe the relationship of the virgin to Christ ... Agatha's *Acts* are more down-to-earth than Agnes' Passion; they are concerned with the virtues to be practised by a virgin in this world, especially humility and steadfastness. They do not advert directly to the virgin's betrothal to Christ. However, the parallels between Agatha and the church – her firm foundation on the Rock, Peter's assistance, the imagery of maternal bounty – suggest that she too is a bride of the Lamb, and moreover the mother of spiritual offspring.[12]

Tavormina argues that by presenting the stories of Agnes and Agatha liturgically in the medieval ceremony for the consecration of virgins, these two saints are held up as role models for the newly consecrated, who are thus inspired to imitate their virtues of innocence, purity, humility and steadfastness in the face of suffering. These two saints were very popular throughout the early and medieval church. Agnes, in particular, was revered because of her youth. Ambrose wrote of her:

She was a martyr at twelve, they say. It was really hideous cruelty which did not spare such tender years. But faith looks all the more powerful when it finds its witness in one of such tender age. There was scarcely room for the deathblow on her tiny body. But though tinier than the sword she still conquered the sword. Normally little girls of that age are hardly able to bear a harsh look from their parents; they shrink from the prick of a pin as if it were a battle wound.[13]

Ambrose holds Agnes up as an example to all Christians, old and young, male and female alike, for her faith, constancy and bravery.

The anonymous *Acts of SS. Perpetua and Felicity*[14] tell of the imprisonment and martyrdom of group of Christians in Carthage in North Africa in 203. This group included a young

---

12. Tavormina, 'Of Maidenhood and Maternity: Liturgical Hagiography and the Medieval Idea of Virginity', p 398.
13. Ambrose, *De uirginibus*, 1.7.
14. English translation in C. White, *Lives of Roman Christian Women* (London: Penguin Classics, 2010), pp 4-17.

Roman matron, Vibia Perpetua, and her slave girl, Felicity. Perpetua had a much-loved baby son, and Felicity had given birth to a baby girl in prison only shortly before. Afraid that according to the law which forbade pregnant women to appear in the arena, she would be denied martyrdom with her companions, they all prayed for her delivery to take place prematurely. When this happened, in spite of the pain and her suffering in giving birth, she was 'relieved that she had safely given birth so that she could fight the beasts, going as it were from one bloody event to another, from the midwife to the gladiator, preparing to wash after childbirth in a second baptism.'[15] The author includes in the story of these martyrs extracts from Perpetua's own account of their time in prison and of her own dreams and also those of her fellow martyr, Saturus.[16] The authenticity of these accounts has been questioned but, as Lefkowitz concludes, even though the *Acts of SS. Perpetua and Felicity* are 'meant to convert and persuade' and so should not be considered 'directly historical or objective', the story 'can tell us much about the working beliefs of the early church and in particular about the experience of a female martyr.'[17] Lefkowitz quotes E. R. Dodds, who 'suggests that unconventional elements in the narrative, such as Perpetua's dreams, are indications of its authenticity.'[18] Lefkowitz's analysis of the account of their martyrdom argues that these women, and Perpetua in particular through her renunciation of her father's emotional pleadings, were endeavouring to free themselves from the expected gender roles and expectations which current society demanded of women and which Christianity in its earliest stages had to some extent reversed. She says:

> It is not without significance that the religion which Perpetua adopts appears to encourage more a-sexual, fraternal rela-

15. Anon, *The Martyrdom of Perpetua and Felicitas*, C. White, *Lives of Roman Christian Women*, pp 14-15.

16. See M. R. Lefkowitz, 'The Motivations for St Perpetua's Martyrdom,' *Journal of the American Academy of Religion*, Vol 44, No 3 (Sept, 1976), pp 417-421.

17. Lefkowitz, 'The Motivations for St Perpetua's Martyrdom,' pp 417-418.

18. E. R. Dodds, *Pagan and Christian in an Age of Anxiety* (Cambridge: Cambridge University Press: 1965), pp 47-53.

tionships between men and women ... Her willingness to die is not only an act of faith and maturity, but in existential terms, a political act against her environment ... We may regret that [the church fathers] did not also wish to realise how Christianity in its earlier stages also met a social need of releasing women from the hierarchical structure imposed by patriarchal society, which the church in its own organisation would increasingly incorporate and emulate.[19]

By expressing so clearly Perpetua's determination to break conclusively with her family, and her father in particular, Lefkowitz argues that the author of these *Acta* is showing the concern women of this period had to free themselves from the limitations imposed on them by sexually defined roles in society. Perpetua's 'diary' is very valuable, being one of the earliest accounts written by a woman. She describes graphically the horrors of their situation and her own anxieties as a mother:

A few days later [after their baptism] we were taken to prison. I was terrified as I had never experienced such a dark place. What a difficult time that was! Stiflingly hot because of the huge crowds; soldiers extorting money; and during the whole time I was there I was tormented with worries about my baby. Then Tertius and Pomponius, those kind deacons who were looking after us, bribed someone to allow us to be moved to a better part of the prison for a few hours so that we could recover a bit. Everyone then left the prison cell and we had a rest. I fed my baby who was weak from hunger. In my anxiety about him I spoke to my mother, tried to comfort my brother and entrusted my son to them, but I suffered because I saw them suffering on my account.[20]

Perpetua continues her account with descriptions of her father's frenzied efforts to persuade her to abandon her faith for the sake of her baby, for the sake of her family, for his own sake, but she remained adamant. Significantly, in her dream:

I was then stripped and I found I was a man. My supporters

---

19. M. R. Lefkowitz, 'The Motivations for St. Perpetua's Martyrdom,' p 421.
20. Anon, *The Martyrdom of Perpetua and Felicitas*, C. White, *Lives of Roman Christian Women*, pp 6-7.

began to rub me down with oil, as is the practice before a contest.[21]

According to the terns of this vision, to fight victoriously in the arena, she had to lose her womanhood and become a man. Current gender perceptions influenced her dream, so that only as a man would she have the strength to overcome the enemy. But in reality, far from turning into men, when Perpetua and Felicity came to the arena, they were delivered to a wild cow, in deliberate and cruel mockery of their sex.

[T]hey were stripped and covered with nets and brought out. The crowd was shocked to see a pretty young girl and another young woman with breasts swollen with milk after recently giving birth. So they were called back and dressed in loose tunics. First, Perpetua was tossed by the heifer and fell on her back. Her tunic had been ripped along the side and when she sat up she pulled it down to cover her thigh, more concerned with her modesty than with the pain. Then she asked for a pin to clip back her hair which had become dishevelled; for it was not right for a martyr to die with her hair in a mess, lest she should be seen to be mourning in her hour of glory. She got up and when she saw that Felicitas had been dashed to the ground, she went up to her and held out her hand to help her up, and the two of them stood side by side ... Perpetua shouted out with joy as the sword pierced her, for she wanted to taste some of the pain and she even guided the hesitant hand of the trainee gladiator towards her own throat. It was as if such an extraordinary woman, feared as she was by the unclean spirit, could not have died in any way except as she wished. You brave and blessed martyrs! Truly called and chosen to share in the glory of our Lord Jesus Christ! Anyone who glorifies and reveres and worships Christ's glory should

---

21. Anon, *The Martyrdom of Perpetua and Felicitas,* C. White, *Lives of Roman Christian Women,* p 11. Interestingly, Clare of Assisi takes up this imagery in her first Letter to Agnes of Prague: 'You also know that one who is clothed cannot fight with another who is naked, because he is more quickly thrown who gives his adversary a chance to get hold of him.' Clare of Assisi, *First Letter to Agnes.*

also read these examples for the edification of the church, for they are no less marvellous than those of the past.[22]

This passage is significant for several reasons: it shows how martyrdom, as well as spanning the division of the sexes so that men and women faced death as equals in God's sight, also levelled the prevailing social and cultural barriers. Perpetua, the young noble matron goes to the aid of Felicity, the slave-girl: 'they stood side by side' – something that would have been unthinkable elsewhere.[23] Sara Parvis, in stressing that Perpetua 'clearly stands out by reasons of birth as well as character'[24] describes how she triumphs over all around her:

> [S]he brings the judicial system down, and brings her companions up, lifting Felicity from the dust to stand beside her, undefeated, *matrona* and slave together.[25]

The *Acts* of these martyrs also show how martyrdom could bring a woman respect and reverence which would have been impossible anywhere else in the society of the day, and show as well a woman exhorting her male companions, which also would have been culturally unacceptable.[26] Margaret Visser suggests that women martyrs were subjected to even greater suffering by being routinely raped before being put to death:

> It is probable that many, even most, early Christian virgins executed for their faith were, in fact, first raped ... These women must often have been first raped and then killed: if so, they suffered a double martyrdom. It is this 'double crown' that we wish the virgin martyr stories would acknowledge, and they do not ... In other words, the powerful 'virgin' archetype is at work here. One reason must be that rape was still held, in the culture, to have the power to render

---

22. Anon, *The Martyrdom of Perpetua and Felicitas*, C. White, *Lives of Roman Christian Women*, p 16-17.

23. See C. White, *Lives of Roman Christian Women*, pp 4-17.

24. S. Parvis, 'Perpetua', *The Expository Times*, Vol 120, No 8, pp 365-372, at p 367.

25. S. Parvis, 'Perpetua', *The Expository Times*, Vol 120, No 8, pp 365-372, at p 371

26. See P. Brown, *The Body and Society: Men, Women, and Sexual Renunciation in Early Christianity*, pp 73-78.

a woman 'shamed', and a 'shamed' hero was a contradiction in terms.[27]

However, as Visser suggests, the probability that these women were routinely raped is rarely recorded because of the dishonour this would have brought them in the society of their day, but if this supposition is true it means that they suffered twice over because of their vulnerability as women.

Both men and women Christian martyrs were seen as the successors of the great men and women of the Old Testament who had 'won acknowledgement through their faith'[28] as well as those who in New Testament times had 'washed their robes white in the blood of the Lamb'[29] and were now examples to the young Christians.[30] Peter Brown states with truth: 'To Augustine and his contemporaries, the martyrs were the *membra Christi par excellence*'.[31] This belief of the early Christian church can be clearly seen in the writings of Origen, among many others:

> For Christian martyrs in the company of Christ completely overcome the principalities and powers; together with him they triumph over them; sharing in his sufferings, they also share in the victories that he has won by his courage in suffering.[32]

So those who endured the sufferings and death of martyrdom in union with Christ were also believed to share in his victory and triumph over death. The day of their death (which in Christian theology became the day of their [heavenly] birth: *'dies natalis'* – 'birthday into heaven') was remembered by their fellow believers as an annual festival. These anniversary days probably coincided with pre-Christian heathen festivals, as 'butchering martyrs was a holiday sport'.[33] The accounts of their

27. M. Visser, *The Geometry of Love* (New York: North Point Press, 2000), pp 236-262.
28. Heb 11:39.
29. Apoc 7:14.
30. Heb 11:32-12:4.
31. P. Brown, *The Cult of the Saints; Its Rise and Function in Latin Christianity* (Chicago: University of Chicago Press, 1982), p 72.
32. Origen, *Exhortation to Martyrdom*, Nn 41-42: PG 11, 618-619.
33. E. Bickersteth Birks, 'Martyrology' in W. Smith and S. Cheetham eds, *A Dictionary of Christian Antiquities* (London: John Murray, 1908), pp 1132-1139 at p 1133.

sufferings were distributed to local churches to be read out loud for the edification and encouragement of new Christians also living under the possible threat of persecution; and their bodily remains ('relics') were treasured with the greatest reverence, often believed to be a source of miraculous healings, and eventually coming to be enshrined in costly reliquaries,[34] often as the objects of long and arduous pilgrimage,[35] or having been filched from neighbouring monasteries by over-zealous monks.[36]

Christians saw their relationship with their heavenly brothers and sisters who had given their lives as martyrs for Christ as fundamentally different to that with those who had not. As Augustine pointed out:

> So in fact at this table we do not commemorate [the martyrs] in the same way as we commemorate others who rest in peace, in order to pray for them also. We commemorate them rather so that they may pray for us, that we may follow closely in their footsteps; for they have reached the fulness of that love than which the Lord said there could be none greater.[37]

So whereas other Christians were prayed *for* when they departed this world,[38] the martyrs were prayed *to* and, because of their violent deaths at the hands of their persecutors rather than forswear their belief in and commitment to the Christ and his teachings, they were believed to have particularly powerful influence before the throne of God in heaven. So the 'white-robed army who shed their blood for Christ'[39] became an example of

---

34. Where the quality and quantity of skilful decoration still bear witness today to how precious the contents were deemed to be by the craftsmen, patrons and devotees responsible for them.

35. On the subject of pilgrimage in this context, see Allie M. Ernst, 'Which Way to the Tomb of Jesus?' in Wendy Mayer, Pauline Allen and Lawrence Cross (eds), *Prayer and Spirituality in the Early Church*, Vol 4 *The Spiritual Life* (Strathfield, NSW: St Paul's Publications, 2006), pp 85-99, at p.96: 'Pilgrims came to touch holy people, holy objects, holy places.'

36. See Brown, op. cit., pp 86-105.

37. Augustine, *On St John's Gospel*, Tract. 84, 1-2: CCL 36, 536-538.

38. See C. Manning, *Early Irish Monasteries*, pp 36-39, at p.- 36: 'Those (stone slabs) with inscriptions almost invariably follow the formula 'OR DO X' ('a prayer for X')'.

39. *Te Deum* (sixth cent. or earlier? See F. L. Cross (ed), *Oxford Dictionary of the Christian Church* (3rd ed E. A. Livingstone, Oxford, 1997) s.v. '*Te Deum*', pp 1592-3.

courage and steadfast faith under persecution and were also regarded as friends and intercessors in heaven, where they were
believed to be now reigning with Christ and watching over fellow believers still struggling in this world: in Tertullian's famous
words, 'The blood of the martyrs is the seed of the church.'
Cyprian expressed the profound regard in which the martyrs
were held, and how they set an example to fellow believers, in
the following eloquent words:

> In confessing your faith you showed the way to your
> brethren, and the confession of the leader was enhanced by
> that of his brethren. While you go before to the glory of eter-
> nal life, you have made many others your companions in
> glory, you have persuaded the people to declare themselves
> Christians by first making profession of your own faith on
> behalf of all. I do not know which to praise you for first: your
> eager and firm faith or the love with which your brothers in
> Christ follow you. Your exemplary courage as a bishop has
> been publicly proved, and your brothers in Christ have
> shown their unity by imitating you. So long as you are unan-
> imous in thought and word it is as if the whole Roman
> Church made a profession of faith.[40]

Thus did the example of the martyrs give courage and
strength to their fellow Christians in time of persecution. Boniface
(c.672-754), a monk of the monastery in Exeter, who went to
Germany to preach the faith in 719 and was eventually martyred in Frisia, expressed this belief vividly thus:

> [W]e have the Fathers of the past, Clement and Cornelius
> and many others in the city of Rome, Cyprian in Carthage
> and Athanasius in Alexandria. Living under pagan emper-
> ors, they steered the ship of Christ, that is the church, his
> beloved spouse. And they did this by teaching, defending,
> working and suffering even to the shedding of their blood.[41]

Here is reflected the honour and reverence the early church
had for those who had given their lives for Christ. In spite of the

---

40. Cyprian of Carthage, *Letter to Cornelius*, Epist. 60, 1-2. 5: CSEL 3, 691-
692. 694-695.
41. Boniface, *Letter* 78: MGH, *Epistolae*, 3, 352. 354.

trepidation expressed further on in this same letter,[42] Boniface himself was later to face martyrdom for the faith and gave his life for his belief in Christ. Boniface was both martyr and monk, and there have always been correlations between the two states.

When the news of the first Franciscan martyrs, Berard and his companions, Peter, Adjutus, Accursius and Odo, who had been killed in Morocco in 1220, reached Clare in her cloister in Assisi, she wanted with all her heart to go there and share their fate, and it was only with great difficulty that her sisters restrained her. During the process of her canonisation, one of the witnesses, Sister Cecilia di Gaultieri Cacciaguerra of Spoleto, who, being one of the first companions to join Clare in San Damiano, had lived with her for nearly forty years, gave the following testimony on oath:

> She also said Lady Clare had such a fervent spirit she willingly wanted to endure martyrdom for love of the Lord. She showed this when, after she had heard certain brothers had been martyred in Morocco, she said she wanted to go there. Then because of this, the witness wept.[43]

Other monastic women actually had the opportunity to give their lives for Christ. Though not as well known as the Carmelites of Compiègne, Josephine Leroux is a martyr of the French Revolution. Anne-Joseph Leroux was born in Cambrai in 1747 and entered the monastery of the Urbanist Poor Clares in Valenciennes in 1769, taking the religious name of Josephine. In 1791 all religious, both men and women, were expelled from that city, and she went to the Ursuline convent, where her sister, Scholastica was one of the community. This house had been allowed to remain open because the nuns ran a school, but the following year it, too, had to close. The city was captured by the Austrian army in 1793 and the nuns returned to their home, but a year later the French forces took the town again. The French victory had been so sudden that no one had had time to escape,

---

42. 'When I consider the example of these men and men like them, I was filled with fear. Dread came upon me and trembling, and the darkness of my sins almost overwhelmed me ...'. Ibid.

43. *The Lady: Clare of Assisi, Early Documents,* Regis J. Armstrong (ed), (New York, London: New City Press, 2006), p 168-169.

but Josephine and Scholastica managed to find refuge with a family in the town who were willing to shelter them. However, they were arrested on 3 September and taken back to the Ursuline convent, which from a school had now become a prison. They were treated particularly harshly, being given neither food nor drink and were court martialled by a commission of inquiry set up to examine their so-called crimes. They were found guilty and executions began immediately. Josephine was beheaded together with five Ursuline sisters on 23 October 1794.

A letter from the sister of Josephine Leroux while they were both still in prison, shows the situation they were in and their own attitude towards their coming martyrdom:

> Without doubt we are going to be given the glory of martyrdom. Do not weep for us but rather ask: O my sisters, what have you done to deserve such a favour? Dear friends, I tell you that the evils we have suffered since leaving you cannot compare with the unutterable delights which the divine bridegroom is preparing for his privileged brides in the glory of martyrdom. Like St Ursula and her companions, we – in a few days – will give our lives for his love and the hope in which we have faith. The consolations we have in view of this favour are inexpressible; they prove the power of grace to us. Without them, we would give way under the weight of our sufferings. Five of us have already gone to the guillotine; they are Mothers Natalie, Laurentine, Ursula, Louise and Augustine. They did not walk, rather they flew to the torture. One of them, wanting to be executed first, was obliged to climb down from the scaffold and then climb up again. They were allowed a bodice and a chemise and had to walk with their hands tied behind their backs. We expect the same thing. I am sure my letter will not reach you until after my death. The judgement of God is unknown, so give me the help of your prayers. In the prison in Douai are Mothers Thérèse, Félicité and Agnés. Here together in this prison are Clotilde and my Urbanist sister and we two religious, Cordule and I. The priests have been executed, and this confirms that our martyrdom is to follow.[44]

44. Letter from Mother Scholastica Leroux, in prison.

This letter reveals a similar attitude to martyrdom as that found among the early generations of Christians and shows that women were still as ready to give their lives with cheerfulness and great courage for their Christian beliefs. It also demonstrates the link between martyrdom and monasticism.

Another French woman who longed to give her life for the Christ, but did not have the opportunity to actually shed her blood was the Carmelite, Thérèse of Lisieux. In her *billet de profession*, a short mediation and/or prayer which it was customary for a young sister about to make her vows to write out and have with her during the profession ceremony, she expressed her desire thus:

> Jesus, I would like to die a martyr for your sake, a martyr in soul or in body; better still in both.[45]

Having been brought up in the almost suffocatingly devout atmosphere of a middle class French family of the mid-to-late nineteenth century, this desire was perhaps not surprising. Later in her short life, she repeated what she acknowledged to be her flight of fancy at much greater length and much more graphically in a letter addressed to her sister, Marie, also displaying her familiarity with the traditional Lives of the Saints on which she had been nurtured and raised:

> But above all I long to shed my blood for you, my Saviour, to the last drop. Martyrdom was the dream of my youth, has been my dream in the sheltered world of Carmel; and yet here too I realise that the dream I cherish is an extravagant one – a single form of martyrdom would never be enough for me, I should want to experience them all. I should want to be scourged and crucified as you were; to be flayed alive like St Bartholomew, to be dipped in boiling oil like St John, to undergo all that martyr ever underwent; offering my neck to the executioner like St Agnes and St Cecily, and, like my favourite St Joan of Arc, whispering your name as I was tied to the stake. When I think of what Christians will have to go through in the days of Antichrist, my heart beats fast, and I

---

45. Thérèse of Lisieux, *Autobiography of a Saint*, trs R. Knox (London: Harvill Press, 1958), p 202.

could wish that all these torments were being kept in store for me.[46]

However, her destined martyrdom was not to suffer any of these torments attributed to the saints of long ago, but to die of tuberculosis – as did so many of her generation –at the age of 24 in the convent infirmary. Another victim was the young Scotswoman, Margaret Sinclair who, having been brought up in poverty and hardship and left school at fourteen to work in a biscuit factory, entered the Poor Clare Monastery in Notting Hill, London, and died of tuberculosis in 1925.[47]

From its earliest days in the deserts of Egypt, Palestine and Syria, monasticism both for men and for women, has been seen as a movement which of its essence seeks silence, solitude and seclusion from the business of purely secular society in order to focus on a life of more concentrated prayer and contemplation. Although frequently in its long history, monastic literature has given the impression that monastics shunned or despised 'the world' (and, at times this has been a fact, not only an impression), ideally, monks and nuns have cultivated a deep concern for the affairs of secular society and have seen themselves as charged with a mission to pray for all these affairs and bring them, and especially all the needy in society, to God. This monastic concern for the 'cultivation' of society, both practical and spiritual, has been well expressed by Benedict XVI, with reference to the writings of St Bernard, in his encyclical on Christian hope *Spe salvi*, which I quote at some length because of its aptness:

> It was commonly thought that monasteries were places of flight from the world (*contemptus mundi*) and of withdrawal from the responsibilities of the world, in search of private salvation. Bernard of Clairvaux, who inspired a multitude of young people to enter the monasteries of his reformed Order, had quite a different perspective on this. In his view, monks perform a task for the whole church and hence also

---

46. Thérèse of Lisieux, *Autobiography of a Saint*, trs R. Knox (London: Harvill Press, 1958), pp 233, 234.
47. Her cause for beatification has since been introduced and she is now officially the Venerable Margaret Sinclair.

for the world. He uses many images to illustrate the responsibility that monks have towards the entire body of the church, and indeed towards humanity; he applies to them the words of pseudo-Rufinus: 'The human race lives thanks to a few; were it not for them, the world would perish ...'. Contemplatives – *contemplantes* – must become agricultural labourers – *laborantes* – he says. The nobility of work, which Christianity inherited from Judaism, had already been expressed in the monastic rules of Augustine and Benedict. Bernard takes up this idea again. The young noblemen who flocked to his monasteries had to engage in manual labour. In fact Bernard explicitly states that not even the monastery can restore Paradise, but he maintains that, as a place of practical and spiritual 'tilling the soil', it must prepare the new Paradise. A wild plot of forest land is rendered fertile – and in the process, the trees of pride are felled, whatever weeds may be growing inside souls are pulled up, and the ground is thereby prepared so that bread for body and soul can flourish.[48]

In this poetic way, both Bernard and Benedict XVI express the function which contemplative monks and nuns have performed for the church and the world down through the centuries. And as well as preparing the new Paradise by 'cultivating' the soil both spiritually and practically, at times of serious crisis when Christian principles were being denied or called into question, they were prepared to make a stand for their beliefs, even to giving their lives.

By totally rejecting ordinary human structures and almost provocatively renouncing worldly institutions, they paradoxically came to represent another kind of power. Their advice was sought in matters of spirituality, salvation, doctrine even social life and political action.[49]

48. Benedict XVI: Encyclical *Spe Salvi: On Christian Hope* (Libreria Editrice Vaticana, Citta del Vaticano: 2007); Eng trs CTS, London: 2007, pp 18-19.
49. J. Chryssavgis, 'From Egypt to Palestine: Discerning a Thread of Spiritual Direction', in J. Behr, A. Louth and D. Conomos (eds), *Abba: The Tradition of Orthodoxy in the West, Festschrift for Bishop Kallistos (Ware) of Diokleia* (Crestwood, New York: St Vladimir's Seminary Press, 2003), pp 299-315, p 299.

Christianity has always given special honour to those who witnessed to their faith even to the shedding of their blood, and for the first four centuries the threat of martyrdom, either actual or potential, was present throughout the Roman Empire. Although Constantine's conversion brought this era of persecution to an end, the monks and nuns who sought solitude in the desert also sought a new kind of martyrdom – that of giving their lives in self-imposed asceticism and sacrifice.

> In his separation from the world, the monk is heir not only to the virgin, but also to the martyr. One of the most interesting aspects of the early treatises on martyrdom is their use of themes and images which would later become associated with the monastic vocation.[50]

The monastic calling has traditionally been seen from the earliest days, as 'white martyrdom' – a total offering of one's life to God, but without the shedding of blood. However, it can, and frequently has in the course of history, provided opportunities for 'red martyrdom'. Even after the first three centuries during which the church was known as the 'church of the martyrs', during the remainder of the first millennium, the monks of Iona, Lindisfarne and Clonmacnoise and Skellig Michael and many other monastic foundations in insular regions were slaughtered by the Vikings, while Boniface and his companions gave their lives as missionaries in the spreading of the gospel.

The persecutions which ravaged the twentieth century also brought a development in the understanding of martyrdom; martyrs in earlier ages had given their lives for what they believed or for the freedom to worship. During the twentieth century, which it has been estimated saw more martyrs than all the previous centuries of Christianity combined, the concept of martyrdom expanded to include the practice of the Christian faith; not simply allegiance to Christ, but the bearing witness to his teaching by living according to gospel values – peace and social justice, human rights, solidarity with the poor and oppressed being some of the issues which put believing Christians

50. M. D. Totah, 'The History of Enclosure' in J. Prou and the Benedictine Nuns of the Solesmes Congregation (Eng ed trs and ed D. Hayes), *Walled About with God* (Gracewing, 2005), p 38.

at odds with their persecutors – often themselves claiming to be pious Christians. These developments have brought with them a new appreciation for the ecumenical dimension of martyrdom – frequently in the last century Catholics, Protestants and Orthodox bore witness together in prison and labour camps, and common Christian belief and practice began to be seen as more important than denominational issues on which they differed. Women monastics have also given their lives down the ages, but with the significant difference that, whereas in the early church, Christian women were frequently martyred in defence of the chastity they had dedicated to Christ,[51] in more recent times women have witnessed to social rights and issues along with men.

This chapter takes examples, two of them from near-contemporary monasticism, and examines these in detail to show that monasticism, although seeking seclusion, is still vitally concerned with secular affairs and monastics have been prepared to give their lives for their beliefs and the freedom to practise those beliefs. It also introduces monasticism as lived in the Orthodox churches, although neither of the two examples can be said to be typical Orthodox nuns: each in their different way, their vision of religious life was nearer to that of the apostolic congregations in Western Christianity. These are women from totally different walks of life, who before their religious profession had been, each in her own way, deeply immersed in the affairs of secular society, and this involvement continued afterwards, eventually claiming their lives. New Martyr Elisabeth was a member by marriage of the Russian Imperial family and this alone would have brought about her death under the atheistic communist regime, but her involvement as a Christian religious woman with the disadvantaged of this world also contributed to her death. She thus joined the ranks of the 'royal passion-bearers', a particularly, but not exclusively, Russian category of sainthood, following in the footsteps of Boris and Gleb, early Russian martyrs whose death was as political as it was religious. Like her younger sister, the Tsaritsa, she was under suspicion because she was German by birth, though there was far less personal

---

51. However, see the reference to Visser's theory quoted above.

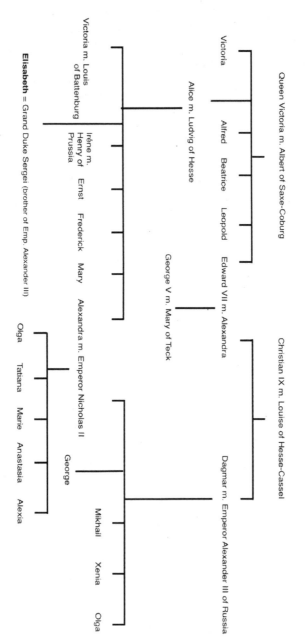

The Houses of Romanov and Hesse (very much simplified)

animosity for the respected Grand Duchess Elisabeth than there was for the hated '*nemka*' – the 'German woman' who was held personally responsible for Russia's downfall.

Princess Elisabeth of Hesse and by Rhine was born in 1864, and was a granddaughter of Queen Victoria, being the daughter of Grand Duke Louis IV of Hesse-Darmstadt and Victoria's daughter, Princess Alice. Their home life was simple, almost to the point of austerity, in spite of their high status. Elisabeth had an upbringing that was typical of the English aristocracy of that time. Having been orphaned at the age of fourteen, she was then brought up mainly in England by her grandmother, Queen Victoria.

Elisabeth grew into a woman of exceptional graciousness and beauty and throughout her life the German Kaiser Wilhelm II, had the greatest regard for her. However, in 1884 Elisabeth married Grand Duke Serge of Russia, brother of Alexander III and uncle of the last Tsar, Nicholas II. Their relationship was described by her niece, Maria Pavlova:

> Uncle Sergei and Aunt Ella never had any children of their own. Their relations towards each other were distinguished by a strained fondness that rested on my aunt's serene acceptance of my uncle's decision in all matters great and small. Proud and timid, both of them, they seldom showed their true feelings and never offered confidences.[52]

The world of Imperial Russia which she entered as a bride of the royal family was one of almost unimaginable wealth and splendour – and great political unrest. Both her English and her German relatives had grave reservations about the wisdom of her marriage both because of the political uncertainties and because of the character of her husband. However, unlike her younger sister who later married the future Tsar Nicholas II, Elisabeth was a great success in court circles because of her beauty, elegance, graciousness and gentle nature. Her niece described her thus:

---

52. Maria Pavlova [the younger], *Memoirs*, quoted in A. Maylunas and S. Mironenko, *A Lifelong Passion: Nicholas and Alexandra, Their Own Story* (London, Weidenfeld and Nicolson, 1996), p 264.

Aunt Ella was one of the most beautiful women I have ever seen in my life, She was tall and slight, of blonde colouring, with features of extraordinary fineness and purity.[53]

But her husband was unpopular and there were rumours about problems in their marriage. It was rumoured that he was homosexual and that the marriage was not happy.[54] However, Elisabeth seemed to have been genuinely fond of him, although according to her niece 'He treated her rather as if she were a child. I believe she was hurt by his attitude and longed to be better understood ... she and my uncle seemed never very intimate.'[55]

Several years after her marriage she converted to Orthodoxy and in the same year her husband was made Governor General of Moscow where the couple moved. He was not a success in this position which, given the political situation, was one of great delicacy. In 1905 Grand Duke Serge was assassinated by a bomb thrown by a terrorist. Elisabeth heard the explosion and was on the scene within minutes and began rescuing the pieces of her husband's body which had been blown far and wide. She later visited her husband's assassin in prison and assured him of her forgiveness.[56]

After this her life changed radically; she sold her jewellery and most of her possessions and adopted a simpler, ascetic lifestyle. With the proceeds she opened the Convent of Martha and Mary in Moscow where in the slums she helped the poor, sick and orphaned. Although she had the greatest regard for the monastic life, and herself lived an extremely ascetic lifestyle, her intention was to reintroduce the order of deaconesses, as she understood the work of her sisterhood to be that of the deacon rather than monastic. In order to carry out her plans, she went to Germany to study the work of deaconesses in the Lutheran Church and also came to England to stay with Anglican reli-

53. Ibid, p 265.
54. V. Cowles, *The Romanovs* (London, Harper and Row: 1971), p 219; C. Zeepat, *Romanov Autumn* (London, Sutton Publishing: 2000), p 132.
55. Maria Pavlova [the younger], *Memoirs*, p 265.
56. See A. Maylunas and S. Mironenko, *A Lifelong Passion: Nicholas and Alexandra, Their Own Story*, pp 258-276 for the memoirs of various members of the Romanov family, the assassin and others.

gious communities who worked in the East End of London. The Holy Synod[57] turned down her original plan fearing that it was too much of an innovation. A revised plan again met with reservations and finally her brother-in-law established the community by his own personal decree. Although the Holy Synod could not agree to her plans, she did receive consistent support from individual bishops. She was, for example, consistently supported by Metropolitan Vladimir of Moscow (later the first of the new martyrs of the Russian Church).

Her original community began in 1910 with six sisters, and it had increased to thirty within the year and continued to grow. Elisabeth was emphatic that her sisters were not nuns: they received a blessing on entering the community, but this was a form of dedication, not the monastic tonsure. She insisted that the nursing sisters had plenty of sleep and food because of their hard physical work, but her own personal regime was ascetic. Her diet consisted largely of vegetables and after a full day of hard work, she often spent most of the night in prayer. In her vision of religious life she wished to combine prayer and action in a suffering world. She opened a hospital where, during the War the injured and the dying were nursed and cared for, irrespective of their nationality. A contemporary Russian described her sisters and her regime thus:

> The nuns were not cloistered but dedicated their lives to visiting the poor and caring for the sick. They also travelled through the provinces, founding new centres. The institution developed rapidly; in a few years all large Russian cities had similar establishments. The Ordinka convent had to be enlarged: a church, a hospital, workshops and schools were added.
>
> The Mother Superior lived in a small, simply furnished three-room house; her wooden bed had no mattress and her pillow was stuffed with hay. The Grand Duchess slept little, a few hours at most, when she was not spending the whole

---

57. The governing body of the Russian Orthodox Church, set up in 1700 by Peter the Great. It was abolished in 1917 and replaced by the Patriarchate. For a full explanation, see T. Ware, *The Orthodox Church* (London: Penguin Books, 1963), pp 126, 128, 137.

night by a sick bed, or praying over a coffin in the chapel. Hospitals and nursing homes sent her their worst cases, and she nursed them herself.[58]

Although her life as a nurse in war torn Russia was admired by many, one commentator wrote that in her stubborn refusal to leave the country or at least accept the offer of safety in the Kremlin, held out to her by the Provisional Government, she 'almost seemed to be seeking martyrdom'; she 'turned down all offers of security and escape.'[59]

Exiled by the Communist government, first to Yekaterinburg, then to Alapaevsk, she was killed on 17 July 1918 along with other members of the Imperial family. When Alapaevsk fell to the White Army in October 1918, her remains, along with those of her companions, were discovered in a mine shaft.

Twenty years later, Maria Skobtsova (born Elizaveta Yurievna Pilenko, 1891-1945) helped Jews in occupied France during World War II and that sealed her death warrant. Although she had been baptised a Christian she became an atheist in her early adult years. She took an active part in the radical intellectual circles of her day (she counted Tolstoy[60] and Blok[61] among her acquaintances), and was a published poet and active socialist, very much involved in local politics (she was mayor of Anapa on the Black Sea). So when she eventually took up monastic life, Mother Maria was far from the traditional image of a nun. After her second marriage failed, she was tonsured as a monastic, on condition she did not have to live secluded in a monastery:

> At the Last Judgement I will not be asked whether I practised asceticism, nor how many bows I have made before the divine altar. I will be asked whether I fed the hungry, clothed the naked, visited the sick, and the prisoner in his jail. That is all I will be asked.

58. F. Yusupov, *Memoirs*, quoted in A. Maylunas and S. Mironenko, *A Lifelong Passion: Nicholas and Alexandra, Their Own Story* (London, Weidenfeld and Nicolson, 1996), p 333.

59. R. K. Massie, *The Romanovs: The Final Chapter* (London, Jonathan Cape: 1995), p 256.

60. Leo Nikolayevich Tolstoy (1828-1910), one of the greatest Russian novelists.

61. Alexander Alexandrovich Blok (1880-1921), a Russian lyrical poet.

She was quite clear in her vision of a form of monasticism which was new in the Orthodox Church: 'I want to create a new form of religious life ... a life in the world ...' After the 1917 Russian Revolution, she emigrated from Russia to Paris. Here she rented a house where she kept open door for refugees, the poor and all the many needy including an increasing number of Jews. When it became known that she was hiding and helping Jews, the house was closed. One of the many stories told about her exploits to assist the Jews was that she went to the *Velodrome d'hiver* where the pro-German French police had imprisoned the Paris Jews, and frequently went in with a dustbin in which she hid and then carried out Jewish children, while pretending to bring out rubbish. Mother Maria was eventually captured and taken to Ravensbrück concentration camp, where she died in the gas chambers on Holy Saturday in 1945. It is said that she exchanged places with another woman condemned to death, a mother with children. Thus her death was a martyrdom very similar to that of Maximilian Kolbe, the Polish Franciscan martyr of Auschwitz. She was canonised by the Russian Orthodox Church on 16 January 2004 and is especially venerated by the Russian Orthodox Archdiocese in France under the Ecumenical Patriarchate. During her lifetime her artistic work included the painting and embroidery of icons. This has special significance for this study in that it was only during the twentieth century that women became recognised as iconographers.[62] While it is not easy to substantiate this remark, as icons are traditionally anonymous, it is true that all the great iconographers of the past have been male (Andrei Rublev; Theophan the Greek, Manuelis Panselinos etc). It was only during the last century that women such as Sister Joanna Reitlinger and Monahia Juliana became known as icon painters. Earlier iconographers' manuals have always assumed that those using them and the rituals involved would be male.

Elisabeth, like the women of late antiquity such as Macrina,

---

62. I owe this observation, along with much of the information in this paragraph, to Dr Elena Ene D-Vasilescu, and I would like to express my gratitude to her for graciously making available to me the results of her research, published as *Between Tradition and Modernity: Icons and Icon Painters in Romania* (VDM Verlag, 2009), and for very kindly answering my questions.

devoted her large fortune to the poor and needy. Maria Skobtsova's holiness was more akin to that of the asceticism of the desert mothers; when travelling, she took nothing with her but a toothbrush. Though so very different in character, circumstances and their interpretation of monastic living, they have been canonised by their respective churches as martyrs for their Christian faith. However, just as their approach to monasticism is controversial, so also it can be debated how fully they deserve the title of 'martyr'; were their deaths at the hands of their persecutors inevitable for reasons other than that of their religious consecration? Were they acts of brutality in war-time or genuine martyrdom?

We have now come almost in a full circle in this study of the place of women religious in the church. In chapter three we traced the connection between martyrdom and monasticism in the early Christian centuries; in this last of the biographical studies we see this connection at work again in the last century: we see women monastics who were prepared to lay down their lives for the Christ and their belief in him and his teaching, as they have been, though perhaps less obviously, all through the Christian centuries.

CHAPTER NINE

Present Day Women's Monasticism –
The Issue of Enclosure

This chapter departs from the study of the biographies of women monastics as used in the preceding chapters and offers a study of an aspect of monasticism that arouses burning interest and strong feeling today: that of enclosure. In order to do this, I will examine how monastic enclosure has been seen by both monks and nuns, but particularly the latter, from the earliest days of monasticism, thus giving a résumé of the conclusions to which this study has come so far. This forms a good basis for a comparison of this understanding and practice with present day legislation as set out in the latest Roman Catholic document on the subject of women's enclosure: *Verbi sponsa*,[1] and its antecedents. In recent decades there has been real progress in our understanding of human dignity which has brought, in its wake, an awareness of the equality of rights between women and men. However, this has not been reflected in Roman legal documentation, which has only given lip service to issues of women's equality. Schneiders notes the reality of the situation:

> Even a religious congregation composed entirely of women could not open or close a chapter, elect a major superior, amend its own constitutions, or receive the vows of its new members without the empowering presence of a man. In short, any matter which was even remotely related to the realm of the sacred was mediated to women by men.[2]

Although for some Congregations there has been progress here, for enclosed monastic communities this is the reality of religious life for women in the twenty-first century. In early Christian society generally, women's position was subordinate

---

1. *Verbi sponsa: Instruction on the Contemplative Life and on the Enclosure of Nuns* (Vatican City, 1999).
2. S. Schneiders, 'The Effects of Women's Experience on their Spirituality', *Spirituality Today*, Summer 1983, vol 35, No 2, pp 100-116.

to men, and monasticism did not succeed in redressing that balance, as has been obvious in the preceding chapters. In spite of this however, earlier generations of women monastics did enjoy some freedom of movement, and were not confined by law for life within their enclosure. In monasticism today, however, although women now enjoy virtual equality with men in all other fields of life, men still exercise control which is more or less absolute. Because of changing sociological and economic conditions in the twentieth century, plus two wars of global magnitude, the place of women has undergone a vast and comparatively rapid change.

> Women's role in society has been a key global concern of the 20th century. Gaining momentum as the century progressed, it has acquired greater credibility as more and more women have taken positions of authority and influence within the structures of public life. Even where pressure for change has been resisted, the women's movement has had an impact on human organisations in all parts of the world and in every walk of life.[3]

However, this has not been mirrored in the church's understanding of the role of women. Some documents issued by the Roman Catholic Church give lip service to these changes, but this has not been born out in practice. The Catholic Church's Canon Law regarding the practice of the enclosure of nuns has only changed minimally since the Middle Ages. This chapter will look at the way monastic enclosure has been lived by women since the beginnings of the monastic movement and compare this with present day legislation and practice.

Such classic monastic texts as the *Historia Lausiaca* of Palladius show that from the very earliest days, even though withdrawal from the world was regarded as being of the essence of the monastic life for women, as well as for men, the first nuns were nowhere required to live under lock and key for life.

> The women lived on one side of the river opposite the men. When a virgin died, the others laid her out for burial, and

3. G. Patterson, *Still Flowing, Women, God and Church* (Geneva: WCC Publications, 1999), p ix.

they carried her body and placed it on the bank of the river.

This incident took place in that monastery: a tailor of the world crossed over through ignorance, looking for work. A young virgin came out – the place was deserted – and heard his story.

In the monastery of Amma Talis in Antinoë, (which is specifically described as being without a lock, the nuns remaining within because of their love for Talis), Palladius is welcomed within the monastic hall and Amma Talis sits by his side, placing her hands on his shoulders 'in a burst of frankness'. Palladius introduces a sister called Taor, who is marked out as different from the other nuns because she does not leave the monastery each Sunday as the others do:

> In this monastery was a maiden, a disciple of hers named Taor, who had spent thirty years there. She was never willing to take a new garment, hood, or shoes, but said: 'I have no need for them unless I must go out. The others all go out every Sunday to church for Communion.'

So it is clear from this anecdotal evidence that it was regarded as normative for the nuns to leave the monastery at least once a week to attend the liturgy in church, and also for liturgical ceremonies such as funerals, while guests were welcomed into the monastic refectory and shared meals with the nuns.

There is also the story of an unnamed Amma, telling of how she and a company of her nuns were travelling and were seen while still at a great distance by a company of monks, also travelling. The monks went to great trouble to avoid the nuns, at which the Amma remarked: 'If you had been perfect monks, you would not have known we were women.'[4]

So in these passages we see women who, although living private and secluded lives in their desert monasteries, had freedom to go to church, to go out of the monastic grounds and converse with others, to travel, and to welcome guests within the monastery. There are many other similar examples from early medieval texts from the Western world such as Bede's *Life of Cuthbert*, where he describes the visit of Cuthbert to 'an estate

---

4. Elm, *'Virgins of God' The Making of Asceticism in Late Antiquity'*, p 267.

belonging to the monastery' of the abbess Aelfflaed where he is asked to converse with Aelfflaed and to consecrate a church. A meal is served for the guests who sit down with 'a goodly number of people' from the estate. There is no indication of any separation between the abbess and her guests and the next day she returns to the main monastery.[5] In Eddius Stephanus' *Life of Wilfrid* he describes a church synod which took place in 706 at an unidentified place 'on the east bank of the River Nidd'.[6] Again, the abbess Aelfflaed was present, even though the River Nidd (in Yorkshire) was a very long way from her own monastery (on the coast of Northumbria).[7] These stories all show that although both nuns and monks realised the need for seclusion and solitude, and often went to extreme lengths to procure these, neither monks nor nuns lived under such a strict interpretation of enclosure that they never left their monastic precincts, never mixed socially with seculars or had converse with others.[8]   Monasticism down through the centuries has always stressed the need for withdrawal from secular life in order to lead a more focused and concentrated life of prayer, but the idea of complete and lifelong obligatory separation was foreign to early monasticism.

This need for seclusion and retreat witnessed by anecdotal and textual evidence is borne out by archaeological investigation. Archaeology reveals that since the earliest days of monasticism in its original homeland in the deserts of the eastern Mediterranean, monastic houses were either built within an already existing walled precinct, or, if such was not available, then became surrounded by high stone or mud brick walls. This

---

5. Bede, *Life of Cuthbert*, (trs J. F. Webb), in D. Farmer ed, *The Age of Bede* (London: Penguin, 1965, repr. 1998), pp 87, 88.
6. Eddius Stephanus, *Life of Wilfrid*, (trs J. F. Webb), in D. Farmer ed, *The Age of Bede* (London: Penguin, 1965, repr. 1998), pp 174- 176.
7. See Map of Monastic Britain (Southampton: Ordnance Survey, 1978).
8. Thus in early medieval Ireland, Samthann, founder of Clonbroney, and closely associated with the strict Céli Dé movement, talks freely to monks and scholars; Ita meets and talks with outsiders, including a young cleric, and is prepared to help a nun with an illegitimate child; Moninna travels freely with her sisters. Even if these stories are telling us more about monasticism at the time they were written down rather than the time they appear to report, they are still portraying what were understood to be appropriate monastic attitudes and acceptable conduct.

was necessary to protect privacy, to keep vegetable plots and domestic animals safe and to deter thieves and cattle raiders. The same building practices obtained when monasticism spread to Europe and the insular world of the early Middle Ages. All domestic settlements were surrounded by an enclosing bank of earth or stone, and this applied to farmsteads and all kinds of secular establishments as well as to monastic sites. When monasticism reached the far West of Europe the monks exchanged the desert of sand for a 'desert in the ocean'[9] and built their hermitages on the many islands and promontories off the west coast of Ireland and Scotland. Archaeological excavation at places such as Nendrum, Armagh, Monasterboice, Melrose and Iona indicate that most monastic settlements, whether individual hermitages or much larger cenobitic houses, were surrounded by an enclosing boundary.[10] However, that something more than simple material shelter was implied is indicated by the presence of the surrounding *vallum* even on island monasteries such as Skellig Michael, Iona, Ardoilean, and Inishmurray, where the sea itself and lack of easy access because of tides and treacherous landing conditions provided more than adequate physical protection. This circular or subcircular enclosing bank or wall came to symbolise the boundary between the sacred and the profane, marking the limits of monastic territory where aggression was not tolerated and where sanctuary and divine protection were accorded to the area within.[11] Visser comments in the general context of church buildings:

> The distinction between an outlined space and the undifferentiated space beyond it is invariably important.[12]

---

9. Adomnán of Iona: *Vita Columbae*, trs R. Sharpe (London: Penguin, 1995), I.6, I.20.

10. For details see M. Herity, 'The Buildings and Layout of Early Irish Monasteries before the year 1000' in *Monastic Studies* 14 (1983), 247-284.

11. For a very comprehensive study of enclosure and the zoning of religious space and its theological implications throughout the Christian world, but particularly in Ireland in the early Middle Ages, see D. Jenkins, *Holy, Holier, Holiest: the Sacred Topography of the Early Medieval Irish Church*, [*Studia Traditionis Theologiae* 4] (Turnhout, Brepols: 2010).

12. M. Visser, *The Geometry of Love* (New York: North Point Press, 2000), p 33. For Sacred Space, see Visser, pp 32-34.

So the holier the place was deemed to be, the more effective the sanctuary and divine protection afforded. This was based partly on the scriptural notion of 'cities of refuge' and the sanctuary thus afforded was frequently taken advantage of by those in need of protection in a violent world.

Bede's description of Cuthbert's hermitage on the Inner Farne illustrates another aspect of the idea of enclosure as it was understood at least by some, if not all early monastics:

> The wall itself on the outside was higher than a man standing upright, but inside he made it much higher by cutting away the living rock, so that the pious inhabitant could see nothing but the sky from his dwelling, thus restraining both the lust of his eyes and of the thoughts, and lifting the whole bent of his mind to higher things.[13]

So enclosure could also have the ascetic element of removing distractions from the sight and mind of the monastic, leaving his thoughts free to concentrate on God and divine things. Poetry attributed to hermits and anchorites is full of the desire and longing for solitude:

> All alone in my little hut without any human being in my company,
> dear has been the pilgrimage before going to meet death ...
> Stepping along the paths of the gospel, singing psalms every hour:
> an end of talking and long stories;
> constant bending of the knee.
> All alone in my little hut, all alone so,
> alone I came into the world,
> alone I shall go from it.[14]

The hermit treasures his solitude and seclusion as affording him the opportunity for uninterrupted prayer and contemplation,[15] and there are many stories from the *Vitae* of the saints

13. Bede, *Historia ecclesiastica gentis Anglorum*, eds B. Colgrave and R. A. B. Mynors (Oxford: Clarendon Press, 1969, repr. 1998).
14. O. Davies and F. Bowie, *Celtic Christian Spirituality* (London: SPCK, 1995), pp 34-35.
15. See D. Ó Corráin, 'Early Irish Hermit Poetry?' in D. Ó Corráin, L.

which illustrate their desire for such places of solitary retreat. Women were strictly excluded from these places as from all male monasteries, as this passage from the ninth century *Rule* of Ailbe states clearly:

> Neither soldiers nor women shall dwell within the monastery. The way of life they follow is both severe and demanding.[16]

Whereas the prohibition of female presence within monastic territory is definite, women monastics could not be quite so uncompromising because a priestly presence was necessary for the liturgical and sacramental life of the community and women needed some male assistance with heavier work around the monastery. Male monastic founders responsible for both monks and nuns had to act with circumspection and prudence; the founder of Monasterboice placed his two monasteries widely apart lest the reputation of his monks and nuns be compromised. Even when a male and a female monastic house were in close proximity, such as Brigid's foundation at Kildare and Carthach's monastery in Lismore,[17] there was strict segregation between monks and nuns.

However, in all these instances of male monastic control of the female, both in the physical and concrete and in the abstract and symbolic, whereas women are excluded firmly from the sacred male territory, there is no suggestion at all of their being controlled by obligatory confinement within their own monastic territory. The First Synod of Patrick states:

> A monk and a virgin, each from a different place, may not stay in the same hospice, nor travel together in the one chariot from house to house nor converse together frequently.[18]

Breatnach and K. McCone eds, *Sages, Saints and Storytellers* (Maynooth: An Sagart, 1989), 251-267 for a different interpretation of hermit poetry, but even if Ó Corráin is correct in his criticism, the 'hermit poetry' still sets out an ideal of solitary and secluded life.

16. U. Ó Maidín, *The Celtic Monk* (Kalamazoo, Michigan: Cistercian Publications, 1996), p 25.

17. 'Half the city was fenced off and no woman was allowed to set foot inside it', J. Ryan, *Irish Monasticism: Origins and Early Development* (Dublin: Talbot Press, 1931, repr. Four Courts Press, 1992), p 144.

18. De Paor, *Saint Patrick's World* (Dublin: Four Courts Press, 1996), p 136.

This passage suggests that both monks and nuns were wont to travel (this is borne out by incidents in the saints' *Vitae*), and this travelling receives no censure; there is no suggestion of disapproval that they would both be outside their monasteries, although their ensuing behaviour is regulated. So although these earlier monastic women enjoyed greater freedom than their secular counterparts, their position was still very subordinate to men. In spite of this, their physical existence was not seen to be co-terminous with their monastic territory, and they enjoyed some freedom of movement outside their monasteries. The possibility of greater freedom for women existed in the monastic life, but it had to be fought for, and bought at a price. Bitel comments:

> It seems that the enclosure not only protected holy women; it also protected men on the outside from impious women ... Once women's sexuality was under control inside the monastic sanctuary, it was no longer threatening to the Christian equilibrium.[19]

So women generally, and women monastics in particular were regarded by churchmen with apprehension, distrust and wariness. They were dangerous and a threat to male virtue, and so had to be kept under control.

However, even in the restricted freedom allowed to them by their male counterparts, there is no indication that monastic women were totally confined within their monasteries for life; there is both ingress to and egress from women's monastic houses. The situation is similar in the monasteries described by Bede in Northumbria: there is no suggestion of an impermeable barrier between nuns and lay people. The only textual evidence we have of a nun vowing never to leave her monastery is that of the repentant nun belonging to Samthann's community who ran off with a cleric, and returned to her monastery after they had been unable to cross a river which had miraculously flooded. The nun then vowed never to leave her monastery again after what she understood to have been miraculous divine intervention.[20]

---

19. L. Bitel, 'Women's Monastic Enclosures in Early Ireland: a Study of Female Spirituality and Male Monastic mentalities', *Journal of Medieval History* 12, (1986), pp 15-36, at 32.
20. Bitel, 'Women's Monastic Enclosures in Early Ireland', *Journal of Medieval History* 12, (1986), pp 15-36, at 33.

The question is: was enclosure seen as a protection for the nuns within, or as a protection for the men outside? Was it necessary that female sexuality be kept under control within the monastic confines, so that it was no longer seen as a threat to the sacred order or to male weakness? The church hierarchy was, on the whole, greatly relieved when nuns were safely within their monastic boundaries and no longer posing a threat to male virtue, but in these early days it had not yet occurred to anyone to enforce their staying and remaining there, and to make this a grave lifelong obligation under pain of 'mortal sin'.

We now move on to the feudal world of the later Middle Ages and examine the situation there. The theology of the Middle Ages continued to regard nuns in a negative light and this was reflected in church and secular law: women were seen as a source of temptation and a danger to male celibacy; their access to holiness was seen in masculine terms. But in spite of this negative outlook, despite the fact of their subordination to men, despite the fact that the parameters of women's lives, secular as well as religious,[21] were set by men, and that even the pattern of their sanctity was dictated in masculine terms – despite all this, monastic women continued to fight for the recognition of their right to order their own lives.

As an example of this: Clare of Assisi was the first woman to write a *Regula* for women in the history of the church, and has frequently been credited with the imposition of enclosure upon women religious. However, her vision of contemplative life was such that she allowed for her sisters to leave the enclosure 'for a useful, reasonable, evident and approved purpose'[22] without specifying minutely what these occasions might be. Clare had lived the greater part of her religious life observing the *Rule*

21. And it has to be borne in mind for a fair assessment of the situation that until comparatively recent times, all adult women lived more private lives than men, and even women in most secular societies lived comparatively secluded lives. The *Collectio Hibernensis* quoted the Synod of Arles: 'Young women you should live thus: knowing nothing beyond home and parents; and, if you should be separated from your parents, you should live an enclosed life, until death, under the authority of a priest'. *Collectio Hibernensis*, Bk 45; Heading 16.
22. Clare, 'The Rule', Regis J. Armstrong (ed), *Clare of Assisi: Early Documents* (New York: Paulist Press, 1988), p 63.

given to her by Cardinal Hugolino (1227-1284), who had been charged with the task of bringing order into the many groups of religious women which were proliferating in the church at that time. He endeavoured to enforce uniformity among these nuns and his legislation on enclosure was particularly stringent. He ruled:

> Therefore, it is proper and it is a duty that all these women who, after condemning and abandoning the vanity of the world, have resolved to embrace and hold to your Order, should observe this law of life and discipline, and remain enclosed the whole time of their life. After they have entered the enclosure of this Order and have assumed the religious habit, they should never be granted any permission or faculty to, leave [this enclosure], unless perhaps some are transferred to another place to plant or build up this same Order. Moreover, it is fitting that, when they die, both ladies as well as servants who are professed, they should be buried within the enclosure.[23]

So Hugolino saw the obligation to remain within the physical boundaries of the enclosure as strictly binding throughout the life of each professed nun and even in death. It is significant that he describes religious profession as 'condemning and abandoning the vanity of the world'. Presumably, this negative vision coloured his conception of the interpretation and observance of monastic enclosure. Clare, however, seems to have had a broader and less restrictive view. Regis Armstrong comments in a footnote to his translation of the *Form of Life* of Clare: 'Clare's balance between flexibility and acceptance of the monastic enclosure is a complex problem.'[24] It would appear to be a great and clearsighted gift, rather than 'a complex problem'. For Clare, enclosure seems to have been a filter to remove unnecessary, useless or distracting material from the lives of the nuns. She wrote in her *Rule* regarding the nun who has just been professed:

> [S]he may not go outside the monastery except for a useful,

23. The 'Rule of Cardinal Hugolino', Regis J. Armstrong (ed), *Clare of Assisi: Early Documents*, p 89.
24. Clare, 'The Rule', Regis J. Armstrong (ed), *Clare of Assisi: Early Documents*, p 63, fn 14.

reasonable, evident and approved purpose ... Let [the extern sisters] not presume to repeat the gossip of the world inside the monastery.[25]

So according to her understanding, enclosure is a filter to remove pointless distractions rather than an impenetrable barrier within which the nuns are contained for life in order to 'condemn the vanity of the world', as it was becoming for other Orders within the church.

However, 'strict enclosure and the status of Bride of Christ, awaiting her Bridegroom'[26] was becoming more and more the norm for nuns and became obligatory for all nuns with the decree *Periculoso* published by Pope Boniface VIII (1294-1303) in 1298.[27] By this decree, confining and constricting attitudes towards nuns that had long existed in the church, such as that of Cardinal Hugolino quoted above, solidified into universal ecclesiastical law. The relevant passage states:

[T]hat no nun tacitly or expressly professed in religion shall henceforth have or be able to have power of going out of those monasteries for whatsoever reason or cause, unless perchance any be found manifestly suffering from a disease so great and of such a nature that she cannot without grave danger or scandal live together with others; and to no dishonest or even honest person shall entry or access be given by them, unless for a reasonable and manifest cause and by a special licence from the person to whom [the granting of such a licence] pertains.[28]

So from the time of the publication of *Periculoso* onwards, on all nuns, whichever monastic Rule they observed and wherever their monastery might be situated, were solemnly bound by the strict law of perpetual cloister and under no circumstances, except those of imminent danger, were they to break this law, either by

25. Clare, 'The Rule', pp 63, 73.
26. Dunn, *The Emergence of Monasticism*, p 57.
27. See E. Makowski, 'Canon Law and Cloistered Women: Periculoso and Its Commentators 1298-1545', *Studies in Medieval and Early Modern Canon Law*, Vol 5 (Catholic University of America Press, 1998).
28. Boniface VIII: Bull *Periculoso*, quoted in Lucas, *Women in the Middle Ages*, p 52.

exiting from their monasteries or by allowing unauthorised persons to enter.

Synodal and conciliar legislation, as well as much anecdotal evidence and the frequently satirical witness of contemporary literature, demonstrate that the Bull *Periculoso* was neither popular nor effective among cloistered women. Continued and repeated episcopal insistence that nuns were not to leave their enclosure except in very specific instances suggests that the decrees of *Periculoso* were not very strictly observed. The frustration of the canon lawyer John of Ayton is very evident:

> But surely there is scarce any mortal man who could do this [enforce claustration]. ... For the nuns answer roundly to these statutes or to any others promulgated against their wantonness, saying 'In truth the men who made these laws sat well at their ease, while they laid such burdens upon us by these hard and intolerable restrictions.'[29]

Both bishops, canonists and the nuns themselves could well repeat the exact same comments today. However, this legislation was repeated yet again at the Council of Trent (Session 25, decree *De regularibus*), and the 1917 Code of Canon Law (Canons 597-603), and remained in force right up to the latter half of the twentieth century. But with the fresh insights of the Second Vatican Council, the possibility of a new understanding of enclosure was hinted at in the Decree On the Up-to-Date Renewal of Religious Life, *Perfectae caritatis* (1965):

> Papal cloister is to be maintained for nuns whose life is wholly contemplative. However, it should be adjusted to suit the conditions of time and place, abolishing obsolete practices after consultation with the monasteries themselves.[30]

Predictably, however, the opinions of nuns on what adjustments 'to suit the conditions of time and place' were necessary and desirable, and what actually constituted an 'obsolete practice' varied enormously and feelings ran high and – frequently – vociferously.

---

29. W. Lyndwood, *Provinciale (seu Constitutiones Angliae)*, with commentary by John of Ayton (Oxford, 1679), quoted by Lucas, *Women in the Middle Ages*, p 54.
30. *Perfectae caritatis*, 16.

In 1969 the Instruction *Venite seorsum* was issued, to legislate 'the norms which in the future will regulate the enclosure of nuns wholly dedicated to contemplation'. Diametrically opposed descriptions have seen it simultaneously as both 'one of the greatest and most beautiful contributions to the church's understanding of enclosure'[31] and also 'undoubtedly one of the most repressive documents to emanate from the Vatican in modern times'.[32] The legislation which it offered, though it continued in theory to govern the lives of enclosed nuns for the next thirty years, did not actually bear out this promise of a wider vision suggested by some portions of *Perfectae caritatis*, but this was the era of experimentation; in practice, all depended on the attitude of the local bishop or vicar for religious, most of whom, if they showed any concern at all, were anxious for contemplatives to expand their horizons, both for their own benefit, and in order to share the richness of their monastic traditions with the local church. Such passages as the following from *Venite seorsum* were as strict as anything in pre-Vatican II days:

> The area of the convent subject to the law of enclosure must be circumscribed in such a way that material separation be ensured, that is, all coming in and going out must be thereby rendered impossible (e.g. by a wall or some other effective means, such as a fence of planks or heavy iron mesh, or a thick and firmly rooted hedge). Only through doors kept regularly locked may one enter or leave the enclosure.[33]

The text continued to specify the 'mode of ensuring this effective separation, especially as far as the choir and parlour are concerned', so that material barriers obtain in these places, and decreed that 'the nuns, novices and postulants must live within the confines of the convent prescribed by the enclosure itself, nor may they licitly go beyond them ...' and added: 'The law of enclosure likewise forbids anyone, of whatever class, condition,

31. M. D. Totah, 'The History of Enclosure' in J. Prou and the Benedictine Nuns of the Solesmes Congregation (Eng. trs ed D. Hayes), *Walled About with God* (Gracewing: 2005), pp 25-108, at p 97.

32. S. Schneiders, *New Wineskins: Re-Imagining Religious Life Today* (New York: Paulist Press: 1986), p 23.

33. *Venite seorsum*, 1969, 3.

sex or age, to enter the cloistered area of the convent except in cases provided for by law.' However, the specific cases which followed were open to fairly liberal interpretation, both for egress from and ingress to the enclosure, and horizons began to widen, imperceptibly at first.

Venite seorsum was the guiding legislation for women's enclosure until the Synod on Religious Life took place in Rome in 1994. By this time it was widely recognised that some reform and new legislation were long overdue, and requests for this came into Rome from enclosed nuns all over the world. The Post-Synodal Apostolic Exhortation *Vita consecrata* raised hopes that new legislation on nuns' enclosure, more in tune with the needs of present day life, would soon be forthcoming, especially as the nuns themselves had been asked to express their wishes in this regard. Consequently, there was widespread disappointment with the subsequent document *Verbi sponsa* (1999). In practice, very little had changed and although the Instruction stated that nuns should 'make decisions regarding all that concerns their religious life with freedom of spirit and a sense of responsibility', in practice, constant recourse to higher superiors (either local or in Rome) for permissions and approval seemed to be unavoidable. However, chinks of daylight were beginning to shine in, and, for the first time:

> For [...] just and grave reasons the Superior, with the consent of her Council or the conventual Chapter ... can authorise a departure for whatever time is needed, not however, beyond one week.[34]

At last there was some limited recognition that the nuns themselves might be in a better position to make decisions about their own lives and their needs in their own particular circumstances than an impersonal authority in far-away Rome.

But opinions and practices regarding enclosure were very diverse; some monastic religious saw a rigid interpretation of enclosure as a *sine qua non* of their way of life, and saw this as having been part of monastic life from the outset:

> From the very beginning, however, an instinctive desire for

---

34. *Verbi sponsa*, 17:2.

more radical separation from the world, and a more pro-
nounced aversion to leaving their hermitage or monastery,
and sometimes for having any contact with the outside
world at all was noticeable on the part of nuns. Spiritual directors of nuns, monastic legislators and ecclesial authorities
sanctioned this impulse by recommending, and then prescribing ever stricter enclosure for nuns This enclosure came
to be protected by specific regulations.[35]

As will have been apparent from the forgoing chapters, this
would seem to be an over-simplification, based on a chicken-
and-egg interpretation of historical evidence. However, the
study continues:

> [W]omen are generally more predisposed than men to a
> purely contemplative, enclosed life. The difference between
> men and women in their relationship to place ... is a reflec-
> tion and an extension of their different relationship to the
> universe ... [W]hen women are called to the monastic life
> they can usually cope with enclosure without any harm to
> their joyfulness and their psychological balance. They are
> able to make the most of the benefits enclosure offers for con-
> templation.[36]

This passage is an unequivocal example of fallacious cultural
expectation masquerading as natural law ('the man goes out
hunting; the woman stays at home'). Once again, empirical
evidence does not bear these statements out. For many women,
they had no choice but to 'make the most of the benefits enclosure offers for contemplation.' And the bald statement that
'women ... can usually cope with enclosure without any harm to
their joyfulness and their psychological balance' overlooks the
distressing number of breakdowns in physical and psychological health of those who were not able to do so and paid the price.
Vatican II tacitly acknowledges this in the decree On the Up-to-
Date Renewal of Religious Life:

---

35. M. Deloffre and F. Lemaître, 'The Spirituality of Enclosure' in J. Prou
and the Benedictine Nuns of the Solesmes Congregation, *Walled About
with God*, p 178.
36. M. Deloffre and F. Lemaître, 'The Spirituality of Enclosure', pp 185, 186.

The manner of life, of prayer and of work should be in harmony with the present-day physical and psychological condition of the members.[37]

But the authors of the above-quoted study posed a very apposite question when they asked:

With the exception of Muslim fundamentalists, no one today would actually think of shutting up a woman behind walls or a grille. Why then does the Church still recommend a discipline for cloistered nuns that she does not require of monks or of other consecrated women?[38]

Why, indeed? Is shutting oneself, or others, away behind heavy grilles, locked doors, high walls, hiding behind veils and archaic customs consonant with the inherent dignity of Christian baptism? The authors provide us with their answer, which is the fruit of the traditionally negative view of sexuality and the subordination of marriage to celibacy and, in its invoking of 'privileged signs' and 'exclusive consecration and love', is insulting to the dedicated and committed Christian laity:

Even beyond its practical utility and its undisputed efficacy, however, enclosure is a privileged sign of the exclusive nuptial consecration of nuns. Just as physical purity encourages and signifies that our heart is reserved for its true purpose, so too enclosure both symbolises and ensures physical and spiritual virginity ... Strict enclosure encourages not only physical virginity, but also the purity of heart which corresponds to exclusive love.[39]

One questions the 'practical utility and undisputed efficacy' of enclosure; every enclosed community has stories, ranging from the highly entertaining to the bizarre, of episodes that took place in 'the old days' when enclosure was enforced in all its strictness and rigour. These episodes did nothing whatever to present female monastic life in a positive and humane light to those involved.

The confusion over the theological understanding and prac-

37. *Perfectae caritatis*, 3.
38. M. Deloffre and F. Lemaître, 'The Spirituality of Enclosure', p 184.
39. Ibid, p 198.

tical interpretation of enclosure shown by the above passages was symptomatic of a much deeper confusion, which affected all religious, not just those committed to the enclosed life, with effects that were much more far reaching. The traditional theology of enclosure had been based on a negative worldview: holiness was only seen as possible of attainment by rejecting 'the world', fleeing from it – either by martyrdom or by a life of seclusion and asceticism in 'the desert', and setting up physical barriers to keep it at bay. This is the attitude which Paul satirises in 1 Cor 5: 9-13. Wayne Meeks comments on this:

> In some later ascetic forms of Christianity, including some that appealed to Paul as an example, 'going out of the world' was the chief preoccupation of a Christian. Here it is treated as an impossibility within an argument of *reductio ad absurdum*.[40]

Vatican II brought with it a positive and world-affirming theology which emphasised the goodness of the world and showed the possibility for all people of finding their way to holiness within this world, not outside it. This realisation has been described by Sandra Schneiders as 'foundation-shaking'.[41] She goes on to comment that by this issue of the rethinking of religious life the Council had reversed the centuries-long 'adversary stance' of the church in relation to the world. No longer was the religious life seen as the only 'call to perfection': the Council proposed a 'universal call to holiness' for all the faithful. So 'how were religious to understand themselves and explain their lifestyle to others without recourse to the fundamental premise that religious life was a higher form of Christian life and commitment?'[42]

In the years immediately following the Vatican Council, reli-

40. W. A. Meeks, *The First Urban Christians: The Social World of the Apostle Paul*, p 105. See also his Note 56, p 233: 'Note that Paul does not even entertain the possibility of the sort of withdrawal practised by some 'pure' groups, notably the Qumran Essenes and the Therapeutae Philo describes in his *Vit. cont.*'
41. S. Schneiders, *New Wineskins: Re-Imagining Religious Life Today* (New York: Paulist Press: 1986), p 25.
42. S. Schneiders, *New Wineskins*, p 25.

gious found themselves in a cleft stick. It had always been understood that religious life was an intensification of the Christian commitment made at baptism: religious men and women were, in a sense, the 'shock troops' of the church, called to a life of 'evangelical perfection' by observing not only the gospel commands which are binding on all Christians, but also its precepts and counsels: the traditional vows of poverty, chastity and obedience made by all religious at their profession. Religious men and women, but especially women, represented the church as she saw herself to be: pledged to a life of separation from 'the spirit of the world', the 'perfect society' separate from the 'secular society' of this material world. This separation was lived out in so many concrete ways, which were the hall marks of religious – the easily recognisable dress, living apart in buildings specially constructed for the purpose and the physical separation of enclosure, following a strictly defined rule of life, and having a concentrated period of training and preparation. But now the church authorities had apparently done a *volte-face* – now in sharp contradistinction to the earlier stance, these documents expressed a view which saw 'the world' as good, even holy – what were religious to do in the face of this 'radical reversal of position in regard to its relationship to the world'?[43] Schneiders comments:

> [T]he adaptations of religious life that were mandated by Vatican II ... have effectively destroyed the mysterious subculture of religious life that evoked a certain fascination in Catholics and nonCatholics alike. Exotic dress, cloistered houses, and quaint if not macabre customs have given way to an ordinary lifestyle that no longer offers potential members instant identity or social status.[44]

No longer were religious the 'spiritual elite', pledged to a life of 'evangelical perfection'. Now they discovered that the laity were being called to holiness, too! Johnson comments on this epoch making pronouncement of the Council:

43. S. Schneiders, *New Wineskins*, p 25.
44. S. Schneiders, 'Religious Life: The Dialectic Between Marginality and Transformation', *Spirituality Today*, Winter 1988 Supplement, Vol 40, pp 59-79.

Vatican II made a remarkable breakthrough, retrieving the ancient awareness of the holiness of the whole living community. At the very centre of the council's *Dogmatic Constitution on the Church (Lumen Gentium)* lies a chapter entitled 'the call of the whole church to holiness'. Here it is emphasised that through baptism human persons are put right with God in Christ. Receiving the Spirit, they become sharers in the divine nature. Lest anyone doubt the result, the council says it plainly: 'In this way they are made holy' (n 40). This holiness, furthermore, is essentially the same for everyone. There is not one type of holiness for lay persons and another for those in religious life or ordained ministry.[45]

The result was that some religious, in weariness and disillusionment, gave up the battle, and turned their backs on a way of life which, for whatever reason, no longer had meaning for them. Some, and this was not necessarily the more elderly among their number, took refuge in a return-to-the-past mentality, where security was to be found in a somewhat legalistic mentality of 'keeping the rules' which had worked, apparently, for previous generations. Others took up the challenge of 're-newal and adaptation', returned to their sources, which for some meant encountering those sources for the first time, and tried to put the spirit and charism of their founders to work actively in the present day world, a world very different from that in which their rules had originally been written. Though feeling at times battered and bruised at the criticism from many sources which became their lot, and the lack of support and understanding they sometimes experienced even from the institutional church, and the fewness of new recruits to take up the torch for future generations, they soldiered on.

At least in theory, on paper, the authorities in Rome were sympathetic. Contemporary documentation from Rome gave some kind of lip-service to the fact that to be a faithful daughter of the church does not always or necessarily mean submissive acquiescence to the (at times unreasonable) requirements of an all male hierarchy. So in one of the later papal documents on the enclosure of nuns the following was stated:

---

45. Johnson, *Truly our Sister*, pp 309-310.

> The church recognises every monastery '*sui iuris*' as possessing legitimate juridical autonomy of life and government in order that it may have its own discipline and be capable of preserving intact its own heritage.
>
> Autonomy favours stability of life and the internal unity of every community, and guarantees the best conditions for the exercise of contemplation.
>
> This autonomy is a right of the monastery, which is autonomous by its own nature, and therefore cannot be restricted or diminished by external interventions. Autonomy does not however mean independence from ecclesiastical authority, but is just, right and opportune in order to protect the nature and proper identity of a monastery of wholly contemplative life.[46]

This document, *Verbi sponsa*, actually recognises explicitly that the church today has a 'new vision and perspective' on the life and contribution which women have to play, and states this categorically:

> In the new vision and perspective in which the church today envisages the role and presence of women, it is necessary to overcome, wherever it may still exist, that form of juridical supervision by Orders of men and regular superiors which *de facto* limits the autonomy of monasteries of nuns.
>
> Men superiors are to carry out their task in a spirit of co-operation and humble service, without creating improper submission to themselves, in order that the nuns may make decisions regarding all that concerns their religious life with freedom and a sense of responsibility.[47]

This was very welcome news to the nuns when it came. Unfortunately, the reality did not always correspond with the theory. Whereas in theory 'monasteries are autonomous and independent of one another' and so 'any form of co-ordination between them, with a view to the common good, requires the free accord of the monasteries themselves and the approval of the Holy See',[48] in actual fact alarming things were taking place.

---

46. *Verbi sponsa* (Vatican City: 1999), para 25.
47. *Verbi sponsa* (Vatican City: 1999), para 26.
48. *Verbi sponsa* (Vatican City: 1999), para 25.

Nuns were moved from house to house by male superiors with no prior warning, without either their own consent or that of the receiving monastery being obtained. Nuns were threatened with the closure of their houses without reasons being given, or even when there were no reasons. Elderly sisters who had given fifty and sixty years of their lives to God were turned out of their own houses. 'Apostolic Visitations' were conducted on instructions from Rome, by persons with little or no appropriate experience of religious life themselves and with no understanding of the way of life of those sisters being investigated. These visitations were conducted under conditions of unreasonable secrecy and the consequent reports were sent to superiors in Rome while the nuns involved were not consulted or allowed to see the reports written about them. Houses and funds were appropriated by male clerics. Nuns were told what to eat, what to wear, how to pray and how to conduct the intimate details of their daily lives by male clerics. These abuses all took place in English houses as a result of male 'apostolic visitations'. Ministerial religious in the USA have also been subjected to apostolic visitations which, although conducted by female religious, showed a similar lack of sensitivity and transparency.[49] In these situations there has been no evidence whatever of the fact that in the documents which were supposed to regulate their lives, nuns were being encouraged to 'make decisions regarding all that concerns their religious life with freedom of spirit and a sense of responsibility'.[50] In 1987, Pia Buxton gave a paper to the Annual General Conference of the Major Religious Superiors of England and Wales. Her paper was entitled 'The Feminine in the Community called Church'. In the course of it, she said:

A lifestyle imposed by men upon women speaks of women

---

49. See the five part essay in the *National Catholic Reporter* from 4-8 January 2010 by Sandra Schneiders; available online at http://ncronline.org/node/16441; http://ncronline.org/node/16463; http://ncronline.org/node/16464;http://ncronline.org/node/16465; http://ncronline.org/news/women/religious-life-sharing-jesus-passion-resurrection. Also S. Schneiders, 'The Effects of Women's Experience on their Spirituality', *Spirituality Today*, Summer 1983, vol 35, No 2, pp 100-116.
50. *Verbi sponsa* (Vatican City: 1999), para 26.

as too weak to live the gospel fully, or too threatening to be given freedom in a man-controlled church.[51]

Whereas in the past, the former premise might on occasion have been thought to be true, today there is no doubt but it is the latter conclusion that has to be drawn. Buxton continued:

> [I]t's no good that the church teaches equality between the sexes, if the names we read and the voices we hear, with few exceptions, are male; and if all the decisions are being made by men, even decisions about what women religious should wear, how enclosed they should be, and what prayers they should say.[52]

If this was true in 1987, how much more true today. Abby Stoner concludes her paper on the place of Beguines in medieval society with a remark which is just as apposite for the place of women in the church today: 'an analysis of attitudes towards "femaleness" and its boundaries sheds a great deal of light on the conditions which enable or deny women the fullest opportunities for participation in their society.'[53]

It is one of the arguments of this study that women's monasticism has always found its dynamism and power of renewal from its interaction and engagement with the currents of secular society and contemporary events (even if this has sometimes meant rejection of that society and its standards). As Chittister remarks:

> The relationship between culture and religious life is tightly woven. Across every period of history, religious life has been a source of social enlightenment, a centre for education, a place of personal liberation as well as a place of spiritual growth. At one point in history, religious life was largely the preserve of intensely committed spiritual people who felt that the road to a better life lay in the negation of this one. In a later period, it developed into a harbour for pious widows.

---

51. Pia Buxton, 'The Feminine in the Community Called Church', talk given at the Annual General Conference of the Major Religious Superiors of England and Wales; published in *Signum*, Documentation Service for Religious, Vol 15, No 7, April 17, 1987, p 11.
52. Ibid, p 10.
53. A. Stoner, 'Sisters Between: Gender and the Medieval Beguines' http://userwww.sfsu.edu/~epf/1995/beguine.html

At another moment in time it provided a centre for devout royalty until, by the 11th century in many places monastic life had become in essence the spiritual monopoly of the nobility, the only people who could afford the dowries necessary to support the communities ... religious life grew out of the soil around it.[54]

Although solitude, quietness and simplicity, with a certain amount of seclusion, have always essentially been seen as an absolute *sine qua non* of monastic life, if enclosure is understood and observed as absolutely as these Roman documents suggest, monastic life for women would a prison sentence for life, be cut off from its surroundings and become increasingly anachronistic, eventually atrophying and dying.[55] Just as secular society needs monastic life, so does monasticism need society.

In early monasticism monks and nuns were governed by the same legislation and this was minimal; in the contemporary setting there is no specific legislation whatever for monks, but for nuns there is an *embarras de richesse* – there is almost too much material. The Conference of Vicars for Religious noted this anomaly and commented on it in their *Open Letter to the Conference of Bishops*, written in 2000:

> We do not understand why a distinction has been drawn between men and women contemplatives or the usefulness of any such division – particularly when men's enclosure has not been considered at all in the document.[56]

---

54. J. Chittister, *The Fire in These Ashes*, pp 5, 6.

55. Schneiders makes the following telling comments regarding Thomas Merton and his evolving desire to 'leave the world' for the sake of 'solitude': 'Toward the end of his life he came to realise that "leaving the world" was more an interior project than a change of geography and that a lifestyle that was obligatory for him because of a personal vocation might not be appropriate for another who shared exactly the same ideals and pursued them with equal zeal and generosity ... But toward the end of his life Merton himself acknowledged that leaving the world was less a geographical than a spiritual project'. S. Schneiders, 'Religious Life: The Dialectic Between Marginality and Transformation', *Spirituality Today*, Winter 1988 Supplement, Vol 40, pp 59-79 at p 59.

56. *Open Letter from the Conference of Vicars for Religious to the Conference of the Bishops of England and Wales*, March, 2000.

As the Vicars for Religious noted, *Verbi sponsa* was concerned entirely with the enclosure of nuns; monks were not mentioned. Today we are in an anomalous position: in earlier ages in society in general and in the church in particular, women's position in life was very subordinate to men, and yet religious women retained at least some freedom and autonomy regarding monastic enclosure. However, in the modern world women have attained emancipation in all walks of life and yet the practice of their monastic enclosure is still regulated by men and they are not regarded as responsible or trustworthy in making their own decisions about their observance of enclosure, except in very limited circumstances. Pia Buxton in the course of her previously mentioned paper, said:

> We have a church that is controlled by men – in fact it is male, celibate and clerical in its decision-making and therefore fundamentally lopsided and unwhole in its stance, in its voice and in its authority system. That imbalance between men and women was challenged by Jesus. Please understand me, I believe that there is a place for celibacy and a need for the clerical, and I think men are wonderful. But this defect in the machinery is making the church an anachronism today instead of a sign. The church will not be credible in our culture if it doesn't change its attitude to women, and this must mean in such visible, audible areas as vocabulary, ministry, liturgy and authority.[57]

The changing fortunes and developments in secular society have constantly brought new challenges, new opportunities and new possibilities for women generally. This has also been true, though sometimes in a qualified way, for religious women. This study has demonstrated throughout how their various responses have kept monastic life alive and thriving through the ages. However, if the challenges, opportunities and possibilities of today are to have their full impact for the religious women of today, there has to be serious questioning about the external

---

57. Pia Buxton, 'The Feminine in the Community Called Church', talk given at the Annual General Conference of the Major Religious Superiors of England and Wales; published in *Signum*, Documentation Service for Religious, Vol 15, N 7, April 17, 1987, p. 4.

practices of enclosure, which interpret 'the world' negatively. In its traditional repressive expression, women's enclosure is an anachronism in the twenty-first century and does not reflect the 'new vision and perspective' in which the church claims to envisage the role and presence of women. This is just one aspect of the theology made explicit by the teaching of Vatican II, which has reversed the centuries-old negative worldview according to which matter and the whole material world were regarded with suspicion and had to be kept at arm's length. It has been this dualistic worldview which has seen all created matter as – at best, a distraction, at worst, as evil – and seen women as the source of all temptation and therefore an evil to be shunned, that has led to the despoliation and exploitation of our planet. Now, we begin to see creation – and maybe even women – in a positive light.

According to this vision, the created world is a theophany – a revelation of God, and once we know the created world in this way, it is an impossibility to treat creation as something to be despised and scorned. So if we see created matter as holy and sacred, the search to 'behold the face of God' which is the monastic life, is not consistent either with a worldview which looks on creation with suspicion, or with an indiscriminate and selfish use of material things. A basic simplicity of lifestyle and a certain austerity and concern for the welfare of this earth have always characterised monastic life: every single thing created is embraced and held in being by the love of God – they are not simply 'good things' provided out of God's love for us, for us to use or abuse as we please. As Elizabeth Theokritoff wrote:

> The material world is thus integral to the divine purpose. It is not disposable packaging for the spiritual, or a mere backdrop to the human drama.[58]

The created world has its own relationship with God, having been created by him and having eventually to return to him.

---

58. E. Theokritoff, 'Embodied Word and New Creation: Some Modern Insights Concerning the Material World', in John Behr, Andrew Louth and Dimitri Conomos (eds), *Abba: The Tradition of Orthodoxy in the West, Festschrift for Bishop Kallistos (Ware) of Diokleia* (Crestwood, New York: St Vladimir's Seminary Press, 2003), p 226.

Each of us, and indeed every single creature, even each micro-
scopic grain of sand, is loved by God in a divine and overwhelming manner. Each and every thing in creation reveals in
itself the evolution of the world towards the fullness of Christ.
So as we integrate our own spiritual lives with the life of the
created universe we learn to recognise in every creature a spark
of divine love, unique to its own self.

> [T]here is not an atom in this world, from the meanest speck
> of dust to the greatest star, which does not hold in its core ...
> the thrill ... of its coming into being, of its possessing infinite
> possibilities and of entering into the divine realm, so that it
> knows God, rejoices in him.[59]

In this perception of creation, the whole of the created world
is sacred. It is not appropriate for us to treat it with disdain or
mistrust: we have a divinely given responsibility towards the
material world and it is where we find God. Fyodor Dostoy-
evsky's Father Zosima speaks about the 'merciful heart which
burns with love for the entire cosmos' because it is God's
creation. We can no longer sing with true authenticity such
hymns as 'O bello Dio, Signor del Paradiso', even if they were composed by saints such as Alphonsus Mary Ligouri, when they
contain lines such as 'No object here below / Awakens my desire
... The world I could despise / Though it were all of gold', or
Francis Stanfield's 'Sweet Sacrament Divine' with its wish that
'Sweet light, so shine on us we pray / that earthly joys may fade
away.' It is precisely in our 'earthly joys' that God sheds his light
upon us and reveals himself to us, not in some 'spiritual' world
removed from our daily, earthly existence. This is Gnosticism
revisited. These hymns, and many more like them, expressed
the spirituality of previous generations, a spirituality which was
somehow detached from the reality of this present world and
underpinned the practice of monastic enclosure for women, but
the theological understanding they articulate is no longer adequate for today.

---

59. Metropolitan Anthony, 'Body and Matter in Spiritual Life', in
Sacrament and Image (London: Fellowship of St Alban and St Sergius,
1987), p 41, quoted in E. Theokritoff, op. cit, p 223.

CHAPTER TEN

Conclusion

In this book we have explored the theme of the religious experience of monastic women and have examined the contribution made specifically by women down through the ages of the church. We have seen the difficulties women have experienced throughout the Christian centuries in having this religious experience acknowledged as authentic. To return once more to Pia Buxton, she has this to say on the way women relate to God and the attitude of (some) of the male saints of the church to this:

> Augustine, Aquinas, Bernard all speak about the spirituality of women and seem to imply that they have none. Mary Ward, who encountered a similar sort of response in the early 17th century wrote: 'There was a gentleman who lately came from England whom I heard say he would not for all the world be a woman because a woman cannot apprehend God – but I smiled for the experience I had to the contrary.'[1]

And all religious women would smile with her. This dynamic woman, Mary Ward, who pioneered both religious life for women and education for girls, founded a religious congregation in England in the early 17th century without enclosure or recognisable habit, which was so unthinkable at that time that the sisters were known as 'galloping girls' and 'Jesuitesses'. She was silenced and was sent to prison because she was inspired to begin a new way of life for women in the church, with an active apostolate. But her work bore fruit after her death and today the 'Institute of the Blessed Virgin Mary' has become the 'Congregation of Jesus', at the forefront of education and of the emancipation of women religious. She was emphatically non-monastic, but she is an inspiration to all women religious in her tenacity of purpose.

This study has followed the course of monastic life for women from the very beginning, understanding it in its very

---

1. Buxton, 'The Feminine in the Community Called Church', p 7.

broadest sense, as the search for God. We have seen women at first living a life of consecrated virginity secluded in their own homes, and then gradually gathering together with others of like mind to form the earliest religious communities, or continuing to live an isolated hermit existence, but now in the solitude of the desert, in Egypt or in Palestine. This basic way of life found different expression with the wealthy, cultured and educated women of late classical society and the monasteries they used their wealth to found in Rome, Asia Minor, and Palestine under the direction of churchmen such as Jerome and Augustine. After the fall of the Roman Empire, the stormy upheavals caused by the subsequent pagan invasions in Northern Europe and the conversion of those pagan tribes to Christianity, monasteries, many of them double, headed by women flourished in Britain, Ireland and Gaul.

We then moved to the Middle Ages when renewed interest in simple gospel living and new economic patterns in the feudal society of medieval Europe gave birth to many new forms of religious life, among them that of the Franciscan friars and their sisters, the Poor Clares. The slowly changing position of women in society during this time, and the increased opportunities for some education, made possible the phenomenon of the medieval mystical tradition, where women had such a prominent part to play. Nearer our own times, the disastrous conflicts which brought the nations of the world, and especially Europe, into such violent and bloody struggles in the twentieth century, did not leave women's monastic life unscathed, and women bore witness with their lives to the teaching of Christ. Just as these wars inevitably brought women in secular society into positions of equality with their men folk, so did they gradually begin to affect the lives of cloistered women

We have seen how women monastics through the ages have had their own very particular contribution to make to the life of the church and we have examined the lives of all these women under the title 'women of the church'. But the question still remains: to what extent were they? Is this title a true reflection of their understanding of their role in the church? Even though most of them would have emphatically seen themselves as such and protested the fact vehemently, there is abundant evidence that the institutional church had severe problems with many of the women who have appeared in these pages and their apparent rejection of, or antagonism towards, ecclesiastical authority.

Many of the desert mothers went for long years without the sacraments of the church or, apparently, without participating in the church's communal worship, even that of the Eucharist; some of the religious women of the late classical era were very high-handed in administrating their large fortunes and although they remained very much under the influence of their male spiritual mentors, they rejected the ideals of the secular society which surrounded them in deciding for themselves how they were going to live their lives: Etheldreda of Ely steadfastly refused to give her two husbands their marital rights, according to the understanding of matrimony as taught by the church; Clare of Assisi and Agnes of Prague fought the highest authority in the church relentlessly and with determination throughout their lives to have their cherished ideals of poverty and non-appropriation recognised by the church. Clare's famous dictum: 'Holy Father, absolve me from my sins but not from following Jesus Christ' echoes in ringing tones down the centuries. Teresa of Avila and other mystics risked the wrath of the Inquisition, and some even faced the prospect of death by burning at the stake rather than deny the reality of the experiences they firmly believed to be supernatural and genuinely of God, but which were called into question by church authorities.

Coming into our own era, Elisabeth Feodorovna several times had her proposed way of life rejected by the Holy Synod (and also had her monastic habit designed by one of the leading artists of her day: 'With a last touch of worldliness, for she had been a woman of extreme elegance and great taste, she had the dress of her Order designed by Nesterov, a Muscovite painter, a long pearl-grey robe of fine wool, a lawn wimple which framed the face and a white woollen veil that fell into long classical folds'[2]). Maria Skobtsova was such a rebel against organised religious life that she only agreed to the monastic tonsure on

---

2. F. Yusupov, *Memoirs*, quoted in A. Maylunas and S. Mironenko, *A Lifelong Passion: Nicholas and Alexandra, Their Own Story* (London, Weidenfeld and Nicolson, 1996), p 333.

condition she would not have to live enclosed and she declared: 'At the Last Judgement I will not be asked whether I practised asceticism, nor how many bows I have made before the divine altar.'

Perhaps at least part of the problem is that the church's image of a faithful woman may at times differ from that of the women themselves, and the church is not always prepared to listen to what the women have to say. In the preceding pages we have seen women of courage, vision and ingenuity who have not always been appreciated by those in ecclesiastical authority, who would have preferred them to be meek, docile and unquestioning. Although Labarge is writing about the nuns of the Middle Ages when she refers to 'the hope of many ecclesiastics that nuns would be submissive, quiet and invisible in their convents', the same could be said of many ecclesiastical authorities today. However, Labarge goes on to comment that: 'the reality was often quite different and much more interesting.'[3] This too, could certainly be said of nuns today.

The women whose lives we have been studying lived at very different times in world history and in the history of the church. Some of them had close relationships with the men who were influential figures in their lives, but the actual boundaries of those relationships differed greatly. Some, such as Paula and Eustochium, acquiesced completely to this male influence; others such as Etheldreda reacted differently according to the status of the men. Etheldreda accepted Wilfrid's spiritual guidance, but refused to let her husband dictate the terms of their marriage. Radegund escaped from a marriage which was brutal and abusive. Clare described herself as the 'Little Plant' of Francis, but in actual fact was a strong and independent woman in her own right. Most of these women refused to let themselves be defined by the men or by the relationship. They were, on the whole, women who set their own parameters and their own agendas, even if these were sometimes influenced by circumstances over which they themselves had little control.

Some clerics (notably those who compose Vatican legislative documentation) seem unappreciative of the fact that, on the

---

3. M. Wade Labarge, *A Small Sound of the Trumpet*, p 101.

whole, religious women love their chosen way of life and are intent on living it with dedication and commitment, not looking for 'loopholes' and ways of circumventing the letter of the law, but ways that will let the Holy Spirit speak through them and their lives to the world of today. They wish to live their lives authentically and with intelligence and in ways that are appropriate and make sense to the world in which we live. We should not be seeking to live in the way that we believe we should through 'loopholes'. The *Open Letter from the Conference of Vicars for Religious* understood this point and makes it clear:

> We recognise that men and women freely offer themselves, as a response to a call from God, to this hidden life and that they, most of all, would wish to maintain a quality of enclosure which frees them to live their elected life.[4]

They rightly understood that 'enclosure' has to be understood as a matter of 'quality' rather than 'quantity' and has to be interpreted as an issue of 'freedom' rather than enforced claustration.

We quoted Joan Chittister in the Introduction to this book; we quote her again in the Conclusion:

> We have not lost the virtues of the past; we have simply shaped them into ones necessary to our own times. Now we must own these new ones and form ourselves in them and carry them proudly. Religious life is not a life being betrayed in this period; it is a life being begun again, under the most difficult of circumstances, with the highest of motives and the most profound, the most brilliant of results. Religious of this period have repopulated the cities of the world with new services, with a new kind of presence, with new voice, with unflagging energy, with total trust and with great cost to themselves as people. Benefactors disappeared, critics decried them, membership declined, and, in some cases, even the church abandoned religious because, ironically, at the direction of the church, they followed the Spirit to the future rather than to the past.[5]

---

4. *Open Letter from the Conference of Vicars for Religious to the Conference of Bishops*, March, 2000.
5. J. Chittister, *The Fire in These Ashes*, pp 174-175.

Just as the women who have figured in this study were raised up by God at critical periods in the history of the church and by their fidelity to the Spirit helped religious life to adapt to the social and cultural needs and pressures of the times, so women religious are struggling to do the same in the church today. Peter Brown, writing of another critical era in the life of the world and of the church, poses the perennial problem like this:

> How to draw on a great past without smothering change. How to change without losing one's roots.[6]

This is the problem monastic women are confronting today. Perhaps the great monastic women of the past can be an inspiration in their fidelity and in their daring to be different, even when the church was not sympathetic to their desires. I have approached this subject as an historian, but always mindful of Chittister's words of warning to historians where she expresses similar sentiments to Brown, but in different terms:

> History is a kind ally to religious life but an albatross of immense proportions at the same time. A sense of history frees religious life from absolutising its 19th-century forms. At the same time, its long history can also constrain religious life to enshrine a past grown quaint but useless.[7]

What I have endeavoured to do in these pages is not to 'enshrine a past grown quaint but useless', but to show how women's monastic life down the ages, by interacting with the society of its own time, has taken different forms through the centuries. Central to this thesis is the argument that in order to do this today, religious life for women must have the freedom to interact with today's society. This in no way negates the essential withdrawal and seclusion required for the contemplative life, but argues that if women are cloistered as absolutely as some interpretations of church law seem to require, then their way of life will atrophy and die.

The women who appear in these pages came from a variety

6. P. Brown, *The World of Late Antiquity AD 150-750* (London: Thames and Hudson, 1971, 1991), p 8.
7. J. Chittister, *The Fire in These Ashes*, p 4.

of social backgrounds, from the highest to the lowest. We have met queens, princesses and grand duchesses, high born ladies of wealth, position, power and influence, rubbing shoulders with slaves and serving women, those with no power at all according to the standards of this world. They were, all of them, women of their own particular times, with all the inherent limitations of specific social and cultural eras that that implies. But the very fact that we know their names and at least some details of their lives as individuals shows that they were also women beyond and outside the restrictions of their own times, not allowing themselves to be confined and restricted by social and cultural restraints. They were women of their own times and women for all times. As such, they have a message for us today.

Perhaps the monastic women of today can take heart from the fact that although the model of religious life traditionally held up to them by male spiritual writers for their imitation has been that of the Virgin Mary as she appeared at Nazareth; humble, obedient, submissive,[8] there is also another model. Feminist theologians today are rethinking the role of Mary and her situation in life. Elizabeth Johnson sets out the new dynamic in marian studies:

> [W]omen have been actively creating a discourse of Mary, friend of God and prophet from female experiences and especially the lives of poor women. Instead of using her to develop a new theology of 'woman' or stressing her stereotypical feminine virtues, this theology opens up space for women to claim their concrete faith history and equal participation in the church. Instead of separating her out as an unreachable paragon, it connects her with the human race, women in particular, seeing her blessedness as a sign of the capacity of all women to bear the image and likeness of God.[9]

And in other places in scripture we find women of spirit, dynamism and fire – in the Old Testament they hastened the coming of the Messiah by their bravery and determination – Jael, Abigail, Esther, Judith. In the New Testament, by word and

---

8. Luke 1:26-38.
9. E. A. Johnson, *Truly Our Sister*, p 321.

by example they spread the message of the kingdom – the woman who was a sinner, the Samaritan woman, the Canaanite woman ... and Mary herself who was the strong and valiant woman who did not desert her disgraced son but stood courageously at the foot of the cross as he died as a common criminal, and was also the praying woman who was present, with several others, at the heart of the church when the Holy Spirit brought the disruptive power of fire and wind to transform the frightened apostles.

One of the most significant, but unfortunately also one of the most contentious, issues at the present time is the role of women in the world and in the church, both present and future:

> The need presently is recognition of women in their capacity to interpret the human venture at its most basic level in the context of the universe and the planet earth. The family, child-bearing and child-rearing, will always be a central focus of human concerns. Yet for women especially a new range of their activities is needed both for themselves and for the larger destinies of the human-Earth venture. We cannot do without those special insights that women offer in every phase of human existence ...
>
> The rise of movements such as feminism and ecofeminism has already altered all the basic professions and social institutions throughout the industrialised countries of the world. As this participation increases throughout the world, as women are liberated from the oppressions they have long endured, as women reach new levels of personal fulfilment, a new energy will undoubtedly be felt throughout the Earth. While we cannot know just what the consequences will be, there is reason to hope that this will be a vast creative and healing energy.[10]

This 'vast creative and healing energy' must spring at least in part from the consequences of the renewed and revitalised monasticism which it is in the power of religious women to offer in and to the church. Throughout the history of the church,

---

10. B. Swimme and T. Berry, *The Universe Story* (London: Penguin Books, 1992), pp 257-258.

women have continued to pray for the spread of the kingdom and to work for it by their courage, zeal and fortitude – their determination to be truly the authentic women God created them to be, and also to be truly committed to the church. Today they continue this tradition: they are committed Christian women seeking to respond wholeheartedly and creatively to the call of the Christ within their minds: the seat of the Logos.[11] They are indeed, totally committed women of that church, and wish to be women who bring new life and richness to the church. The church would be far poorer if she did not have religious life, but how women religious construe themselves and their *modus vivendi* is at a crucial stage in its evolution. If religious life for women in its specifically monastic form is to survive into the future, we have to have the courage to face hard questions, to which, as yet, we have only partial answers.

---

11. I am indebted for this phrase to Professor Tom O'Loughlin.

Bibliography

BIBLICAL SOURCES
Holy Bible: New Revised Standard Version (London, Harper Collins: 1998).

PRIMARY SOURCES
Anon, *Account of the martyrdom of the holy martyrs of Carthage*, Chap 18. 20-21: edit. Van Beek, Noviomagi, 1936.

Anon, *Acts of the Martyrdom of Justin & Companions*, Chap 1-5: PG 6, 1566-1571.

Anon, 'The Monastery of Tallaght,' ed E. J. Gwynn, and W. J. Purton, *Proceedings of the Royal Irish Academy* 29 C (1911), pp 115–179.

Anon, 'The Rule of Ailbe of Emly', trs J. O'Neill, *Ériu* 3 (1907), pp 92-115.

Anon, 'The Rule of Carthage', trs MacEclaise, *Irish Ecclesiastical Record* 27 (1910), pp 495–517.

Anon, 'The Teaching of Máel Rúain' and 'The Rule of the Céli Dé', ed E. J. Gwynn, *Hermathena* 44, Second Supplemental volume (Dublin: Hodges, Figgis & Co, 1927).

Anon, 'Two Monastic Rules', trs J. Strachan, *Ériu* 2 (1905), 227-229.

Anon., *Sacrum commercium sancti Francisci cum domina Paupertate* (The Sacred Exchange between Saint Francis and the Lady Poverty) in Regis Armstrong, J. A. Wayne Hellman, W. J. Short (eds), *Francis of Assisi: Early Documents* Vol 1: *The Saint* (New York: New City Press: 1999), pp 521-554.

Ambrose, *De uirginibus*, 1.7.

Anon, *Vita sanctissimi Ceolfridi abbatis [auctore anonymo]*, ed. C. Plummer, *Venerabilis Bedae opera Historia I* (Oxford: OUP, 1896), 388-404.

Basil, 'The Long Rules', in *Ascetical Works*, trs M. Wagner (Washington: Catholic University of America Press, 1962).

Bede, *Historia ecclesiastica gentis Anglorum* (eds B. Colgrave and R. A. B. Mynors; Oxford: Clarendon Press, 1969, repr. 1998).

Bede, *Life of Cuthbert*, (trs J. F. Webb), in D. Farmer ed, *The Age of Bede* (London: Penguin, 1965, repr. 1998).

Benedict, *Regula*, trs Justin McCann (London: Sheed and Ward, 1976).

Benedict, *Regula*, trs D. Ph. Schmitz (Maredsous, 1962 [third edition]).

Cassian, *De institutis coenobiorum*, ed M. Petschenig, CSEL 17 (Vienna: Academia Litterarum Caesarea, 1888).

Catherine of Siena, *Dialogue: On Divine Revelation*, Ch 167, *Gratiarum actio ad Trinitatem*: ed Lat, Ingolstadii 1583, f 290v-291.

Clare, *Testament*, Regis J. Armstrong (ed), *Clare of Assisi: Early Documents* (New York: Paulist Press, 1988).

Cyprian, *Letter* 6, 1-2. CSEL 3, 480-482.

Eddius Stephanus, *Life of Wilfrid*, (trs J. F. Webb), in D. Farmer ed, *The Age of Bede* (London: Penguin, 1965, repr. 1998).

Eusebius of Caesarea, *Hist. Eccl.* 5. 1. 1-63.

Eusebius of Emesa, *Homilia* 7, 13 (Amand de Mendieta, 784).

Francis of Assisi, 'The Later Rule', Regis J. Armstrong and Ignatius Brady (eds), *Francis and Clare; the Complete Works* (New York: Paulist Press: 1982).

Gregory of Tours, *The History of the Franks*, trs Lewis Thorpe (London: Penguin Books, 1974).

Ignatius of Antioch, *Letter to the Romans*, Cap. 4, 1-2; 6, 1-8,: Funk 1, 217-223.

Óengus mac Óengobann, *Félire Óengusso (The Martyrology of Óengus the Culdee)*, W. Stokes ed, London, (Henry Bradshaw Society 29, 1905; repr. Dublin: DIAS, 1984).

Palladius: *Historia Lausiaca*, trs and annotated by Robert T. Meyer (London: Longmans, Green and Co, 1965).

Peter Damian, *Serm 3, De sancto Georgio*, PL 144, 567-571.

Clare of Assisi: Early Documents, Regis J. Armstrong, ed, (New York: Paulist Press, 1988).

The Lady: Clare of Assisi, Early Documents, Regis J. Armstrong, ed, (New York, London: New City Press, 2006).

Bernard of Clairvaux on the Song of Songs 1-4 (Kalamazoo: Cistercian Publications, 1971-80).

Decretum Gratiani

Hadewijch: *The Complete Works*, trs.Mother Columba Hart, CWS (London: SPCK, 1980).

Julian of Norwich: *Revelations of Divine Love*, trans. C. Wolters, (London: Penguin Books, 1966).

Julian of Norwich, *Showings* (trs and ed Edmund Colledge and James Walsh) (New York: Paulist Press, 1978).

Matthew of Paris, *Chronicles of Matthew of Paris: Monastic Life in the Thirteenth Century*, trs and ed R. Vaughan (Gloucester: Alan Sutton Press, 1984).

Mechtild of Magdeburg, *The Flowing Light of the Godhead*, trs C. M. Galvani, ed S Clark, (New York: Garland, 1991).

Origen, *Exhortation to Martyrdom*, Nn 41-42: PG 11, 618-619.

Teresa of Jesus, *Conceptions of the Love of God* in *The Complete Works of St Teresa of Jesus* Vol II, trs and ed E. Allison Peers (London: Sheed and Ward, 1946).

Teresa of Jesus, *Autobiography*, trs E. Allison Peers (New York: Doubleday, 1991).

Teresa of Jesus, *The Way of Perfection*, trs and ed E. Allison Peers (New York: Doubleday: 1991).

Teresa of Jesus, *The Interior Castle*, ed E. Allison Peers (New York: Doubleday: 1972).

Tertullian, *De cultu feminarum, Corpus Christianorum, Series Latina*, vol 1, (Turnholt: Typographia Brepols, 1954).

Thérèse of Lisieux, *Autobiography of a Saint*, trs R. Knox (London: Harvill Press, 1958).

SECONDARY SOURCES

Anson, J., 'The Female Transvestite in Early Monasticism: the Origin and Development of a Motif', *Viator* 5, (1969), pp 1-32.

Bartoli, M., *Clare of Assisi*, trs Frances Teresa Downing (London: Darton, Longman and Todd, 1993).

Bartoli, M., *Chiara: Una donna tra silenzio e memoria* (Edizioni San Paolo, 2001, 2003), Eng. trs F. T. Downing, *Saint Clare; Beyond the Legend* (Cincinnati: St Anthony's Messenger Press, 2010).

Baumstark, A., *Comparative Liturgy*, B. Botte ed, trs F. L. Cross (Westminster: Newman, 1958).

Beard, M., 'The Sexual Status of Vestal Virgins', *The Journal of Roman Studies*, Vol 70 (1980), pp 12-27.

Beer, F., *Women and Mystical Experience in the Middle Ages* (Woodbridge: The Boydell Press, 1992).

Behr-Sigel, E., 'Mary and Women', *Sobornost: Eastern Churches Review* 23 (2001).

Benedict XVI: Encyclical *Spe Salvi: On Christian Hope* (Libreria Editrice Vaticana, Citta del Vaticano: 2007); Eng. trs by CTociety, London: 2007.

Bindoff, S. T., *Tudor England* (London: Penguin, 1976).

Bitel, L. M., 'Women's Monastic Enclosures in Early Ireland: a Study of Female Spirituality and Male Monastic mentalities', *Journal of Medieval History* 12, (1986), pp 15-36.

Blamires, A., (ed), *Woman Defamed and Woman Defended: An Anthology of Medieval Texts* (Oxford: Clarendon Press, 1992).

Bolton, B., 'Mulieres sanctae', in *Studies in Church History*, Vol 10 (Oxford, Blackwell, 1973), pp 77-95.

Bowie, F. (ed, trs O. Davies), *Beguine Spirituality: Mystical Writings of Mechtild of Magdeburg, Beatrice of Nazareth and Hadewijch of Brabant* (New York, Crossroad Publishing Company, 1990).

Bradshaw, P., *The Origins of the Daily Office* (Alcuin Club Annual Reports, 1978).

Bradshaw, P., *Daily Prayer in the Early Church*, Alcuin Club Connections 63 (London: SPCK, 1981).

Bradshaw, P., *The Search for the Origins of Christian Worship: Sources and Methods for the Study of the Early Liturgy* (London: SPCK, 1992).

Bradshaw, P., *Two Ways of Praying* (Nashville, Tennessee: Abingdon Press, 1995).

Bradshaw, P., *Early Christian Worship: a basic introduction to ideas and practice* (London: SPCK, 1996).

Brakke, D., *Athanasius and Politics of Asceticism* (Oxford: Clarendon Press, 1995).

Bray, D. A., 'The Manly Spirit of St Monenna' in R. Black, W. Gillies and R. Ó Maolalaigh (eds), *Celtic Connections: proceedings of the tenth international congress of Celtic Studies* (East Linton: Tuckwell Press, 1999).

Breviarium Romano-Seraphicum, Ex Decreto S. Concilii Tridentini Restitutum (Augustae Taurinorum, MCMXXVI).

Brianchaninov, I., *The Arena: An Offering to Contemporary Monasticism* (Madras: Diocesan Press, 1970).

Brock, S. P., 'Early Syrian Asceticism,' *Numen* 20 (1973).

Brown, P., *The World of Late Antiquity AD 150-750* (London: Thames and Hudson, 1971, 1991).

Brown, P., *The Cult of the Saints: Its Rise and Function in Latin Christianity* (Chicago: University of Chicago Press, 1981)

Brown, P., *The Body and Sexuality: Men, Women and Sexual Renunciation in Early Christianity* (New York: Columbia University Press, 1988).

Brown, R., 'The Genealogy of Jesus Christ' (Matthew 1: 1-17), *Worship* 60 (November 1986), pp 482-490.

Bruce, J., Prophecy, *Miracles, Angels and Heavenly Lights? The Eschatology, Pneumatology and Missiology of Adomnán's Life of St Columba* (Carlisle: Paternoster Press, 2004).

Brundage, J. A., *Medieval Canon Law* (London, Longman: 1995).

Bullough, V. L., 'Transvestites in the Middle Ages', *American Journal of Sociology* 79, (1974), pp 1381-1394.

Buxton, P. 'The Feminine in the Community Called Church', talk given at the Annual General Conference of the Major Religious Superiors of England and Wales; published in *Signum*, Documentation Service for Religious, Vol 15, No 7, April 17, 1987.

Callam, D., 'Clerical Continence in the Fourth Century', *Theological Studies*, Vol 41, (1980), pp.3-50.

Canon Law: Letter and Spirit; A Practical Guide to the Code of Canon Law (London: The Canon Law Society of Great Britain and Ireland, 1995).

Carney, M., *The First Franciscan Woman: Clare of Assisi and her Form of Life* (Quincy University, Illinois: Franciscan Press, 1993).

Carver, M. (ed), *The Cross Goes North: Processes of Conversion in Northern Europe, AD 300-1300* (York: York Medieval Press, 2003).

Casey, M., 'Thoughts on Monasticism's Possible Futures' in P. Hart (ed), *A Monastic Vision for the 21st Century: Where Do We Go From Here?* (Michigan, Kalamazoo: Cistercian Publications, 2006), pp 23-42.

Castelli, E., 'Virginity and its Meaning for Women's Sexuality in Early Christianity', *Journal of Feminist Studies in Religion*, Vol 2, No 1 (Spring, 1986), pp 61-88.

Chittister, J., *The Fire in These Ashes: A Spirituality of Contemporary Religious Life* (Kansas City: Sheed and Ward, 1995).

Chitty, D. J., *The Desert a City: An Introduction to the Study of Egyptian and Palestinian Monasticism under the Christian Empire* (New York: St Vladimir's Seminary Press, 1999).

Chryssavgis, J., 'From Egypt to Palestine: Discerning a Thread of Spiritual Direction', in J. Behr, A. Louth and D. Conomos (eds), *Abba: The Tradition of Orthodoxy in the West, Festschrift for Bishop Kallistos (Ware) of Diokleia* (Crestwood, New York: St Vladimir's Seminary Press, 2003), pp 299-315.

Churton, T., *The Gnostics* (London: Weidenfeld and Nicolson: 1987).

Clark, E. A., (ed and trs), *The Life of Melania the Younger: Studies in Women and Religion* (Edwin Mellen Press, 1984).

Clark, E. A., 'Women', in E. Ferguson (ed), *Encyclopedia of Early Christianity* (Chicago, St James Press: 1990), pp 940-943.

Clark, E. and H. Richardson, *Women and Religion: The Original Sourcebook of Women in Christian Thought* (San Francisco, HarperCollins; rev ed 1996).

Clark, G., *Women in Late Antiquity: Pagan and Christian Lifestyles* (Oxford, Clarendon Press, 1993).

Clément, O., *The Roots of Christian Mysticism* (London: New City, 1993).

Cohn-Sherbok, D., *Judaism: History, Belief and Practice* (London: Routledge, 2003).

Collicutt McGrath, J., *Jesus and the Gospel Women* (London, SPCK, 2009).

Condren, M., *The Serpent and the Goddess: Women, Religion and Power in Celtic Ireland* (San Francisco: 1989).

Cooper, K., 'Insinuations of Womanly Influence: An Aspect of the Christianization of the Roman Aristocracy', *The Journal of Roman Studies*, Vol 82 (1992), pp 150-164.

Cowles, V., *The Romanovs* (London, Harper and Row: 1971).

Crichton, J. D., H. E. Winstone, and J. R. Ainslie (eds), *English Catholic Worship* (London: Geoffrey Chapman, 1979).

Crichton, J. D., *Christian Celebration* (London: Geoffrey Chapman, 1981, 1985).

Crichton, J. D., *Understanding the Prayer of the Church* (London: Geoffrey Chapman, 1976, 1993).

Cross, F. L. (ed), *Oxford Dictionary of the Christian Church* (3rd ed by E. A. Livingstone, Oxford, 1997).

Dalrymple, J., *Costing Not Less Than Everything* (London: Darton, Longman and Todd, 1991).

Davies, O. and F. Bowie, *Celtic Christian Spirituality* (London: SPCK, 1995).

de Bhaldraithe, E., 'The Three Orders of Irish Saints: New Light from Early Church Studies', *Milltown Studies* 61, (2008), pp 58-83.

De Gank, R., *Life of Beatrice of Nazareth* (Cistercian Fathers Series, Number 50), (Kalamazoo, Michigan: Cistercian Publications, 1991).

De Gank, R., *Beatrice of Nazareth in her Context* (Cistercian Studies Series, Number 121), (Kalamazoo, Michigan: Cistercian Publications, 1991).

De Gank, R., *Towards Unification with God* (Cistercian Studies Series,

Number 122) (Kalamazoo, Michigan: Cistercian Publications, 1991).

Delehaye, H., *The Legends of the Saints* (Sociéte des Bollandistes, 1955, repr. Dublin: Four Courts Press, 1998).

Dekkers, E., 'Were the Early Monks Liturgical?' *Collectanea Cisterciensia* 22 (1960), pp 120–137.

Demacopoulos, G. E., *Five Models of Spiritual Direction in the Early Church* (Notre Dame, Indiana: University of Notre Dame Press, 2007).

Deming, W., *Paul on Marriage and Celibacy: The Hellenistic background of 1 Corinthians 7* (Cambridge, CUP, 1995).

de Paor, L., *Saint Patrick's World* (Dublin: Four Courts Press, 1993, 1996).

Dodds, E. R., *Pagan and Christian in an Age of Anxiety* (Cambridge: CUP, 1965).

Donahue, A., 'Cenobites', in *New Catholic Encyclopaedia* 3 (Washington: 2003 [second ed]), p.334.

Douglas, M., *Purity and Danger* (London, Routledge and Kegan Paul: 1966).

Downing, F. T., *This Living Mirror: Reflections on Clare of Assisi* (London, Darton, Longman and Todd, 1995).

Duchesne, L., *Christian Worship: its Origin and Evolution* (London: SPCK, 1904).

Dunn, G. D., 'The Elements of Ascetical Widowhood: Augustine's *De bono viduitatis and Epistula* 130' in W. Mayer, P. Allen and L. Cross (eds), *Prayer and Spirituality in the Early Church*, Vol 4: *The Spiritual Life* (Strathfield, NSW: St Paul's Publications, 2006), pp 247-256.

Dunn, M., *The Emergence of Monasticism* (Oxford: Blackwell, 2000).

Dyer, J., 'Monastic Psalmody of the Middle Ages', *Revue Bénédictine* 99 (1989), 41–74.

Ehrensperger, K., *That we may be Mutually Encouraged: Feminism and the New Perspective in Pauline Studies* (London: T & T Clark, 2004).

Elm, S., *'Virgins of God' The Making of Asceticism in Late Antiquity* (Oxford: Clarendon Press, 1994).

Epp, E. J., *Junia: The First Woman Apostle* (Augsburg Fortress Publishers: 2005).

Epp, E. J., 'Junia' in Daniel Patte (ed) *The Cambridge History of Christianity* (Cambridge: CUP, 2010), p 668.

Ernst, A. M., 'Which Way to the Tomb of Jesus? Martha as Myrrhbearer in Image, Text and Liturgy' in W. Mayer, P. Allen and L. Cross (eds), *Prayer and Spirituality in the Early Church*, Vol 4: *The Spiritual Life* (Strathfield, NSW: St Paul's Publications, 2006), pp 85-99.

Farmer, D. F., ed and trs, 'The Anonymous History of Abbot Ceolfrith' in *The Age of Bede* (London: Penguin, 1965, repr. 1983, 1988, 1998).

Farr, C. A., 'Worthy Women on the Ruthwell Cross: Woman as Sign in Early Anglo Saxon Monasticism in Karkov, Ryan and Farrell (eds), *The Insular Tradition* (Albany, New York, 1997).

Fell, C., *Women in Anglo-Saxon England* (London: British Museum, 1981).

Ferguson, E., 'Martyr, Martyrdom' in E. Ferguson (ed), *Encyclopedia of Early Christianity* (Chicago: St James Press, 1990), pp 575-580.

Follett, W., *Céli Dé in Ireland: Monastic Writing and Identity in the Early Middle Ages* (Woodbridge: Boydell and Brewer, 2006).

Fortini, A., *Francis of Assisi* (trs H. Moak) (New York, Crossroads: 1981).

Fuchs, E. 'Marginalization, Ambiguity, Silencing: The Story of Jephthah's Daughter', *Journal of Feminist Studies in Religion*, Vol 5, Pt 1, 1989, pp.35-45.

Fujita, N., *A Crack in the Jar: What Ancient Jewish Documents tell us about the New Testament* (New York, Paulist Press: 1986).

Gibbon, E., *The Decline and Fall of the Roman Empire* (London: Penguin Classics: 1985).

Goehring, J. E., 'Monasticism' in E. Ferguson (ed), *Encyclopedia of Early Christianity* (Chicago, St James Press: 1990), pp 612-619.

Gould, G., 'Women in the Writings of the Fathers: Language, Belief and Reality' in W. J. Sheils and D. Woods (eds), *Women in the Church* (Oxford: Blackwell, 1990).

Gribomont, J., 'Cenobitism' in *New Catholic Encyclopaedia* 3, pp 334-5.

Haddon, A. W., 'Canonization' in W. Smith and S. Cheetham eds, *A Dictionary of Christian Antiquities* (London: John Murray, 1908), p 283.

Hale, R., 'Monasticism' in P. Sheldrake (ed), *The New SCM Dictionary of Christian Spirituality* (London: SCM Press, 2005).

Hall, D., *Women and the Church in Medieval Ireland* (Dublin: Four Courts Press, 2003).

Hart, P., (ed), *A Monastic Vision for the 21st Century: Where Do We Go From Here?* (Michigan, Kalamazoo: Cistercian Publications, 2006).

Hartung, E. F., 'St. Francis and Mediaeval Medicine', *Annals of Medical History* 1935, 7, p. 85-91.

Herity, M., 'The Buildings and Layout of Early Irish Monasteries before the year 1000' in *Monastic Studies* 14 (1983), 247-284.

Hollis, S., *Anglo-Saxon Women and the Church: Sharing a Common Fate* (Woodbridge: The Boydell Press, 1992).

Horner, T. J., 'Jewish Aspects of the Protoevangelium of James', *Journal of Early Christian Studies*, Vol 12, No 3, Fall 2004, pp 313-335.

Horowitz, M. C., 'The Image of God in Man: Is Woman Included?' *The Harvard Theological Revue*, Vol 72, No 3/4 (Jul-Oct, 1979), pp 175-206

Hunter, D., 'Resistance to the Virginal Ideal in Late-Fourth Century Rome: The Case of Jovinian', *Theological Studies* 48 (1987), pp 45-64.

Hunter Blair, P., *Northumbria in the Days of Bede* (London: 1976, repr. Felinfach: Llanerch Publishers, 1996).

Hymns for Prayer and Praise (Norwich, The Canterbury Press, 1996).

Imbert-Gourbeyre, A., *La stigmatisation* (Bellet: Clermont, 1894).

Irvin, D., 'The ministry of women in the early church: the archaeological evidence', *Duke Divinity School Review* 45. 2 (1980), pp 76-86.

Jankulak, K., *The Medieval Cult of St Petroc* (Woodbridge: The Boydell Press, 2000).

Jenkins, D., *Holy, Holier, Holiest: the Sacred Topography of the Early Medieval Irish Church, Studia Traditionis Theologiae* 4 (Turnhout, Brepols: 2010).

Johnson, E. A., *She Who Is: The Mystery of God in Feminist Theological Discourse* (New York, Crossroad: 1992).

Johnson, E. A., *Truly our Sister: A Theology of Mary in the Communion of Saints* (New York; London: Continuum: 2003).

Johnston, E., 'Transforming Women in Irish Hagiography', *Peritia* 9, (1995), pp.197-220.

Kadloubovsky, E., and G. E. H. Palmer, *Writings from the Philokalia on Prayer of the Heart* (London: Faber and Faber, 1951).

Kardong, T. G., *Benedict's Rule, A Translation and Commentary* (Collegeville, MN: The Liturgical Press, 1996).

Keller, D. G. R., *Oasis of Wisdom: The Worlds of the Desert Fathers and Mothers* (Collegeville, MN: Liturgical Press, 2005).

Kelly, F., *A Guide to Early Irish Law* (Dublin: Dublin Institute for Advanced Studies: 1988).

Klawiter, F. C., 'The Role of Martyrdom and Persecution in Developing the Priestly Authority of Women in Early Christianity: A Case Study of Montanism', *Church History*, Vol 49, No 3 (Sept 1980), pp 251-261.

Knowles, D., *What is Mysticism?* (London: Burns and Oates, 1967).

Knowles, D., *Christian Monasticism* (London: Weidenfeld and Nicolson, 1969).

Kodell, J., 'The Celibacy Logion in Matthew 19:12', *Biblical Theology Bulletin*, Feb 1978, vol 8, No 1, pp 19-23.

Koehler, L., *Saint Elizabeth the New Martyr* (NY: The Orthodox Palestine Society, USA, 1988).

Koester, H., 'The Divine Human Being', *Harvard Theological Review*, Vol 78, No 3/4 (Jul-Oct, 1985), pp 243-252.

Kraemer, R. S., 'The Conversion of Women to Ascetic Forms of Christianity', *Signs*, Vol 6, No 2, Studies in Change (Winter, 1980), pp 298-307.

Kraemer, R. S., *Her Share of the Blessings: Women's Religions Among Pagans, Jews and Christians in the Greco-Roman World* (NY: OUP, 1992).

Lacarrière, J., *The God-possessed* (London: George Allen & Unwin, 1963).

Ladner, G. B., *The Idea of Reform: Its Impact on Christian Thought and Action in the Age of the Fathers* (Cambridge: MA, 1959).

Leclercq, J., F. Vandenbroucke and L. Bouyer (eds), *A History of Christian Spirituality* (3 Vols) (London: Burns & Oates, 1968).

Leddy, M. J., *Reweaving Religious Life: Beyond the Liberal Model* (CT: Twenty Third Publications, 1990).

Lefkowitz, M. R., 'The Motivations for St Perpetua's Martyrdom,' *Journal of the American Academy of Religion*, Vol 44, No 3 (Sept 1976), pp 417-421.

Leyser, H., *Hermits and the New Monasticism; A Study of Religious Communities in Western Europe, 1000-1150* (London, Macmillan Press: 1984).

Losada. I., *New Habits: Today's Women who Choose to Become Nuns* (London, Hodder and Stoughton: 1999).

Lossky, V., *The Mystical Theology of the Eastern Church*, Eng. tras Fellowship of St Alban and St Sergius (London: James Clark & Co, 1957, repr. 1968, 1973).

Louth, A., *The Origins of the Christian Mystical Tradition: From Plato to Denys* (Oxford: Oxford University Press, 1981, repr. 2007),

Lucas, A. M., *Women in the Middle Ages* (London: The Harvester Press, 1983).

Luckman, H. A., 'Celibacy' in P. Sheldrake (ed), *The New SCM Dictionary of Spirituality* (London, SCM Press: 2005), pp 182-182.

MacMullen, R., 'Women in Public in the Roman Empire', *Historia: Zeitschrift für Alte Geschichte*, Vol 29, No 2 (2nd Qtr., 1980), pp 208-218.

MacNiocaill, G., *Ireland Before the Vikings*, (Dublin: Gill and Macmillan, 1972).

Maher, M., (ed), *Irish Spirituality*, (Dublin: Veritas, 1981).

Makowski, E., 'Canon Law and Cloistered Women: Periculoso and Its Commentators 1298-1545', *Studies in Medieval and Early Modern Canon Law*, Vol 5 (Catholic University of America Press, 1998).

Malone, M. T., *Women and Christianity*, vol. 2: *From 1000 to the Reformation,* (Dublin: The Columba Press, 2002).

Map of Monastic Britain (Southampton: Ordnance Survey, 1978).

Márkus, G., *Adomnán's 'Law of the Innocents': Cáin Adomnáin* (Glasgow, Blackfriars Books: 1997).

Martimort, A. G.,'The Liturgy of the Hours', in I. H. Dalmais, P. Jounel and A. G. Martimort (eds), *The Church at Prayer* 4, *The Liturgy and Time,* (Collegeville, Minnesota: Liturgical Press, 1983), 153-275.

Martimort, A. G., 'The Assembly', in I. H. Dalmais, P. Jounel and A. G. Martimort (eds), *The Church at Prayer* 4, *The Liturgy and Time,* (Collegeville, Minnesota: Liturgical Press, 1983), pp 77-206.

Mateos, J., 'The Morning and Evening Office', *Worship* 42 (1968), 31-47.

Mateos, J., 'The Origins of the Divine Office', *Worship* 41 (1967), 477-485.

Massie, R. K., *The Romanovs: The Final Chapter* (London: Jonathan Cape, 1995).

Matter, E. A., *The Voice of My Beloved: The Song of Songs in Western Medieval Christianity* (University of Pennsylvania Press, 1990).

Maylunas, A., and S. Mironenko, *A Lifelong Passion: Nicholas and Alexandra, Their Own Story* (London, Weidenfeld and Nicolson, 1996).

Mayr-Harting, H., *The Coming of Christianity to Anglo-Saxon England* (London: Batsford, 1972, 1977).

McGinn, B., *The Presence of God: A History of Western Christian Mysticism*, multiple vols. (New York: Crossroad / Herder, 1991-).

McNamara, J. A., 'Sexual Equality and the Cult of Virginity in Early Christian Thought', *Feminist Studies*, Vol 3, No 3/4 (Spring-Summer, 1976), pp 145-158.

McNamara, J. A., *Sisters in Arms* (Massachusetts: Harvard University Press, 1996).

Meeks, W. A., 'The Image of the Androgyne: Some Uses of a Symbol in Earliest Christianity', *History of Religions* 13, (1974) pp 165-208.

Meeks, W. A., *The Origins of Christian Morality: The First Two Centuries* (New Haven: Yale University Press, 1993).

Meeks, W. A., *The First Urban Christians: The Social World of the Apostle Paul* (New Haven, Yale University Press: 2nd ed 2003).

Meier, J.P., *A Marginal Jew: Rethinking the Historical Jesus*, Vol 1: *The Roots of the Problem and the Person* (New York, Doubleday: 1991).

Merton, T., *Pre-Benedictine Monasticism* (Kalamazoo, Michigan: Cistercian Publications, 2006).

Mews, C. J. (ed), *Listen, Daughter: The Speculum Virginum and the Formation of Religious Women in the Middle Ages* (New York: Palgrave, 2001).

Millar, L., *Grand Duchess Elizabeth of Russia* (Redding, CA, 1991).

Morris, C., *The Tudors* (London: Fontana / Collins, 1977).

Mosshamer, O., *The Priest and Womanhood* (Cork: Mercier Press, 1964).

Mueller, J., *The Privilege of Poverty: Clare of Assisi, Agnes of Prague and the Struggle for a Franciscan Rule for Women* (Pennsylvania: Pennsylvania University Press, 2006).

Murphy-O'Connor, J., *Paul: A Critical Life* (Oxford: Oxford University Press, 1996).

Neil, B., 'On True Humility: An Anonymous Letter on Poverty and the Female Ascetic' in W. Mayer, P. Allen and L. Cross (eds), *Prayer and Spirituality in the Early Church*, Vol 4: *The Spiritual Life* (Strathfield, NSW: St Paul's Publications, 2006), pp 233-246.

Neuman de Vegvar, C., 'Saints and Companions to Saints: Anglo-Saxon Royal Women Monastics in Context' in P. E. Szarmach (ed), *Holy Men and Holy Women: Old English Prose Saints' Lives and their Contexts* (New York: State University Press, 1996).

Newman, B., *From Virile Woman to Woman Christ: Studies in Medieval Religion and Literature* (Philadelphia: University of Pennsylvania Press, 1995).

Ní Dhonnchadha, M., '*The Lex Innocentium*' in M. O'Dowd and S. Wichert (eds), *Chattel, Servant or Citizen: Women's Status in Church, State and Society* (Belfast: Historical Studies xix, 1995).

Nikodimos of the Holy Mountain and Makarios of Corinth, *The Philokalia* 1-4, trs G. E. H. Palmer, P. Sherrard and K. Ware, (London: Faber and Faber, 1979–1984).

O'Caroll, M., *Theotokos: A Theological Encyclopedia of the Blessed Virgin Mary* (Wilmington: Michael Glazier, 1982, 1983),

Ó Corráin, D., 'Early Irish Hermit Poetry?' in D. Ó Corráin, L. Breatnach and K. McCone (eds), *Sages, Saints and Storytellers* (Maynooth: An Sagart, 1989), pp 251–267.

Ó Corráin, D., 'Women and the Law in Early Ireland' in *Chattel, Servant or Citizen: Women's Status in Church, State and Society* (Belfast: Historical Studies xix, 1995).

Ó Cróinín, D., 'A Tale of Two Rules: Benedict and Columbanus' in M. Browne and C. Ó Clabaigh (eds), *The Irish Benedictines* (Dublin: The Columba Press, 2005), 1-24.

Ó Cróinín, D., 'Merovingian Politics and Insular Calligraphy: The Historical Background to the Book of Durrow and Related Manuscripts', in M. Ryan (ed), *Ireland and Insular Art AD 500-1200* (Dublin:Royal Irish Academy, 1987), pp 40-43.

O'Dwyer, P., *Céli Dé: Spiritual Reform in Ireland 750-900* (Dublin: Editions Tailliura, 1977, repr. 1981).

Ó Fiannachta, P., 'The Spirituality of the Céli Dé' in M. Maher (ed), *Irish Spirituality*, (Dublin: Veritas, 1981), 22-32.

O'Loughlin, T. 'Marriage and Sexuality in the Hibernensis', *Peritia* 11 (1997), pp 188-206.

O'Loughlin, T., *St Patrick: the Man and his Works* (London: SPCK: 1999).

O'Loughlin, T., *Celtic Theology* (London: Continuum, 2000).

O'Loughlin, T., *Journeys on the Edges* (London: Darton, Longman and Todd, 2000).

O'Loughlin, T., 'The Early Church' in D. Cohn-Sherbok and J. M. Court (eds), *Religious Diversity in the Graeco-Roman World* (Sheffield: Sheffield Academic Press, 2001), 124-142.

O'Loughlin, T., 'Collectio Canonum Hibernensis, Book 46' in A Bourke *et al* (eds), *The Field Day Anthology of Irish Writing*, IV: *Irish Women's Writings and Traditions* (New York University Press, New York: 2002).

O'Loughlin, T., 'The *Didache* as a Source for Picturing the Earliest Christian Communities: The Case of the Practice of Fasting' in *Christian Origins, Worship, Belief and Society*, The Milltown Institute and the Irish Biblical Association Millenium Conference, K. O'Mahoney (ed), *Journal for the Study of the New Testament Supplement Series* 241 (Sheffield: Sheffield Academic Press, 2003), 83-112.

O'Loughlin, T., *Discovering St Patrick* (New York: Paulist Press, 2005).

O'Loughlin, T., 'Gnosticism' in P. Sheldrake (ed), *The New SCM Dictionary of Spirituality* (London, SCM Press: 2005), pp 323-325.

O'Loughlin, T., *Liturgical Resources for Advent and Christmastide*, Years A,B, and C (Dublin, The Columba Press: 2006).

O'Loughlin, T., 'Treating the "Private Mass" as Normal: Some unnoticed evidence from Adomnán's *De locis sanctis*', in *Archiv für Liturgiewissenschaft* 51 (2009), pp. 334-344.

O'Loughlin, T., *The Didache: A Window on the Earliest Christians* (London: SPCK, 2010).

Ó Maidín, U., *The Celtic Monk* (Kalamazoo, Michigan: Cistercian Publications, 1996).

Ó Murchú, D., *The Prophetic Horizon of Religious Life* (London: Excalibur Press, 1989).

Orr, S., 'Women and Livelihoods in 1st Century Palestine: Exploring Possibilities', *The Expository Times*, 121 (11), 2010, pp 539-547.

Pagels, E., *The Gnostic Gospels* (London: Pelican, 1982).

Parvis, S., 'Perpetua', *The Expository Times*, Vol 120, No 8, pp.365-372.

Patterson, G., *Still Flowing, Women, God and Church* (Geneva: WCC Publications, 1999).

Peters, M., 'The Beguines: Feminine Piety Derailed,' *Spirituality Today*, Spring 1991, Vol 43 No 1, pp 36-52.

Perkins, P., 'Gnosticism' in E. Ferguson (ed), *Encyclopedia of Early Christianity* (Chicago: St James Press, 1990), pp 371-376.

Peterson, I., 'Clare of Assisi: Hidden Behind which Image of Francis?' in J. M. Hammond (ed), *Francis of Assisi, History, Hagiography and Hermeneutics in the Early Documents* (New York: New City Press, 2004), pp 39-63.

Peterson, J. M. (ed and trs), *Handmaids of the Lord: Contemporary Descriptions of Feminine Asceticism in the First Six Christian Centuries* (Kalamazoo, Michigan: Cistercian Publications, 1996).

Petroff, E. A. (ed), *Medieval Women's Visionary Literature* (Oxford: Oxford University Press, 1986).

Pike, N., *Mystic Union: An Essay in the Phenomenology of Mysticism* (Ithaca: Cornell University Press, 1992).

Prou, J., and the Benedictine Nuns of the Solesmes Congregation (Eng. trs ed David Hayes), *Walled About with God* (Gracewing: 2005).

Ranke-Heinemann, U., *Eunuchs for the Kingdom of Heaven: Women, Sexuality and the Catholic Church* (London: Penguin Books, 1990).

Ratzinger, J., *Jesus of Nazareth, Part Two, Holy Week: From the Entrance into Jerusalem to the Resurrection* (trs P. J. Whitmore), (London: Catholic Truth Society, 2011).

Rhee, H., 'Spirituality of female Martyrs: Virginity and Spiritual Motherhood' in W. Mayer, P. Allen and L. Cross (eds), *Prayer and Spirituality in the Early Church*, Vol 4: *The Spiritual Life* (Strathfield, NSW: St Paul's Publications, 2006), pp 133-148.

Ritari, K., 'Saints and Sinners in Early Christian Ireland: Moral Theology in the Lives of Saints Brigid and Columba', *Studia Traditionis Theologiae* 3 (Turnhout: Brepols, 2009).

Robinson, W., 'Mary: The Flower and Fruit of Worship', in J. Behr, A. Louth and D. Conomos (eds), *Abba: The Tradition of Orthodoxy in the West, Festschrift for Bishop Kallistos (Ware) of Diokleia* (Crestwood, New York: St Vladimir's Seminary Press, 2003), pp 193-205.

Rumsey, P. M., 'The Different Concepts of Sacred Time Underlying the Liturgy of the Hours', *Worship* 78 (2004), 290-309.

Rumsey, P. M., *Sacred Time in Early Christian Ireland* (London, T & T Clark, 2007).

Rumsey, P. M., 'All Praise be Yours, My Lord, for All Creation: Francis and Clare and Ecology', *The Cord*, Vol 61, No 1 Jan/March 2011.

Ryan, J., *Irish Monasticism: Origins and Early Development* (Dublin: Talbot Press, 1931, repr. Dublin: Four Courts Press, 1992).

Ryan, M. (ed), *Ireland and Insular Art AD 500-1200* (Dublin:Royal Irish Academy, 1987).

Salisbury, J., *Church Fathers: Independent Virgins* (London: Verso, 1991).

Salisbury, J., 'The Latin Doctors of the Church on Sexuality', *Journal of Medieval History* 12 (1986), pp 279-289.

Salmon, *The Breviary Through the Centuries*, (Liturgical Press, Collegeville, Minnesota, 1962).

Schneiders, S., 'The Effects of Women's Experience on their Spirituality', *Spirituality Today*, Summer 1983, vol 35, No 2, pp 100-116.

Schneiders, S., *New Wineskins: Re-Imagining Religious Life Today* (New York: Paulist Press: 1986).

Schneiders, S., 'Religious Life: The Dialectic Between Marginality and Transformation', *Spirituality Today*, Winter 1988 Supplement, Vol 40, pp 59-79.

Schneiders, S., *Religious Life In a New Millennium*, Volume 1: *Finding the Treasure* (New York: Paulist Press: 2000).

Schneiders, S., 'Religion and Spirituality: Strangers, Rivals or Partners?' Santa Clara Lecture, Vol 6, No 2, 2000.

Schneiders, S., *National Catholic Reporter*, January 4th-8th 2010; http://ncronline.org/node/16441; http://ncronline.org/node/16463; http://ncronline.org/node/16464;http://ncronline.org/node/16465; http://ncronline.org/news/women/religious-life-sharing-jesus-passion-resurrection.

Simpson, C. J., 'The Stigmata: Pathology or Miracle?' *British Medical Journal*, Vol 289, Dec 1984, pp 1746-1748.

Skobtsova, M., with a preface by O. Clement, *Mother Maria Skobtsova: Essential Writings* (Maryknoll: Orbis Books, 2003).

Smith, W., and S. Cheetham (eds), *A Dictionary of Christian Antiquities* (London, John Murray, 1908), pp 401-2.

Smith, J. A., *Ordering Women's Lives: Penitentials and Nunnery Rules in the Early Medieval West* (Aldershot: Ashgate, 2001).

Southern, R. W., *The Making of the Middle Ages* (London: Hutchinson, 1967).

Stearns Davis, W. (ed), *Readings in Ancient History: Illustrative Extracts from the Sources* (Boston: Allyn and Bacon, 1912-13), Vol. II: *Rome and the West*.

Steinberg, D. (ed), *The Future of Religious Life: The Carondelet Conference* (Collegeville, Minnesota: The Liturgical Press, 1988).

Stevenson, J. B., 'The Monastic Rules of Columbanus' in *Columbanus: Studies on the Latin Writings* (Woodbridge: The Boydell Press, 1997), 203-216.

Stoner, A., 'Sisters Between: Gender and the Medieval Beguines', http://userwww.sfsu.edu/~epf/1995/beguine.html

Swimme, B., and T. Berry, *The Universe Story* (London: Penguin Books, 1992).

Taft, R., *The Liturgy of the Hours in East and West: The Origins of the Divine Office and its Meaning for Today* (Collegeville, Minnesota: Liturgical Press, 1986, 1993).

Tavormina, M. T., 'Of Maidenhood and Maternity: Liturgical Hagiography and the Medieval Idea of Virginity', *American Benedictine Review*, Vol 31, 1980, pp 384-399.

Taylor, J., 'St Paul's Missionfield: the World of Acts 13-28' in *Proceedings of the Irish Biblical Association* 21 (Dublin, 1998), pp 9-24.

Thekla, *Mother Maria, Her Life in Letters* (London: Darton, Longman and Todd, 1979).

Theokritoff, E., 'Embodied Word and New Creation: Some Modern Insights Concerning the Material World', in J. Behr, A. Louth and D. Conomos (eds), *Abba: The Tradition of Orthodoxy in the West, Festschrift for Bishop Kallistos (Ware) of Diokleia* (Crestwood, New York: St Vladimir's Seminary Press, 2003).

Turner, D., *The Darkness of God: Negativity in Christian Mysticism* (Cambridge: Cambridge University Press, 1995, 1996, 1998, 1999).

Underhill, E., *Mysticism: a study in the nature and development of man's spiritual consciousness* (London: Methuen, 1911).

Van den Goorbergh, E. A., and T. H. Zweermen, *Light Shining Through a Veil: On Saint Clare's Letters to Saint Agnes of Prague* (Peeters, 2000).

Vanderlip, D. G., *Christianity According to John* (Philadelphia: Westminster Press, 1975).

Van Dijk, S. J. P., and J. Hazelden Walker, *The Origins of the Modern Roman Liturgy* (London: Darton, Longman and Todd, 1960).

D-Vasilescu, E., *Between Tradition and Modernity: Icons and Icon Painters in Romania* (VDM Verlag, 2009).

Vatican, Second Ecumenical Council of the, A. Flannery (ed.), (Dublin: Dominican Publications, 1975, 1977).

Venarde, B., *Women's Monasticism and Medieval Society* (Ithaca and London: Cornell University Press, 1997).

Venite Seorsum: Instruction on the Contemplative Life and the Enclosure of Nuns (Vatican City, 1969).

Verbi Sponsa: Instruction on the Contemplative Life and on the Enclosure of Nuns (Vatican City: 1999).

Vita Consecrata; Apostolic Exhortation of John Paul II (London: Catholic Truth Society, 1996).

Waddell, H. (trs), *The Desert Fathers* (London: Constable, 1936).

Wade Labarge, M., *A Small Sound of the Trumpet* (London: Hamish Hamilton, 1990).

Walker, G. S. M. (ed), *Sancti Columbani Opera* (Dublin: Institute for Advanced Studies, 1957, 1970,1997).

Walker Bynum, C., *Holy Feast and Holy Fast: The Religious Significance of Food to Medieval Women* (Berkeley: University of California Press, 1987).

Ward, B., *Harlots of the Desert: A Study of Repentance in Early Monastic Sources* (Kalamazoo: Cistercian Publications, 1987).

Ward, B. (trs), *The Desert Fathers: Sayings of the Early Christian Monks* (London: Penguin Classics, 2003).

Ware, T., *The Orthodox Church* (London, Penguin Books, 1963).

Warner, M., *Alone of all her Sex: The Myth and the Cult of the Virgin Mary* (Picador: 1990).

Warr, C., 'Representation, imitation, rejection: Chiara of Montefalco (d. 1308) and the passion of Christ' in C. Meek and C. Lawless (eds), *Studies on Medieval and Early Modern Women 4; Victims or Viragos?* (Dublin: Four Courts Press, 2005), pp. 89-101.

Wayne Riddle, D., 'Early Christian Hospitality: A Factor in the Gospel Tradition', *Journal of Biblical Literature*, Vol 57, 2 (June, 1938), pp 141-154.

Wemple, S., *Women in Frankish Society: Marriage and the Cloister 500-900* (Philadelphia: University of Pennsylvania Press, 1981).

White, C., *Lives of Roman Christian Women* (London: Penguin Classics, 2010).

Wolters, C., *Julian of Norwich: Revelations of Divine Love* (London: Penguin Books, 1966).

Wood, C. T., 'The Doctor's Dilemma: Sin, Salvation, and the Menstrual Cycle in Medieval Thought', *Speculum*, Vol 56, No 4 (Oct., 1981), pp 710-727.

Wood, M., *Domesday: A Search for the Roots of England* (London: BBC Publications, 1986).

Wood, J. M., *Women, Art and Spirituality: The Poor Clares of Early Modern Italy* (Cambridge: Cambridge University Press, 1996).

Wooding, J., 'Monasticism' in Christopher Snyder (ed), *Early Peoples of Britain and Ireland, An Encyclopedia* (Oxford: Greenwood World Publishing, 2008), pp. 395-402.

Woolfenden, G. W., *Daily Liturgical Prayer: Origins and Theology* (Aldershot: Ashgate, 2004).

Yorke, B., 'The Adaptation of the Anglo-Saxon Royal Courts to Christianity', in M. Carver (ed), *The Cross Goes North : Processes of Conversion in Northern Europe AD 300-1300* (University of York: York Medieval Press, 2004), pp 243-257.

Zeepat, C., *Romanov Autumn* (London, Sutton Publishing: 2000).

Index

Praise for *Women of the Church*

I wish this important book the very best and know it will be a big help to many, both monastics in the strict sense and women religious in general as well as many of our lay sisters and brothers.

Sandra M. Schneiders, IHM, Professor of New Testament Studies and Christian Spirituality

In this book, Patricia Rumsey raises radical issues from a firm Christian feminist standpoint, which will probably produce interesting questions that need to be addressed. The author herself is an enclosed contemplative nun with long experience and she speaks with authenticity and simplicity about what she has genuinely lived herself. This is a courageous and challenging book; it is stylish and scholarly in its presentation.

Sr Anne-Lise StrØm, OP, Prioress of Lunden Kloster Contemplative Dominicans, Oslo, Norway.

Patricia Rumsey gives us a rare insight into the experience of monastic women living within a male-dominated context. She offers a passionately-felt and vigorously-worded argument from a feminist perspective for a more inclusive understanding of the structures and purpose of monastic life. While monastic women choose to embrace prayerful silence on behalf of the world, the silencing of their opinions, experience and desires for rightful self-determination is a loss to the whole church. While some may find its viewpoint provocative, this book is a long overdue addition to the debate on the nature of contemporary religious life.

*Dr Gemma Simmonds CJ
Director, Religious Life Institute*

Praise for *Women of the Church*

This is a book that has been extensively researched. It is well documented and provides an introduction to monastic life as lived by women down through the ages. It shows how monastic women have made, and continue to make, a valuable and much overlooked contribution to the whole monastic tradition. The author writes for the interested non-specialist but also as an encouragement to those students who wish to pursue further research. The book clarifies how extensively historical and social factors have influenced monastic women in their interpretation of their ways of life and how many of these women have freed themselves from traditional gender roles and expectations. The author discusses the issue of enclosure perceptively, pointing out that it was not until after Vatican II that any new understanding and practice of enclosure emerged. It remains true that women in the Church are still subordinate to men. This prompts the writer to ask, "Can the Church be credible in today's world if it continues this practice?"

The author's easy style of writing is another contributory factor that makes this book not only informative but an interesting and enjoyable read.

Pauline Cowie, LSU